Remembering Dvinsk
Daugavpils, Latvia

Part 1. Dvinsk, The Rise and Decline of a Town

Original in Yiddish by Yudel Flior

Translated by Bernard Sachs

Part 2. In Memory of the Community of Dvinsk

Original in Hebrew – Edited by Tamar Amarant

Translated by Amy Samin

Part 3. Appendix of Images

Collected and edited by Eilat Gordin Levitan

Published by JewishGen

An Affiliate of the Museum of Jewish Heritage - A Living Memorial to the Holocaust
New York

Remembering Dvinsk - Daugavpils, Latvia

Layout: Joel Alpert
Image Editor: Martha Forsyth
Cover Design: Nili Goldman
Translation Project Coordinator for In Memory of the Community of Dvinsk:
Ilana Lutman
Indexing: Lorraine Rosengarten

Published by JewishGen, Inc.
An Affiliate of the Museum of Jewish Heritage
A Living Memorial to the Holocaust
36 Battery Place, New York, NY 10280

"JewishGen, Inc. is not responsible for inaccuracies or omissions in the original work and makes no representations regarding the accuracy of this translation. Digital images of the original book's contents can be seen online at the New York Public Library Web site."

The mission of the JewishGen organization is to produce a translation of the original work and we cannot verify the accuracy of statements or alter facts cited.

Printed in the United States of America by Lightning Source, Inc.

Library of Congress Control Number (LCCN): 2016944514
ISBN 978-1-939561-41-1 (hard cover: 322 pages, alk. paper)

Cover photographs courtesy of Hagit Porat

JewishGen and the Yizkor-Books-in-Print Project

This book has been published by the **Yizkor-Books-in-Print Project,** as part of the **Yizkor Book Project** of **JewishGen, Inc**.

JewishGen, Inc. is a non-profit organization founded in 1987 as a resource for Jewish genealogy. Its website [www.jewishgen.org] serves as an international clearinghouse and resource center to assist individuals who are researching the history of their Jewish families and the places where they lived. JewishGen provides databases, facilitates discussion groups, and coordinates projects relating to Jewish genealogy and the history of the Jewish people. In 2003, JewishGen became an affiliate of the **Museum of Jewish Heritage - A Living Memorial to the Holocaust** in New York.

The **JewishGen Yizkor Book Project** was organized to make more widely known the existence of Yizkor (Memorial) Books written by survivors and former residents of various Jewish communities throughout the world. Later, volunteers connected to the different destroyed communities began cooperating to have these books translated from the original language— usually Hebrew or Yiddish—into English, thus enabling a wider audience to have access to the valuable information contained within them. As each chapter of these books was translated, it was posted on the JewishGen website and made available to the general public.

The **Yizkor-Books-in-Print Project** began in 2011 as an initiative to print and publish Yizkor Books that had been fully translated, so that hard copies would be available for purchase by the descendants of these communities and also by scholars, universities, synagogues, libraries, and museums.

These Yizkor books have been produced almost entirely through the volunteer effort of researchers from around the world, assisted by donations from private individuals. The books are printed and sold at near cost, so as to make them as affordable as possible. Our goal is to make this important genre of Jewish literature and history available in English in book form, so that people can have the personal histories of their ancestral towns on their bookshelves for themselves and for their children and grandchildren.

A list of all published translated Yizkor Books in the project with prices and ordering information can be found at:
                    http://www.jewishgen.org/Yizkor/ybip.html

Lance Ackerfeld, Yizkor Book Project Manager

Joel Alpert, Yizkor-Book-in-Print Project Coordinator

JewishGen
Yizkor Book Project

This book is presented by the
Yizkor Books in Print Project
Project Coordinator: Joel Alpert

Part of the
Yizkor Books Project of JewishGen, Inc.
Project Manager: Lance Ackerfeld

These books have been produced solely through volunteer effort
of individuals from around the world. The books are printed and
sold at near cost, so as to make them as affordable as possible.

Our goal is to make this history and important genre of Jewish
literature available in English in book form so that people can have
the near-personal histories of their ancestral towns on their bookshelves for themselves and for their children and grandchildren.

Any donations to the Yizkor Books Project are appreciated.

Please send donations to:
Yizkor Book Project
JewishGen
36 Battery Place
New York, NY 10280

JewishGen, Inc. is an affiliate of the
Museum of Jewish Heritage
A Living Memorial to the Holocaust

Title page of the 1974 Class project by the 8th grade of the Kol Haverim Junior High
School of Haifa In Memory of the Community of Dvinsk

ל ז כ ר

ק ה י ל ת

דבינסק

Translation of Title page of the 1974 Class project by the 8th grade of the Kol Haverim Junior High School of Haifa <u>In Memory of the Community of Dvinsk</u>

To the Memory

of the Divinsk

Community

Foreword

This *New Dvinsk Yizkor Book* is a compilation of three sources. First is a reprint of the 1965 book *Dvinsk – The Rise and Decline of a Town* by Yudel Flior, translated from the Yiddish by Bernard Sachs. Second is the translation of the 1974 class project *In Memory of the Community of Dvinsk*, to memorialize the Latvian town of Dvinsk by the 8th grade of the Kol Haverim Junior High School of Haifa; it is a fine collection of history, recollections of former residents, essays, historic photographs, and artwork by the students. Third is an appendix of historic photographs assembled by Eilat Gordin Levitan.

It is the desire of the Yizkor-Books-In-Print project that this new compilation of material in English serve as a fitting memorial for the Jewish Community of Dvinsk.

Acknowledgements

This book, being a compilation of three sources required cooperation from numerous people.

For Dvinsk – <u>The Rise and Decline of a Town</u>, we'd like to thank Roy Flior, grandson of the author Yudel Flior who granted us permission to reprint the translation of the Yiddish book. Much gratitude to Owen Pell who arranged to have scanned the book and to Martha Forsyth, who modified the scans so that they were more readable.

For the 1974 class project In Memory of the Community of Dvinsk by the 8th grade of the Kol Haverim Junior High School of Haifa, thanks to Ilana Lutman, Translation Project Coordinator and to Amy Samin, the translator and Joel Gardner who donated the translation to JewishGen. Many thanks to those students who by now have reached maturity and to who this project was likely very important.

Thanks finally to Eliat Gordin Levitan, who had assembled the appendix of historic photographs of Dvinsk.

Special thanks to Owen Pell, who suggested the publication of this book on Dvinsk.

Dedication

This book is dedicated to my father-in-law, Nathan Hersh Seril (Nahum Hirsch ben Chaim Zelig), who came to America from Dvinsk, and in honor of the rest of Nathan Seril's family, which includes beloved relatives who perished in the German invasion of the USSR and the ensuing Holocaust.

Owen Pell

Latvia and vicinity with Dvinsk shown
Map by Rachel Kolokoff Hopper

Geopolitical Information:

Daugavpils, Latvia: 55°53' North Latitude, 26°32' East Longitude

Alternate names: Daugavpils [Latvian], Dvinsk [Rus], Denenburg [Yiddish], Dünaburg [Ger], Dyneburg [Polish], Daugpilis [Lithanian], Dźvinsk [Belarussian], Dźwińsk [Polish], Daŭhaŭpils, Daugapils, Daugpiļs, Daugava, Dynaborgs, Dynaburg, Dinaburg, Deneburg, Duenaburg, Dwinsk

	Town	District	Province	Country
Before WWI (c. 1900):	Dvinsk	Dvinsk	Vitebsk	Russian Empire
Between the wars (c. 1930):	Daugavpils	Daugavpils	Latgale	Latvia
After WWII (c. 1950):	Daugavpils			Soviet Union
Today (c. 2000):	Daugavpils			

Jewish Population in 1900: 32,369 (1897), 55,680 (1914)

Notes: Russian: Двинск / Даугавпилс / Динабург. Belarusian: Дзьвінск. Yiddish: דענענבורג / דענעבאַרג / ווינסקד
In SE Latvia; second-largest city in Latvia.

Nearby Jewish Communities:

Grīva 3 miles SSW
Skrudaļiena 8 miles ESE
Ilūkste 11 miles WNW
Silene 13 miles SE
Višķi 15 miles NE
Zarasai, Lithuania 15 miles SW
Eglaine 16 miles WNW
Dubinovo, Belarus 18 miles ESE
Plyussy, Belarus 20 miles ESE
Okmyanitsa, Belarus 22 miles SE
Zarachye, Belarus 24 miles SE

Rimše, Lithuania 24 miles S
Krāslava 25 miles E
Dukštas, Lithuania 25 miles SSW
Salakas, Lithuania 26 miles SW
Subate 26 miles WNW
Braslaw, Belarus 26 miles SE
Opsa, Belarus 27 miles SSE
Dusetos, Lithuania 28 miles WSW
Obeliai, Lithuania 29 miles W
Slobodka, Belarus 29 miles ESE
Preiļi 30 miles NNE

Notes to the Reader:

Also please note that all references within the text of the book to page numbers, refer to the page numbers of the original Yizkor Book.

The original book can be seen online at the NY Public Library site: http://yizkor.nypl.org/index.php?id=2113

A list of this book and all books available in the Yizkor-Book-In-Print Project along with prices is available at:

http://www.jewishgen.org/Yizkor/ybip.html

Table of Contents

Dvinsk – The Rise and Decline of a Town by Yudel Flior	Pages 1-89

In Memory of the Community of Dvinsk	Original Page Number
This booklet was published with the assistance of the Dov Aloni Memorial Fund	
Remarks of the School Management	1
Yad Vashem, the Remembrance Authority of the Holocaust and its Heroes	2
Scroll of Remembrance	3
Dear Pupils…	4
Introduction	5
The Memorialization of the Dvinsk Community	6
The Community of Dvinsk	7
The Youth Television Broadcast on Dvinsk	8

Dvinsk in the Past	
Dvinsk in the Past	10
The Foundation and Development of the City of Dvisnk	11
The Jews of Dvinsk	13
The City's Rabbis	14
The Synagogues in Dvinsk	15
The Political Parties in Dvinsk	16
Jewish Activity in Dvinsk	18
Industry and Commerce in the City	19
Cultural Life in the City	20
The Jewish Community in the City	20
The Hebrew School in Dvinsk (photo)	21
Haim Nachman Bialik's Visit in Dvinsk (photo)	21
The Self-Defense Organization in Dvinsk at the Start of the Twentieth Century	22
Jewish Cultural and Religious Life in Dvinsk at the Start of the Twentieth Century	23
The Zionist Movement and the Youth of Dvinsk	24
The Community of Dvinsk	25
Dvinsk, My City	27
My City, Dvinsk	28
The Community of Dvinsk	29

Dvinsk – City of the Jews	30

Dvinsk Today

How Does Dvinsk Look Today?	39
Dvinsk Then and Now	40
Dvinsk Today	41

Dvinsk During the Holocaust

The Ghetto in Dvinsk	44
The Dvinsk Ghetto	46
The Ghetto of Dvinsk	50
The Camp Ganbin and Liberation	55
The Metamorphosis of a Young Man of Dvinsk from the Old Left	57
Yizkor [Memorial Prayer]	61
Yizkor [Memorial Prayer] – 29 years after the destruction of the Jews of Latvia	62
To Them!	

Appendix of historic photographs
Assembled by Eilat Gordin Levitan

DVINSK

THE RISE AND DECLINE OF A TOWN

YUDEL FLIOR

Translated from the Yiddish
by
Bernard Sachs

DIAL PRESS
Johannesburg

CONTENTS

1. DVINSK BEGINS TO STIR   11

2. COMMERCE — BIG AND SMALL   20

3. BEGGAR'S OPERA   33

4. THE MARKETS   43

5. DIE VOLKMENSCHEN   54

6. THE RELIGIOUS WORLD   64

7. THE SECULAR WORLD   80

8. THE WORKING CLASSES   94

9. THE RED YEARS   105

10. THE RISING STORM   116

11. FLOOD TIDE   129

12. THE REACTION   142

13. WAR AND REVOLUTION   155

14. THE FIRST WORLD WAR   168

15. REVOLUTION AND AFTER   182

Introduction

Dunaburg — Dvinsk — Daugavplis : These were the varied names that the town of my birth was known by. Its history was bound up with these names. I have humbly taken it upon myself to let the world know something of its chequered story.

Who am I? I am no expert with the pen; or a historian who has delved deeply into the archives; or an academician to go burrowing in the encyclopaedias to discover the origins of this town, and how the first Jews came there.

That's how it is! I make no claims to be a professional writer. I am no journalist, carry no title, do not flaunt long hair; neither do I wear spectacles to make myself scholarly. I am a simple man of the people—a house painter, in fact. And when you will read my book on Dvinsk, which has been a hallowed name in Jewry, and find literary shortcomings or some historical inaccuracies—then I crave your forgiveness. I am writing of what my eyes have seen and my ears have heard from reputable people, whose testimony can be fully relied on.

I was born in Dvinsk, and lived there for 43 years. But I have to confess that until the age of twelve I knew very little about the town. For during my childhood and cheder days I lived in Altstadt, called Rypoli in Russian—which means Paradise. Altstadt, though five miles from Dvinsk proper, was part of the town. I did not have occasion to visit Dvinsk more than five times a year—usually when my parents took me there to purchase a cap for me.

For one reason or another, neither a doctor nor a cap-maker were to be found in Altstadt. That there was no doctor caused little concern to the Jews of Altstadt. For was there not the good Lord above to cure all our ills? On top of it, he was ably assisted by his earthly representative, Rav Moshe Aharon, who could exorcise evil spirits. But apart from these two lacks, Altstadt possessed everything—tailors, boot-makers, butchers. As for those who had dedicated their lives to matters sacred—why, we had more of them than any other four places put together. To this day I have not discovered why it was that Altstadt had been without a cap-maker. After all, caps did not grow on trees. And since you, dear reader, will no doubt be curious to know why I required so many caps, I must forthwith proceed to tell you.

For the six months from Succas to Pesach I used up one cap only, like any other boy from Altstadt. But in the hot summer days I went through four caps. The reason was that when the green vegetables made their appearance in the neighbouring gardens, I would indulge in such escapades as climbing over the fences and liberally help myself to the tiny onions, red carrots lifting themselves gaily from the earth, and radishes so fresh and appetising to the eye that I simply could not resist them. Besides, there were the orchards where luscious apples and pears, and red cherries would claim my attention and divert me from the strait and narrow. And since I was blessed with Jewish good fortune, which is a byword, it invariably happened that I was caught, doled out a goodly number of blows—and had my cap taken from me, to crown it all.

Now it is common cause that a Jewish child it not permitted to pass his days without wearing a covering on his head, like a "shaigetz". That is why I knew that very shortly after losing one cap in an orchard, I would be taken to Dvinsk to be fitted with another cap that both sat neatly on my head and matched my bright, youthful face. If my parents could have safely detached my head, and taken it by itself to Dvinsk, they would gladly have left me behind in Altstadt.

But there was certainly no question of allowing me to go through life without a cap. For at the age of ten I had already commenced the study of the Gemarra—I was, what you would call, a "ballebatischer kind". Experts were impressed with my aptitude. It was predicted that I would grow up to be among the greats of Israel—perhaps a Rav. And, truth to say, the Rabbinical symptoms were there for every one to see—a high forehead, a paunchy stomach, a splendid appetite. Also I could sleep through a whole day of twenty four hours, was indolent to a degree, and, let it also be noted—I was not totally hopeless at my studies.

Yes! I am Dvinsk-born. Nothing much to boast about to the great, wide world, who know only too well that the inhabitants of Dvinsk are often spoken of in terms not very flattering—Dvinsker hooligans, is only one of the blemishes for which the town is very widely known. For all that, I have no reason to blush for my hometown. For it was also a centre of Torah and general culture, Yeshivas and schools, charitable bodies and workers' trade unions.

How is it, then, that in all my humility I have taken it upon myself to write this book about a town full of so many complexities and themes? The answer is that I have had a weakness for writing since the time I was a child ten years old. And nothing could keep me back.

And now I must express my grateful thanks to you, dear reader, for the time you are prepared to give to getting to know what my book is about.

YUDEL FLIOR

Johannesburg,
3 January, 1956.

Chapter One

DVINSK BEGINS TO STIR

In the days of old, Dvinsk was known as Dunaburg. Centuries have rolled by, and the name of Dunaburg can still be heard. At one time the town belonged to Poland. Then it was taken over by Sweden, who lost it to Russia. Ivan the Terrible, Tsar of Russia, gave it back to the Poles. In 1772, Catherine the Great of Russia conquered Poland and annexed large stretches of land and many towns, among which was Dvinsk. The Poles left behind them many landmarks—a Catholic Church and a cemetery in the district known as Slabodki.

The name Dvinsk is derived from the River Dvina, on which the town is situated. The Dvina takes its rise in a small lake not far from the sources of the Volga and Dnieper. It moves with increasing momentum through the towns of Vitebsk, Polotsk, Dvinsk and Jacobstad, taking in its forward sweep numerous townlets and villages. Thus it flows for 640 miles before it finally plunges into the Gulf of Riga, in the Baltic. It drains an area of 33,000 square miles.

In normal times, the Dvina around Dvinsk was of a width not exceeding 1,400 feet. But in spring it went into flood, flowed much more strongly and over a much greater width. It often happened that when the ice thawed, the ice floes swept over its bank into Griva, on the other side of the River. I can recall two serious floods—one in 1906 and another in 1924, when the raging waters swept into the suburb of Gayok and wrought much havoc.

There is no definite historical evidence regarding the arrival of the first Jews in Dvinsk. It is well known that in the olden days every Jewish community kept records of its main activities and significant happenings,

such as an outbreak of fire, epidemics, floods — also of
lesser events, such as a Jewish conversion to Christia-
nity, or when a Jewish youth absconded with a "shikse".
The record was handed down from generation to
generation. These older generations are no longer
there, and the records have vanished with them. All
that is left to tell us something of Jewish life and
striving there, is the old cemetery beyond Lake Soonia,
situated just outside Altstadt. The guardian of the
cemetery, Reb Avram Chaim, had discovered tombstones with scarcely legible lettering, establishing that
Jews were buried there in the sixteenth century.

At one time when much bigger towns were scarcely
known, Dvinsk had already established itself throughout Russia as an important railway centre. For it was
situated midway between St. Petersburg and Warsaw.
The train used to stop at Dvinsk to pick up wood, fuel
and water, and the workmen from the big railway depot
would give the train a thorough check-up before it
moved on. The train to and from Germany also
stopped at Dvinsk. The Petersburg station was two
miles out of town. Passengers drove to and from the
station in cabs during the summer, and in sledges in the
winter. In 1906, the railway line was extended from
the Petersburg Station to the town proper. This branch
line was known as the Peredatche.

And then there was the Riga Station, situated right
in the heart of the town. The main thoroughfare
leading to this Station was known as Riga Street. It
lay on the railway line linking Riga with Orel. The
third railway station was on the line from Libau, and
was known as the Kalkoener Station. It was situated
about five miles from Dvinsk, next to Griva. To reach
it in summer, you had to cross the Dvina by ferry; and
in winter it was frozen over and you could cross it by
foot.

When Russia defeated Poland in war, in 1772, one of

the first things the authorities did was to expand the fortress on the outskirts of the town, near where Altstadt stood. The military did not want to have a populated area near the fortress, and they decreed that no further expansion encroaching on the fortress area would be permitted. Thus it was that the inhabitants started spreading towards the sand-dunes, some distance away from the fortress. This was probably the beginning of Dvinsk proper. As was to be expected, the Jews started building synagogues in this developing area. One of them they named the Sandy Synagogue, and the other Novgorodsker Synagogue—that is, the Synagogue of the new town.

The number of people who transferred to the new part was not large at first. Twenty-four streets crossed each other at right angles. On the one side the town was skirted by the Riga railway-line, and on another side was the Esplanade where the open fields spread as far as Altstadt and the fortress. On the third side a dyke had been erected to prevent the Dvina flooding the town. Where the dyke ended, a tarred road curving away from the Dvina and bounding the fourth side of the new town, became a paved highway that carried on to St. Petersburg.

On the other side of this main highway was the suburb of Gayok, where was to be found a fair concentration of Jews. It was the site of the saw-mills belonging to the brothers Mizrach, Gurevitch's Brewery, flourmills, and a number of factories. The power station was also situated in Gayok. At one point near the highway stood a complex of red buildings, which made up the famous gaol of Dvinsk.

The streets were wide and cobbled, and the pavements were of brick. The houses were mainly wooden and single-storeyed. But structures on the main Riga Street, and where the commercial part of the town was situated, were of brick and mostly double-storeyed. When insurance companies began operating there, and the wooden houses began to burn down in disquietingly large numbers, the owners who had greatly benefited from these fires started rebuilding more imposing structures of brick that often reached four storeys. It is estimated that before the First World War, the population of Dvinsk amounted to 90,000 souls. While there are no vital statistics to check up on, I would hazard a guess that half the population was Jewish.

The largest suburb of Dvinsk was known as Pletzer, which the Russians called Novo Stroyenia—New Structures. It was not altogether a fitting name, as they were by no means new, and were very modest structures. In fact, the beams of the houses had more often than not rotted away, and the walls seemed warped and desolate with age—as in a painting of Chagall. Pletzer was situated on the other side of the Riga railway line. To reach it the railway had to be crossed. The number of times the interfering booms came down was indicative of the heavy railway traffic round Dvinsk.

Pletzer was a huge area. There had been no proper planning and it sprawled chaotically in every direction. Proper paving was scanty, and the streets were either submerged in mud or in sand. Half the Jews of the town lived in this suburb, mostly from the lower economic strata—workmen, casual employees, traders, and the lumpen elements. In this welter could be located Zacks's match factory, where there worked 800 men, women and children. Then there was Grieliche's tannery, employing 500 hands. Waldenberg's tannery employed 300. Pletzer was adjacent to the summer resorts known as Tserepova, Mayak and Strop.

An arid, desolate stretch of field lay between Dvinsk and Altstadt, and it was quite a trial to cross it. In summer the sand, fine, yellow and soft, overlay it. And when the rains came it was turned into a muddy swamp, which squelched menacingly as you sank into it ankle-deep. Along the road itself there was not a shed, a house, a roof where you could seek shelter from the heavy rains, moaning winds and snowstorms. It was with considerable reluctance that you took it upon yourself to go to town from Altstadt. In most cases it was considered too forbidding to be lightly undertaken —and you remained at home seated by the warmth of the fire. In 1905, there were 200 Jewish families in Altstadt. By 1914, only half of them had remained on.

Under half the population of Dvinsk was made up of fanatical Old Believers Staravera who were a breakaway Russian religious sect. Then there were the Letts, Poles and some Germans. The Old Believers did not shave their beards, and smoking was a deadly sin. They were persecuted by the Tsar. They were not allowed to build houses of worship, and they had to congregate in private houses to perform their religious ritual. Five thousand of the Old Believers lived in Altstadt, and 20,000 in Pletzer and the outlying villages.

About fifty wandering Gypsies would descend on Altstadt with the arrival of summer. They were colourful, and not only brought life and merriment to Altstadt but also an epidemic of thieving. One of the eminences of Dvinsk was the Crimean tobacconist by the name of Tursu, where you could buy cigarettes called Livadia. And there were a number of bakeries owned by Turks. One of them, Pandul, would proudly stroll down the main street with his nineteen children, as if to let the world know of his accomplishment.

There was a part of Pletzer, near the barracks of the Ivanogorodski Regiment, where the Jews of the underworld lived. In this area were to be found the cripples, the deformed, the diseased, street musicians, cardsharpers, horse-traders, and straight horsethieves. And these denizens of the underworld had around them their stooges, relatives and friends. It was called Na Peshkach—On The Sands. The women plied their disreputable trade and reaped profits. For the turbid, filthy stream from the city congregated in the cheap brothels of Na Peshkach, a word that was never mentioned in respectable places.

A large number of the Jews of Dvinsk lived in Griva. It was not a suburb of Dvinsk, but a town of its own across the Dvina. One main street ran through the centre of it, from which there branched off a number of curving, narrow lanes. Despite its smallness, Griva carried the flattering title of Gorod—that is, Town. It did not belong to the Province of Vitebsk, like Dvinsk, but was part of Courland. The Courlanders were a proud lot, and the Jews of Griva likewise regarded themselves as a notch above the Jews of Dvinsk. Jews were not allowed to live there, except for those who were already there in 1880. Then a new generation grew up, who were little concerned with their Courland associations. These Jews came to work in Dvinsk and mingled freely with the Jews there on terms of complete equality.

Most of the Jews of Griva took to commerce. As Jews were not allowed to own land, surreptitious partnerships were established with the non-Jews. Land was bought in the name of the Lettish peasant. The Jew paid for seed and maintained the peasant until he sold the produce of his land, which was then equally divided between the two. It can safely be said that it was not the peasant who did the Jew down. The Jews of Griva also traded in timber. There were few productive workers among them. Many of their daughters came to Dvinsk to work as shop assistants. The sons hung on to their parents.

The fortress was situated on the Dvina, near the huge iron bridge. It was built to guard against an attack from Germany, which was regarded a potential enemy. The invader would have to cross the Dvina under heavy fire from the fortress, and their progress could, if necessary, be impeded by the demolition of the bridge.

The fortress was first started towards the end of the sixteenth century. There were a number of additions and technical improvements through the years. The Russian word "kreposht", for fortress, actually means "powerful." And it can be said that the name was justified in the case of Dvinsk fortress, which military experts for a long time considered to be impregnable. The fortress consisted in the main of solid, towering walls, surrounded by ramparts made up of sand-mounds to render the shells of the enemy ineffective. The walls served as emplacements for the cannons. Around the fortress a deep moat had been dug, the flooding of which would halt the attacker. The moat was spanned by four wooden bridges, which could be demolished at short notice. These four bridges led to four heavy iron gates, one on each side of the fortress, and they were constantly guarded by sentries.

Before the First World War the 25th Division, numbering 25,000, was stationed in Dvinsk. It was made up of four regiments of infantry, a brigade of light artillery, and a brigade of heavy artillery. In addition, there were companies of cavalry as well as sappers. A reserve of 5,000 soldiers was stationed just beyond the Petersburg Station. Of the four regiments of infantry, only one—the Ostrovsky, with their black caps—was stationed inside the fortress. The Orievsky Regiment, with their blue caps, were lodged in the buildings owned by Chaim Lurie, opposite the Dubro-vinski Park. The Liflandskee Regiment, distinguished by their flaming red caps, were lodged in barracks owned by Sacha Hurwitz, in the suburb of Gayok. There was not enough room to house the whole regi-ment, and a few companies took up lodgings in quarters owned by Apter. The Ivanogorodski Regiment, with their white caps, were stationed in the suburb of Pletzer, opposite the cemetery.

This does not yet complete the catalogue of military doings around Dvinsk. For during summer a military camp lasting three weeks was held on the Polygon, a huge field less than a mile outside Dvinsk. This camp was made up of artillery drawn from distant towns.

Night and day, cannons roared and belched flame and smoke. Some Jews of Dvinsk wished they could earn from Purim to Pesach the fortune it cost Tsar Nicholas II in wasted shells alone.

The Army filled the town with every species of officer —from the modest ensign to the important-looking general, together with their wives and children, doctors and nurses. The young and hot-blooded officers kept in luxurious comfort their coquettes and chansonettes —women genteel as well as low-living. It was the task of Dvinsk to provide this massive conglomeration of people with provisions, clothes, luxuries and all other requirements. And that is where the Jews came in.

The army gave out all its work to contractors, who were Jews without exception. The huge concentration of soldiers lodged there had to be fed with bread, meat, sour cabbage, barley for porridge, tea, sugar and pork. The horses had to be provided with oats, teff, lucerne and meal. And then there was the army hospital, always full of the ailing and the sick. Not only were the sick of Dvinsk Garrison hospitalised there, but also those of the neighbouring towns.

The contractors Dovid Potash and Bentse Rafaelovitch provided the garments for the soldiers. They employed over 300 Jewish girls and they were still short of workers to cope with the heavy demand. The reason was that the girls preferred to work for less in the tiny rooms of the tailoresss Chaie Dobbe, because of the peace and quiet that reigned there—as against the clothing factories, with their shouting and noise and the stamping feet of soldiers coming there to fit garments.

Four hundred worked in the fortress itself, making boots for the army. There were also sub-contractors, who milled around the big contractors—agents, shop-keepers, brokers, cab-drivers, wagoners, butchers, fish-mongers. They were all on the make. Half the town lived on the garrison.

The fortress grew bigger and bigger with the passage

of the years. Barracks were continually being built to house the growing number of soldiers. And then there were also the dwellings for the officers, stables for horses, clubs, workshops. Construction was going on inside and outside. 200 building workers were constantly on the go inside the fortress. My own father Mordecai Flior was one of the contractors. For 30 years he carried out contracts for glazing and painting inside the fortress. It was a hive of industry. Sand, brick, woodwork, stones, glass and much else was being carted endlessly up and down the avenue leading from the town to the fortress. The Jews earned handsome profits for their active participation in these goings-on. Thieving in the army itself was widespread, and gripped everyone—from the officer of the highest rank to the private soldier. The illegal transactions were mainly conducted in a place called Talkoets, on the outskirts of Dvinsk, on the way to the fortress.

In a town where the soldiers were ubiquitous, robbery and murders were almost unknown. Petty thieving, and mild cases of robbery were, however, not infrequent. The town had every reason to be thankful for this absence of crime to the head of the garrison —a German, a Baron from Dresden, who was friendly with the rich Jews of Dvinsk. The Mayor of Dvinsk was also a German—Viver by name.

Chapter Two

COMMERCE — BIG AND SMALL

Commerce was the soul of Dvinsk. Apart from the army, the factories helped greatly to promote commercial activity. Wholesalers a n d shopkeepers abounded. You encountered them wherever you turned. The warehouses of the wholesalers were brimful of goods. They sold to the shopkeeper, who in turn sold it by the pound and the yard to the mass of the people. There were all kinds and grades of traders—small storekeepers, who traded in provisions mainly, and smaller ones still who, one way or another, displayed their meagre stocks from the tiniest of shops, consisting mainly of an open door onto the street. How they earned a living from these tiny enterprises, is a mystery.

Dvinsk was renowned for its textiles—so much so that they called it, somewhat extravagantly, the Little Lodge and Little Manchester. The wholesalers trading in textile goods were concentrated in two blocks in the centre of the city—Wofsy, Mehring, Slachter, Coblenz, Rabinowitz, Finkelman and fifteen others, all Jews who rode the crest of trade in that part of the world. There were 10 to 15 assistants to help in each of these wholesale houses. Travellers journeyed as far afield as villages and towns 130 miles away, offering their wares. The wholesale merchants formed a combine, and they often purchased all the textile goods turned out in a Moscow factory, which they sold at excessive prices because of their monopolistic manoeuvrings. Other wholesalers traded in hardware, paint, leather, haberdashery, provisions and tobacco. The hardware store of the richest Jew in Dvinsk, Moshe Wittenberg, employed about 50 assistants—all of them long-bearded, middle-aged Jews, with "kapottes". They knew what they were about, and the flow of the profits was steady and unending.

I, myself, was employed in the hardware store of Moshe Yawitz, at the corner of Riga and Vladimir Streets. It was thoroughly up-to-date, carrying a great variety of stocks—ironware, nickel, enamelware —from a needle to a samovar. There were six assistants, apart from myself. I was apprenticed there for three years. In Moshe Yawitz's store I was able to acquaint myself with life and people—all types, shapes of noses, colours of hair. I observed, without being observed. For who, in any event, would take any notice of the youngster who cleaned the floor and emptied the dust-bins ?

Opposite the store was situated the Gastchina Rad. To reach it you had to climb 11 stone steps. And then you found yourself on a spacious platform which was a whole block in length, and covered by a roof. Located there were the biggest haberdashery stores, owned by the brothers Lourie and Kalman Finkelstein; the textile store of Minna Yoffe, a woman who held her own in the fierce competition, and the pharmacies of Astrinsky, and Aronowitz. On the other side was the old Gastchina Rad, where more humble storekeepers, about 20 of them, sold their wares—mostly cloth and haberdashery.

On Alexandernevsky Street, where young men and their girl-friends promenaded in the night, could be found perfumeries and jeweller shops. The mistresses and beloved of the officers knew these establishments very well. Wasbutzky's high-class store employed 30 assistants, smartly-dressed, becoming young girls and personable young men. In the same street was to be found Movsohnson's bottle-store, and Rublevsky's Restaurant, known throughout the whole of Dvinsk for its excellent fare. And round about this time, the first ladies' salon opened up—a sure sign that Dvinsk was on the march. In that whole melee of commercial activity, there were only four Christian store owners to be found. Shatrov's store confined its clientele to non-Jews—barons, officers and a few select from the non-Jewish upper strata. Then there was Kamkoff's huge provision store, and Shevilkoff, who owned a hardware store. But he could not compete with the more nimble and resourceful Jews, and he was forced to sell out. Formakoff had built up a large bottle-store. But he himself was over-fond of the commodity he was selling, and it resulted in his downfall.

Apart from these giant undertakings, the town was studded with stores of the middle-range, who did a big turn-over on credit, more especially with the railway workers and civil servants. Names of defaulters were immediately circulated among the storekeepers and their credit facilities were forthwith terminated. On the whole, these middle storekeepers were able to eke out a tolerable existence.

Let us now descend the scale, and we arrive at the humblest of all commercial entrepreneurs—the small man who opened a door on the street, as the saying had it. Lacking resources, he could offer no credit, but was able to attract the custom of the passersby whose purchases did not exceed more than a few kopkes. The wives were usually in charge of these humble stores, as the men had to seek work elsewhere to supplement their meagre earnings. Girls often helped in these stores for other reasons. For in those parts, one who was at home in commerce could more easily attract a suitor.

In the suburbs and tiny side-streets—wherever a Jew owned a house, and had a daughter—he would take one room of the house, break through a door to the street, build up an approach, and open a store in the name of his daughter. The mother of the home, more often than not, gave a hand—baking bread, and on the Thursday, with the Sabbath approaching, chicken-fries and white bread. The whole day long, the daughter in charge sat at the entrance sewing and knitting to impress the world with her capacities. Others sat there reading, mostly Ozer Blaustein's melodramatic novels, so as to give the impression of being cultivated.

The girl storekeepers near the soldiers' barracks were experts at the game, which had all kinds of shadowy aspects to it. The soldiers made their purchase for cash. Quite often they sold for a bagatelle things they had pilfered from the army stores. Some of the more refined spirits among these girl storekeepers would lament—"One gets up with a soldier, and one goes to bed with a soldier!" They regarded themselves on a higher status than a girl factory worker, and they looked down on them condescendingly. People often wondered what a Jew could be doing in a shop totally bereft of stocks. "I keep my door open, and put my trust in God," was the reply one gave in answer to the question how he made a living.

One of the reasons why Dvinsk became a big commercial town, is that it was an important railway centre. Through its numerous stations roared all day and night trains coming from, and going to the major cities of Western Russia. Merchants came there to buy and sell from as far afield as the regions of Pskov and Vilna. Towns in the neighbourhood such as Resitza, Korsevka, Lutzin, Kreslava, Vishky, Prail, Sebezh were so closely linked commercially with Dvinsk, that they were like the rooms of one big house.

Early Sunday morning the business people who came to buy had already made their appearance in the town. The shop assistants were pulling them importunately to the warehouses and stores. The petty traders who sold to the villages and farms had a keen look in their eyes, as they were about to make their purchases from the wholesalers. The better-off ones owned a fine looking horse and cart, travelling from village to village. They built shelving on their wagons, on which they placed their large variety of wares for the peasant to buy. They not only sold their wares, but also bought farm products from the villagers. Often they resorted to barter when the peasant had no ready cash. And then there were those who tramped on foot from farmhouse to farmhouse. They had a hard life of it. With the aid of a rope they carried on their shoulders their wares in a wooden box, like a soldier carrying his pack. On Monday morning they left for the outlying villages and walked as much as 25 miles. On Thursday, they returned so as to be in time to sell the products they had acquired in the villages, before the Sabbath was upon them.

There was little doing during the summer, when the peasants were busy ploughing, harrowing and sowing, preparing for the coming season. Their farming methods were still antiquated. The wife led the horse, and the man exerted all his strength to drive the plough deeper into the ground. The sons, too, helped all they could. It was work, work, work. And at the end of the day's work he was too exhausted to bother with the Jewish trader. Early the next morning he was up with the crowing of the cock. The soil was fertile and rich in the Dvinsk neighbourhood—dark, good soil that brought forth much produce. Some of the villages came almost right up to the town itself. The fields behind the Esplanade were known for their large crops of potatoes and rye. Beyond Griva and Kalkoen, they specialised in cabbages and cucumbers. Following the example of these peasant farmers, the Jews of Dvinsk took to planting vegetables in the tiny gardens fronting their houses. The peasants were mostly Letts. The land which they tilled belonged to Count Zybert Platov, and stretched about as far as Riga, some 135 miles away. Land was a preserve from which the Jews were excluded, and so they were driven to the towns where their energies went into commerce and manufacturing.

The trains that started out from Libau threaded their way across Lithuania and finally came to a halt at the Kalkoener Station. To reach Dvinsk, the passengers had to cross the Dvina. This they did by ferry-boat, at a cost of one kopek, approximately a farthing. There was a slightly bigger toll if the luggage was heavy. Other passengers would combine and hire a cab to take them across the iron bridge into the town.

Dvinsk was a trading centre that attracted the Jews of Lithuania, who lived on a much lower social and economic level. They would catch the train coming from Libau at Shavel, Ponevezh, Rakeshik and other small places, and Dvinsk was their destination. I have often travelled on this train, and it was quite an experience to see these Litvakes making merry during the journey with plenty of "Lechaims" and also many a "Leshana Habo b'Yerusalaim," as the vodka brought with it an exuberance of spirit. When the sun sank in the far west, and darkness approached, the Jewish passengers foregathered in one carriage and offended the ears of the peasant passengers with a hearty "Maariv".

Quite a number of Jews who lived not more than 30-40 miles from Dvinsk, did not avail themselves of the train—why feed Tsar Nicholas, may he be cursed, with another 50 kopeks! And on top of it, develop dizziness with the train's swaying! Five or six Jews would often hire a wagoner and make for Dvinsk. They rode and they walked. For more often than not, the horse was too emaciated and exhausted to pull up an incline—and he needed some assistance to make headway. It was more like a funeral procession as they pushed the wagon and gesticulated with their hands at every third step. There was much to talk about, and to complain about. It took four times as long as the train journey, but they had plenty of time on their hands. "In any event, the hours do not belong to us—they belong to God."

But don't think that it was all hardship along these roads with their animal-drawn vehicles. Soon a "kretzme" came into view and the spirits picked up.

The horse was given a sack of oats, which was tied round his neck to keep him fully occupied. The Jews entered the "kretzme", ordered drinks and good food, and it was "Layehudim!" This was life, this was "chavershaft". It made the world go round. There was no need to hurry. After one day passed, there were plenty more that the good Lord could draw from the bag. Who wants to grab the whole world in one day, in any case?

These Lithuanian "baalebatim" had come to Dvinsk not only to trade, but for a whole lot of other reasons. Look at them as they get off the trains! There goes one with a three-quarter coat, as well-tailored as you will get it in any city given to fashion. He wears a hat of silk and velvet. He carries a cane with a silver knob. At his side is his daughter, in a long silken dress, holding the train so as not to drag it through the dust of the street. In the other hand she carries a handbag and parasol. And then there is Yankel, at whose side a youngster of 14 is hurrying to keep pace. They are on the way to the Yeshiva, where Yankel will enrol his son and make a great "lamden" of him. Behind them is the trader walking in highly-polished "shtivel", a multi-coloured scarf encircling his neck. They came, all of them, young and old, bearded and clean-shaven. They distributed themselves among the boarding-houses.

When shortly after Pesach the ice began to melt, the rafts could be seen floating down the river, all day and all night. These rafts started out where the Dvina has its source near Smolensk, and they drifted with the current all the way down to Riga. The rafts were made up of logs, fifty feet in length. They were lashed together by rope, one next to the other, till the width was also approximately fifty feet. Those who did the steering built a straw hut on the raft to protect them and their wives, who usually accompanied them, from the elements. They were mostly from the lower strata of society—the uncouth and unkempt from the villages. The Jews called them "kadolnikis". To this day I do not know from where this term derives. In favourable weather it took three weeks for the rafts to reach Riga from Smolensk, a distance of 600 miles. It was a severe physical strain on both the men and women.

You could hardly blame them for anchoring the raft when they came to a big town. They did so by hammering pylons into the ground and tying the rafts to them securely with rope. And you could hardly blame these hardy men, when they headed for the bar to re-energise themselves with strong drink. They usually walked down the streets in groups of ten, with loaves of bread and herring, from which they tore chunks with their teeth. On the way back they carried with them provisions to last them for the next portion of their journey.

The timber merchants, or their assistants, would go by train ahead of the drifting rafts to make sure that they were coming down the river, according to schedule. Quite often it happened that whole rafts were sold illicitly, or were stolen. It required quite a deal of careful supervision to ensure that the rafts reached their destination safely. You may ask how it is possible that something so bulky as a raft could be stolen. The answer is that thieves are ingenious enough to do anything. When the "kadolnik" saw a bottle of brandy, there was nothing for him to do but to drink it. He would drink and sing—"Brothers, let us drink and be merry, for our lives are short, and we are dead a long time." They drank without limit.

The "kadolnikis" went into a stupor with drink, and sank into oblivion. This was the opportune moment for those bent on mischief. They rowed in boats to the raft and cut the ropes anchoring them, so that everything came loose and the logs floated down the river. The thieves moved ahead and drew the floating lumber to the edge of the river with iron hooks. When the "kadolnikis" sobered up, and discovered that their rafts had disappeared, they sent up the agonising cry—"Lord, have mercy on us!"

There were huge pine forests in the neighbourhood of Dvinsk. One of the smaller forests was situated not far from the fortress. Beyond Pletzer was the Tsera-pover Forest. Then there was the Mayak Forest, which later was turned into the Nicolaevski Park. The biggest of them all was the Stropper Forest, where plots were sold for summer residences. The Pogulanki Forest was eight square miles in extent, and was entirely owned by Count Zybert Platov. It was famous throughout the whole of Russia as a holiday resort. The wealthy from all over came there to enjoy their holidays and peace. It was said that a certain juice extracted from the trees had medicinal value. Whether it was good for the ailments of the rich I cannot say definitely, but it was certainly very good for Dvinsk.

Wagon-loads of dairy products and fruit, poultry and vegetables were sent night and day into Pogulanki —anything to tickle the palate of the rich holiday makers. One who owned a hotel in Pogulanki did not have to work more than four months in the year—and he had plenty.

The district had a large water supply. Rivulets beginning in the Tserapover Forest sped along for a short distance and fell into the Dvina. Then there were the Soonia and the Stropper Lakes, which had a plentiful supply of fine fish. When the Dvina flowed, and its waters spread over Griva and Kalkoen, the earth drank the water deeply, and it yielded much fruit.

The very rich of Dvinsk lived in palatial residences. They mostly found themselves around Vladimirska Street, near the Dubrovinski Park. That is where the Mayor of the town lived, and the Commissioner of Police. The General in charge of the garrison also had his residence in that part of the town. And there could be found the wealthiest of the Jews—Wittenberg, Friedland, Gluskin, the family Gurevitch, Rafaelovitch, Potash and the brothers Mizrach, and also the Christian wealthy. The two finest hotels—the Bolshoi and the Central—situated in that part, were patronised by the officers of higher rank and their womenfolk. The houses of the rich possessed every amenity. There was no luxury that was beyond the reach of those who dwelt there.

Those on a lower social rung, the upper middle-class like my employer, Moishe Yawitz, lived in more modest dwellings. His home consisted of three bedrooms and a dining-room. His three daughters occupied one of the bedrooms, and his two sons the other one. As can be seen, there was quite a gap between the very rich and the not so rich. He did not even have a proper bathroom in the house. Most of these smaller merchants had their dwellings on top of their businesses. It was a way of keeping a proper watch on them. They were built of brick, and were double-storeyed.

The smallest of the merchants had to wage a difficult struggle to eke out an existence. The young couples occupied a room in the home of the parents. And they lived in this way, till they saved enough to lease a house of their own. The lowest strata of petty traders, cab-drivers and wagoners made the Esplanade their domain. Their homes were tiny, and often three families lived there. One of the advantages of living on the Esplanade was that it was near to the place where they earned their living. All in all, there was no family in Dvinsk that did not have a roof over its head, despite the not very high level of economic activity in those regions.

I have so far mainly written about the Jews of Dvinsk. But that is not the whole story. For we were only half of the population. Let me now say something about the Christian half of Dvinsk. They polarised themselves into the extremes—those who were clean and

resourceful, and the ne'er-do-wells.   From amongst the
latter, came the criminals and social misfits, who spent
more time in the gaols than in their homes.   These
lumpens lived a twilight existence in the suburbs of
Dvinsk.

On the other hand, there were the steady-going
elements who worked hard and honestly for their
bread—carpenters, joiners, bricklayers, plasterers,
masons, tile-makers, road and bridge builders.   A few
were bootmakers.   They were mostly Russians who
belonged to the Old Believers (Staraveras).   Since the
religion of the Old Believers permitted them to con-
sume alcohol, they indulged with all the necessary zeal.
For all that, they retained a sense of decency and
decorum.   They were fine specimens of manhood—
broad shoulders, fine beards, and the top of their heads
clean-shaven.   They nearly all possessed small dwellings of their own, surrounded with vegetable gardens.
Four or five pigs more often than not lay about the
backyard and made up their other possessions.   The
more prosperous among them even owned a cow.
They all helped the domestic economy.   The wives
looked after the garden and household.   The sons,
seldom given to study, would work side by side with
the fathers.

The Old Believer provided no dowry for his daughter.
But he would give her several dresses and a valuable
home-made fur coat, so that when she made her
appearance to meet a potential suitor at the specially-
prepared celebration, the guests could see her in her
splendid turn-out.

The wedding celebrations of the Old Believers were
of a protracted and complex character.   They centred
around the Christmas festivities.   Seven weeks before
Christmas, the Old Believers commenced a partial fast
as a form of penance.   They were totally forbidden
meat and dairy products, and they subsisted on
potatoes, herring, bread and vegetable oil.   The fast
came to an end with Christmas.   The following seven

weeks was a period of festivity and merriment, known as the "Maslenitza". By day, and right into the early hours of the morning, they abandoned themselves to song and dance, to the accompaniment of balalaikas and concertinas. Every Friday afternoon of these seven weeks, there would foregather suitors dressed in the best fur-coats. They arrived in sledges that were a delight to the eye, drawn by gaily-caparisoned horses. And they would meet the young girls who had come of age, and amenable to a suitor's advances, parading in their velvet and silken dresses that drew all-round admiration. The Gastchina Rad was the matrimonial venue.

Then there were also friends and relatives of these suitors and potential brides, who came from forty miles away and further, to view the spectacle. The Rad became so overcrowded, that spectators over-flowed into the Vladimir and Riga streets, and cab-drivers had to make a detour to be able to reach their destination. When a suitor chose his bride, he would take her into his sledge and drive her to an open-air celebration of dancing and feasting. At these goings-on tens and hundreds plighted their troth in marriage. They rejoiced till late into the night, and then departed for their homes. In this way they were observing the marriage injunctions of the Old Believers.

The Jews got on well with the Old Believers. They gave them plenty of credit, and there were no disputes or quarrels. But there was a group among the Old Believers known as "Chazernikes", trading mostly in pigs, who were hostile to the Jews. And they were all too ready to join in any manifestation against the Jews, even to the extent of a pogrom.

It was not easy to distinguish the Poles from the Russians. When in the open, they spoke Russian. But in their massive church, which was situated in Riga Street, they offered up their prayers in their own lan-guage. The Poles in Dvinsk felt a sense of guilt, which they tried to relieve with prayer, because this soil on which they were standing had been lost by Poland to Catherine the Great.

The Poles were mainly of the proletariat, employed in industry—in the factories of Grilechis and Mizrach; and in the building industry and other undertakings that called for physical strength.

The other Russians (Provoslavni), that is, those who were not Staraveras, were haughty in manner, belonging as they did to the ruling race. They were the white-collar brigade, occupying the most important positions in the civil service and the financial world. A large number were employed in the railway depot.

Very little was heard of the Germans. All that was known of them was that their church was half-full for Sunday morning prayer. The Letts were mainly engaged in agricultural pursuits. They were most prominent on the market-place. There were some amongst them who owned a fair amount of land; the poorer Letts became their tenants. These Letts spoke mostly Russian when they visited the town.

Chapter Three

BEGGARS' OPERA

Autumn. The townspeople are returning from their summer holiday recess. Rosh Hashanah is approaching. The Jews are examining their outfits—if they are sufficiently new and becoming for the importance of the occasion. The extra farmhands are on the way to the fields to help with the reaping and the gathering of the harvest. On the first day of Ellul, the Shofar that has been laid aside since the last Yom Kippur is tried out by the Baal Kriah. The Psalm Ledovid Uri is read in the synagogue. In the outlying areas, the Jews are getting ready to make their purchases in Dvinsk for the Holy Days.

On Sunday morning, when the worshippers were in the churches, the shops were all closed. The massive church stood out majestically in the Old Park. In front of the church was the huge square, where the military and the fire-brigade held parades. The splendid edifice in Riga Street that was the Polish Church, was an echo of an age that had passed. The church bells pealed away incessantly, the priests chanted their prayers, and the young shop assistants were on edge, twirling their keys in their eagerness to open the stores as soon as the church services were over. Clandestine sales have been going on all the time. But the shop owner has his eye on the street, ready to throw the doors wide open for the purchasers to enter en masse.

The Sunday services generally concluded about noon. But it all depended on the extent of the supplications one had to offer up to the Lord on high. As with us Jews, there were times of the year when services were more protracted. There were Sundays when the priests, overcome by zeal, carried Icons as they led a procession round the church, blessing the soil. It would irk the Jewish merchants no end to lose a whole hour of trade. When the religious fervour had subsided, the shop assistants removed the iron bars from the doors and windows, the shutters were taken down, and the customers came in droves to make their purchases. The religious pall had lifted from Dvinsk, and brisk commercial activity followed.

The countless number of doors I, myself, have opened in that time! And the number of shutters I have removed! In the six months before I had become apprenticed to Yawitz, I had changed jobs twice. There we sold tools to workmen, samovars to the peasants, pots and pans to women. There was plenty doing in the way of trade, but there was some undercurrent drawing the mass of buyers towards Talkoets. Why? Let me tell you something about Talkoets.

I do not know to this day where the name originated. It was a kind of Petticoat Lane, where anything and everything was bought and sold—old clothing not much better than rags, worn-out boots, broken furniture, chipped and cracked plates and cutlery. In a word, all the debris discarded from the homes of the wealthy found its way to the Talkoets market-place. There was no fixed price or value. Nearly every offer was accepted—and there could be no regrets or claims on the part of the purchaser. Tiny rooms opening out onto the streets were dignified by the name of store. Their stocks consisted of small quantities of cloth and haberdashery.

But most of the transactions were effected in the spacious closed-in courtyard, which could hold a much larger number. At various points in this courtyard sat bootmakers repairing boots and goloshes, and pairing up a diversity of single shoes looking for mates. Then there were Jews seated at machines, patching up the trousers of the soldiers. As one tailor pressed a pair of trousers, he addressed the waiting soldier with—

"Look—it's like new!" In another corner is the Jewish carpenter Mordecai, his spectacles affixed to his ears with wire and string. He is busy mending the leg of a bed. He first hammers, and then spreads out the putty over the crack. Other Jews are standing nearby, advising him how to go about things. Every trades-man can be found there—cap-makers, locksmiths, tin-smiths. They are busy sandpapering, planing, sawing. Keys are fitted into locks. And above this febrile activity, there issues the cry from a peasant—"Lord help me, I've been robbed!"

There was no need to be envious of the traders of Talkoets. The main profit was derived from their illicit transactions—"linke schaires", as the Jews knew it. There were even some extremists who had taken a vow not to handle anything that was not illicit. Most of their stocks came from the fortress. It was said that they would have bought a naked General, provided he was stolen. Everybody knew them. Among them were a number who had prospered and bought a seat of honour in the synagogue.

From time to time, the police chief Yermolovitch, accompanied by his assistant, Yurke, paid a formal visit to Talkoets and he reported back to his superiors that everything was in a perfect state of order. The Jews of Talkoets spoke in the highest terms of Yermolovitch, for it was generally known that he had "taking ways", and that he would not prove bothersome.

The first eminent figure you were bound to encounter when visiting Talkoets was Itzke Katarinschik, on whose hurdy-gurdy stood a bird. His favourite song was—"Defke vles ja Zanei"—"Maids in the forest—I in pursuit of them." The peasants who have bunched round him all agreed that he is a wonderful musician. Kopkes are thrown at him from every direction. Itzke is very versatile. Not only is he a musician, but he is also a clairvoyant who for five kopeks can foretell the future. And who is there that would not like to know what lies ahead in a world so full of uncertainty. The

five kopkes are passed to him. He turns the handle of
the hurdy-gurdy, and the little bird pulls out a card on
which can be read what the future foretells. The peasant studies the card very closely, and moves hurriedly
away without disclosing its contents to his friends.

Not far from Itzke, stood Elke Zigan on a box." Red,
you win—Black, you lose!" he keeps calling out, holding a deck of cards in his hand which he endlessly
shuffles. The peasants around him eye him quizzically.
One of them with a confident look in his eye, who is
Elke's stooge, comes up and stakes half-a-rouble on a
card. Elke turns up the card. It is red. A smile
spreads over the face of the peasant. "Turn up one for
a rouble," he calls out. The red card that shows
up again brings delight to the peasant. The onlookers
are agog at the ease with which money can be won.
They draw their hard-earned roubles from their
pockets. Elke's pockets are soon bulging with notes
and silver. The peasants draw on their last resources
in a vain effort to recoup themselves.

At another strategic point, Hirschke Kadoolnik has
taken up his position. He, too, has a deck of cards in
his hand. His finger-ends are capped with thimbles
to reassure the peasants that there is no possibility of
any fraudulent manipulation of the cards. Hirschke's
reputation is not good. The peasants are staring at
Hirschke as if mesmerised. This is the moment Yocke
Zigan, brother of Elke, and Shainke with the Golden
Hands have been waiting for. They weave in and out
of the crowd of peasants, and with deft fingers extract
a purse, a watch, or a rouble note, from the pockets.
Some youngsters, employed by Yocke and Shainke, are
also on the prowl, and they reap their share of loot from
the unwary peasants.

A cry pierces the air: "Thieves! I've been robbed!"
"Who's been robbed?" asks Hirschke. "Thieves!
Thieves!" the peasant repeats, even more loudly. But
there is nothing to be done about it. Yocke, Shainke,
and the rest have as if disappeared from the face of the

earth. Suspicion spreads throughout the crowd. Loud altercations are followed by fisticuffs. A policeman suddenly appears on the scene, and orders everyone to disperse in the name of the Tsar.

By two o'clock the trading and bargaining reaches a climax. Voices are raised, gesticulations are more emphatic. J e w i s h traders are carrying several pairs of highly-polished "shtivel", slung over their shoulders. Others have hoisted jackets high on a wooden stick. Anything and everything is on offer. Purchases and exchanges are effected at a more feverish pace. One peasant is trying on a pair of "shtivel". He pats them with his hand and asks the little Jew Berl —"How much?" "12 rouble, 15 kopecks," Berl says. "4 roubles," the peasant offers. "He's a buyer!" Berl mumbles to himself in Hebrew. And then the hard bargaining commences, accompanied by gesticulations and pleadings. Finally, the peasant agrees on five roubles cash, and one rouble on credit to be paid within a week. The Jew blesses him that he should wear them in good health.

"Do you really think he's going to pay you the rouble?" Berl's friend, watching the proceedings, asks.

"That's the last of my worries," answers Berl. "He'll have the satisfaction of boasting that he's cheated a Jew—and may the good God send me ten more such customers every day."

At another spot, a peasant complains bitterly to a Jewish trader that he has sold him a samovar without a tap.

"Stupid, what am I going to do with a tap—without a samovar?" The Jew tries to pacify him. Words are exchanged, then threats, followed by wild curses. A policeman is on the spot as if from nowhere. The peasant is persuaded to hand over two more roubles, in return for another tap, and he calms down. He pulls two roubles from his pocket, and the Jew hands him a tap which he has taken from another of his samovars. They wish each other good fortune and long life. Everyone is happy—and the Jew is two roubles to the good.

The sun is now setting. The trading tempo has slackened, and the peasants are departing for their homes. Another Sunday of trading at Talkoets has come to an end.

The Jews from the villages are steadily arriving in Dvinsk with horse and cart and wagons. Each village had its own favourite lodging-house. There was a special lodging-house for the Rakishker, Ponodeller, Preiler, Nova-Alexandrovsker, and many others.

The lodging-house was generally owned by a religious Jew. A "yarmulke" sits on his head, and his woollen "Arbe Kanfoth" is visible from his open "zoopitse". His wife, plump and heavy-bosomed, is wearing a grey apron and a handkerchief over her head. She welcomes the guests effusively. "My guests, my very good guests," she fawns. "A whole summer has passed, and I have not set eyes on you." And then after eyeing the young girl the village trader has brought with him— "Is this your daughter, Reb Chaim Rafoel? Why, what a beauty—like a princess. Leave her over with us, and we'll find her a worthy and handsome suitor in no time."

Reb Chaim Rafoel smiles to express his pleasure. "Do you really know of a suitor of means and standing? Let me hear more—I'm ready to conclude a bargain if the right one comes along. But remember—no poor workman for my daughter. Good family background counts most with me—and I'm ready to pay the price for value."

After they had brought their wares into the lodging-house, they were offered a hot glass of tea. They drank it with zest, smacking their lips sweetened by the loaf-sugar they keep sucking noisily. And then they hurried off to the Beth Hamedrash for morning prayers. When they returned they found some people waiting for them. There were the Yeshiva Bocherim who wanted to hear news of their families. There might also be regards and, who knows, perhaps a little cheese or some other delicacy from mother to tickle the palate. The young girls who had left their villages to come and work in Dvinsk, are there to ask a friend to take back a few roubles to their families. The traders were all the time plying their goods with fervour. There was no time to waste.

And then there suddenly makes his appearance the celebrated "shadchen" Naphthali, who has matched up a record number of Jewish couples in his day. His beard is a bright red, and on his head sits a formidable bowler-hat. His kaftan just fails to close about his portly stomach. Rain or sunshine—he is carrying his umbrella. For the umbrella to a "shadchen" is what the reed-pipe is to the shepherd. The trader is conscious of the importance of the moment, and behaves accordingly. He conducts the "shadchen" into a private room, where a full discussion can be held under four eyes. Herring and "kichel" and a bottle of vodka are brought in to help establish a warm atmosphere. The door is locked, and the discussion goes forward in meaningful whispers. When they conclude, and are about to take leave of each other, the trader urges the "shadchen" to explore more fully the lie of the land from the relations. Boys from poor homes have assembled outside the lodging-houses, in the hope of earning a few kopkes by carrying loads of skins and other goods to the fur merchant Zilberman.

While waiting for the midday-meal to be served up, they sat around the room and talked garrulously about various happenings of the day. The mistress of the house waxed eloquent in praise of her dishes. The food is brought as they seat themselves around the table. "Do you see this fish?" she asks, pointing to a plate. "They were so lively when I bought them that they jumped from my hands. They come from your Lake Salokki."

"I wonder," says one of the traders, "if the fish told you anything about the "yarmulke" I lost when I was bathing in Lake Salokki a fortnight ago." One "lechaim" follows another. And then they regale themselves with fish, brawn and a portion of beef. Grace is said. With some considerable difficulty they raise themselves from the table, and take to their beds for an afternoon siesta—until it is time for Mincha.

The young girls, who have come with their fathers from the villages, have decked themselves out in their very best and are presenting themselves for approval to the mistress of the lodging-house. They put all kinds of questions to her: Are their dresses fashionable? What are they wearing in Dvinsk? And much else. And if the mistress expressed satisfaction, the girls would make for the town for the world to behold them.

As the Holy Festivals approached there was a great deal more congestion in the lodging-houses, mainly from the religious ones. They came to buy "lulovim" and "esrogim"; "shochtim" bought new "chalofim"; the young ones bought colourful materials, and came to terms with tailors and tailoresses to make them into suits and dresses according to the latest fashions. Women came from the village to seek interviews with the Gaon, Reb Meir Simcha. They wanted their dreams interpreted by him, and that he should bless them—or even just gaze upon his divine countenance.

And they also came to visit the graves of parents who had passed on. Children were brought to the doctors to have their ailments attended to. And youths who were about to be called up for military service, visited the doctors to have some physical ailment, such as a hernia, artificially inflicted on them so as to get exemption from military service. Ageing girls and women, widowed or divorced, came carrying a cushion, a blanket, and a couple of dresses—offering themselves as domestic servants. With the approaching Holy Days, work was plentiful. They were mostly from the

Lithuanian villages, for the girls from Dvinsk preferred working in a factory to domestic service.

On Thursdays, with the Sabbath approaching and goodwill beginning to warm the hearts of every Jew, the shnorrers of Dvinsk made the most of their opportunity. If Mendele Mocher Shforim had been in Dvinsk on Thursday afternoons, his celebrated work, "Fishke der Kroomer", would have been a much more voluminous study than it turned out to be. Bands of beggars, in every state of degradation, crowded round the doors of the shops beseeching the owners to let them have a "ndove" for the Sabbath. The leader of one group of these mendicants was an old Jew in tatters, carrying a staff in his hand. He was followed by a dozen women, the epitome of Jewish poverty. Some carried sucklings in their arms to emphasise their dire need. Behind them followed children a little older, who were getting to know the ropes of this ancient profession. The merchants in their shops, and their wives at home, were anticipating their arrival, and had prepared for it by changing a rouble into kopkes, which were distributed among this procession of the destitute. There was no question of refusing them an alm. For they reacted with an endless spate of curses, the savage character of which soon made the hardest hearted yield. These groups and bands of mendicants swept up and down the town. There were the individualists amongst them who preferred to operate on their own, or at most in pairs. They may have belonged to the social debris, but they were not lacking in ingenuity. Many a beggar would exchange his rags, and sally forth for a second round in his new guise. It was not often that he was apprehended, so resourceful were they in the manipulation of their rags to establish a new personality. And there were also the truculent ones amongst them. When an assistant was deputed to give them a kopke and see them on their way, it often happened that they complained to the owner at the insult to which they had been subjected by the meagreness of the alm. If the owner was in a good mood, he would restore their "amour propre" with two more kopkes.

There were also a number of enterprising among them, who had secretly amassed quite a handsome reserve. Take Chana die Koole: One day she lost her Siddur near the Planover Minyan. She raised a shattering hue and cry, the agony of which disconcerted everyone. The explanation was soon forthcoming. When the Siddur was picked up, it was found that there were five crackling 100 rouble notes hidden inside a slit made in the covers.

Chapter Four

THE MARKETS

Not all people enjoy the same standard of living, or eat food of the same quality. The rich man eats roast duck—the poor man has to make do with a sheep's head. Still, everyone must eat. Dvinsk did not have to bring its agricultural products from the Ukraine, the granary of Russia. The soil of the district was fertile and brought forth plentifully. Poultry, beef, and fish from the lakes were readily available. The peasants brought their produce to market in a steady flow of wagons and carts.

Let me now recall personal painful memories of the market-place. Every Friday, it was one of my duties to take two baskets and a sack and accompany my employer's wife, Madame Lapinski, to the market. Lapinski was my employer before I went over to Yawitz. You may ask how it was that I, a learned youth apprenticed to become an assistant, and with a career as a merchant ahead of me, could have been called upon to do such menial work as to drag myself from one market to another, with baskets and sack in hand. The answer is that I had absconded from my first employer, Yaacov Sosin. This brought sorrow to my mother, as it meant the loss of the commission she had paid to the agent for securing employment for me. It followed that I had to submit to every indignity in my second place of employment. I scrubbed the floors of the store, made the fire in the stove, poured paraffin into the lamps. All that I took in my stride. But when Madame Lapinski ordered me about wilfully, I resented it. I had to assist her maid with domestic work, carry the poultry to the "Shochet". And I was assigned every out of the way errand. On Friday mornings she would greet me with—"Late again, eh!"—even when I was well on time. And then I followed behind her as we wended our way from market-place to market-place, a sense of degradation eating into me.

The market-places stretched over an immense area. Even on a cold and frosty morning, the peasants used to arrive very early so as to be able to take up their positions at the most advantageous points. By 5 o'clock in the morning they had already come in large numbers and were busy preparing for the day. They stacked their wares neatly in the wagon and awaited the arrival of the purchasers. They did not have to wait long.

The Jews were all agog at the prospect of trade. They were soon weaving their way through to the wagons, blowing into a fowl's behind, tasting a pat of butter. These were known as the "perekupstchiki"— go-betweens. They bargained and gesticulated no end —went away to frighten the peasant into submission, and returned to effect a deal when it was sufficiently keen. And then the women would make their appearance. They were known as "genzlerkes". They purchased poultry and dairy products with a view to reselling. They not only bargained with the peasant, but vented curses on him when he proved obdurate— "To charge such prices for poultry that cost him nothing to feed!" was a cry that was often heard from these "genzlerkes".

By ten o'clock the market was packed to capacity. They were all milling around each other—peasants, middlemen, housewives. A youth is dragging a sack-full of goods, another an earthen potfull of beans. The Friday is never long enough for the housewife. The purchases have to be made in good time for the Sabbath, the cooking has to be done. Even so, they let time pass, bargaining till they themselves are exhausted, and the peasant with them.

The unemployed of the town were frequenters of the market-place. What point was there to sit and mope at home over their misfortune! At the market-place there was plenty doing. They did not come to buy—needed nothing—and had nothing with which to buy. One of them is coming along with a walking-stick in his hand, picks a straw from a wagon and places it between his teeth to test it. He casts a glance in the direction of someone he has recognized. There is plenty to talk about with a friend. He is envious of the brute peasant, who sits on his wagon like a lord and keeps raking in the money.

The Christian women did not go to the market the way the Jewish women went. They were living in the suburbs, had their own small gardens, and bred poultry for their own use. Others had connections with the villages through friends and relatives, and so were able to obtain farm products direct. As for the working-classes, they had not the cash to buy on the market. They depended on credit, which they obtained from the small shopkeeper.

There were Jews who in the early hours of the morning drove out along the road to meet the peasants bringing their goods to market. They would buy a calf, bundles of flax, and pig skins. The Jew would bring the peasant into his house and regale him with food and vodka. Most of the traders lived on the outskirts of Dvinsk, in the suburbs of Gayok, Pletzer and Griva. The market would not have been the same without Itzke Katarinschik, and his musical fare was always a great attraction for the peasants. Very popular was his song—

> The presents that I have given away,
> Are not so precious
> As the ruby lips I have kissed.

The hearts of the peasants melted as they listened to these songs of love and romance, which Itzke rendered very feelingly, accompanied by his hurdy-gurdy. Elke Zigan was also there with his table and pack of cards.

His brother Yocke and Shainke with the Golden Hands are on the prowl for a victim. Hirschke One-Eye whispers into the ear of a peasant. The peasant follows him into Chanke's house, where the shutters are closed for very good reason. By noon, sales have been completed and the peasants begin to disperse. Within half-an-hour there appear the convicts from the Dvinsk gaol, escorted by green-hatted soldiers. They climb down from their wagons, and with brooms and spades proceed to clear the market-place of all refuse and debris.

The fish and vegetable market was on the outskirts of Dvinsk, near the Esplanade. The Municipality had seen to it that the obscene curses and shouts inseparable from a fish-market should not besmirch the town proper. To reach the fish-market you had to pass through a huge gate. The women bought the fish at the market, and their husbands greatly enjoyed the dishes they made for them. For what is there more congenial in this world than to sit comfortably at your table, partaking of a Sabbath repast of beautifully prepared fish, singing a song of praise to the Lord on high who has provided fish, meat, and a plum-pudding. The love that the Jew has for good food is legendary. Did they not reject as unpalatable the honey cakes made from the manna, recalling their days in Egypt when their flesh-pots were full and fish was plentiful? No wonder the women took the greatest care when preparing their fish for the Sabbath.

As you passed through the gate leading to the fish-market, you had to run the gauntlet between two lines of beggars—women and children with their hands out-stretched; a blind Jew scraping out a tune on his fiddle, and singing a doleful melody about the Kishinev Pogrom to tear at your heart-strings; and still more hands outstretched. Hands! hands! hands! It is not easy to pass them by, however hardhearted you may be.

If the Good Lord has sent enough money to buy fish for the Sabbath, he will also send the extra kopke for the needy beggar. Along the line you encounter a pale-faced, haggard woman. She holds a wrapped-up child in her arms, and with heartrending cries begs an alm for a poor, tiny orphan. "Orphan be damned!" calls out another beggar. "It's a log of wood—not an orphan. Be damned to her for her lies. She's disgracing us!" Curses and shouts are hurled at each other. And if you will investigate more closely, you will find that the blind can see, the dumb can speak, and the lame can walk.

The floor of the fish-market was of cement, and was constantly being flushed with water to keep it clean. The roof was mounted on concrete pillars. The men and women wore high boots and aprons to which the scales of the fish clung. The fish were packed high in huge wooden boxes, which you reached by passing through a narrow passage. "Buy fresh fish for the Sabbath!" was the cry that met you. There were all kinds of fish on display—the expensive pikes for the rich; and for the poor tiny little mud-fish known as smelts, which were so smelly that they had to be cooked or made into paste. And there were also the in-between breams and carps for the middle-range. You could tell the social category of the customers by the fish which they bought.

You can't fool a Jewish woman with fish. She opens the ear of the fish, and if she sees a stain of yellow she'll throw it back into the box. "What are you fiddling about with, you lousy bitch?" the fishmonger spits out at her. And if she answers that the fish is stale, the fishmonger really lets go. "Have you come here to buy? Admit it, you've come to steal. Can't I see it? Be off with yourself, you slut." The woman customer is taken aback at the verbal assault unleashed, and she hastily moves on. But by next Friday she has forgotten all about it, and the chances are that she will again be examining the fish at the same stall.

Of all the fishmongers only two or three were not degraded and vulgarised by their calling. These had their regular clients among the well-to-do, and they delivered the orders to their homes. Fishmongers were noted as heavy drinkers, and every now and again they would betake themselves to Chaike Tanz's pub. At midday the market used to empty out. The best fish had already been disposed of. The poorer clients waited for this moment to buy up the fragments and left-overs, for the fishmonger, who had no ice-boxes to keep the fish wholesome over the Saturday, had to get rid of all his stock. Poor quality fish and left-overs were also sold in bulk to the pubs and lodging-houses, where the mistress could boast that the fish she had bought were so fresh and lively that they kept leaping from her hands.

Adjacent to the fish-market was the vegetable market. Old and middle-aged women, known as market-women, were the owners of stands. Their vegetables were stacked in wooden boxes, and their total stock was not more than two roubles in value. How they eked out an existence is a puzzle to me to this day. The boxes stood under the blue sky, and in winter they shivered in the bitter cold. They would sit there, clad in cast-off men's coats, with a charcoal fire to warm themselves. They were also known as "bool-besitzerkes", and they had to pay a rental. If they defaulted, a policeman came and took away a sack of potatoes to the police station in lieu of the rent, brushing aside the woman running after him to try and recover it. The man who owned the market and collected the rent did not know the meaning of pity, and he was nicknamed the "Malchamovves."

The women would call out at the approach of a customer: "Sour or sweet cabbage, your ladyship! Frozen apples, dear good one!" But they were also capable of a change of mood, and then they could curse better than any fishmonger. "Boolbesitzerke" became a word with which to call a woman of ill-repute. As was the case with the fish, the remnants of the vegetables were sold in bulk to the pubs and the lodging houses.

The meat-market, unlike the main market-place, was situated right in the heart of the town. The butcher-shops making up the market were built around a square. Some of the doors opened onto the street, and others onto the courtyard. The butcher, or his wife assisting him, wore white overalls which were smeared over with dried-out blood. Their high boots were soiled with blood and feathers. Among the butchers there were some powerfully built Jews. They could take a drink, but there were few drunkards amongst them. On the whole, they were a well-ordered body of men. They had their regular customers, and were fairly free with credit. There were few among them who did not make a living.

The butcher-shops were crowded out on Friday mornings. Friends and neighbours, having made their purchases, would examine each other's baskets to see what kind of bargains had been effected, and pronounce their views like experts. Women from as far away as Altstadt used to do their shopping at the meat-market. As a rule, everything was conducted in an orderly fashion.

If a horse could have spoken, he would have wanted to know why the horse-market was stuck away beyond Talkoets and beyond the boundary of the town ; why the market-place was not cleaned up by the convicts the way they cleaned up the ordinary market-place under an escort of soldiers; and also why all the rubbish of the town was dumped onto the horse-market. And then again, the horse would have wanted to know why, for no reason at all, they whipped him across the buttocks. Looking him in the teeth was reasonable enough, or to groom him down once in a while—but why this random whipping across the buttocks ?

The horse-market was at its busiest in autumn and winter, for during these two seasons the horses did little work on the farms. A peasant found it to his benefit to sell the horse during this slack period on the land, and then buy him back when spring came round again. In this way, he would save on the horse's food. They came to the market-place when the morning was well underway. The first to arrive were the "borisnikes". The "borisnik" was the expert on horses, and the go-between in the sales effected. In addition to the commission he received, he was treated to a bottle of liquor known as "boris". That is how the word "borisnik" was derived. I cannot vouch for the accuracy of it, but the "borisnik" Yona had assured me that it was so.

The "borisnikes" were a mixed lot of horsetraders, horsethieves and some gypsies. Until they were caught, there was no reason to be ashamed of being in their company. They were a healthy, powerfully-built body of men. Some came from the villages in the neighbourhood of Dvinsk either by train or sledge. On the way to market, they stopped at more than one inn to offer up a blessing, glass in hand. They also knew how to put away a good meal. Eventually, they would make their entry into the market-place, carrying a whip in their hand, and they took delight in whipping the horses across the buttocks. As the horse reared, they opened his mouth and examined his teeth. And then they looked round for buyers. Without a "borisnik" as an intermediary, it was very difficult to buy a horse. There were about twenty of them in Dvinsk, and came mostly from a few families. Notable amongst them were the three Petruk brothers and their old father, Simon. But more often than not, one of the brothers did not make his appearance for the reason that he had been arrested for horse-stealing and lodged in the Dvinsk jail.

Even at the age of 70, Simon was most ingenious in his handling of horses. For instance, he knew how to groom a horse, and to do much else in the way of changing his colour and his looks, so that not even the owner would recognise him. Give him a horse as black as night, and under his expert treatment he would develop white patches on his body. The black hair of the mane and the tail would likewise turn a most natural grey. Even the teeth took on a different shape and lustre. As one wag had it—Simon owned a beauty parlour for the smartening up of the horse's looks. More often than not, these horses treated by Simon were brought clandestinely to him in the dead of night.

The "borisnikes" used to say of the brothers Petruk that they had a genius for picking the most intricate lock of a stable in which a horse was to be found. There were others among the "borisnikes"—the Pozoimer, Spoongans, Kadaliskes — who tried to emulate the Petruks in the art of acquiring horses in unusual circumstances, which the law frowned upon. But all were agreed that the Petruks stood head and shoulders above them.

By ten o'clock, horses by the hundred had been brought to the market-place from outlying parts— townlets, villages, farms. The cab-drivers and wagoners were milling round them, feeling them, inspecting them. There were also agents from Germany who had come a long way to make a deal, and the hired buyers of the big horse-traders—Sholem Behr Kourland and Moishe Wofsi. There was much back-slapping and hearty drinking of toasts. Everything was right in this world of buying and selling. And amongst those milling around, scrutinising closely every animal, were the peasants and Jews who were looking for those horses that had been stolen from them. But their luck was usually out. Horsethieving had been raised to a fine art in this part of the world.

The gypsies were the most expert in assessing the value of a horse—and they were also acknowledged as the finest horsethieves. Accompanying them, were their children and wives who were expert in the art of fortune-telling with a pack of cards. The children were trained in the gentle art of picking pockets.

The feverish trading continued for something like five hours.   And when it had subsided, the "borisnikes" betook themselves to the saloons, where they indulged heavily in "boris", the name by which vodka was known to them.

Chapter Five

DIE VOLKMENSCHEN

The horse played a notable part around Dvinsk. There were any number of people who extracted a livelihood from the horse. At the Gastchina Rad, at almost any time of the day, you could see about fifty middle-aged Jews, their clothes in rags and tatters. They were covered in flour, dirtied with tar, and they smelt of kerosene. These were the wagoners who owned powerfully-built horses, and wagons which were known as "drongas". The flat bottom of the "dronga" was made of a number of wide planks on which could be placed large loads of goods. It often happened that the loads were so heavy that the horse could not pull up an incline or a hill. The wagoner would dismount, and with his powerful shoulder help the horse along. It was customary for a passer-by to lend a helping hand. It was not exceptional for one single wagon to be loaded with one hundred bags of salt, each weighing two hundred pounds.

It was not always that the wagoner had a wagon-load of goods to take to some place. And then he would stand there, with his arms folded and a doleful look on his face, waiting for something to turn up from a warehouse. It was not unusual for the wagoner, his family and the animal to do without food. For it often happened that he set off in the morning with nothing in his pocket, and returned home in the evening with exactly the same amount in his pocket. On these sorrowful days, he would curse his fate. But on days when there was more doing, he would nip over to Chaike Tanz, toss down a glass of vodka, and dispose of a herring. When the wagoner grew old and could no longer labour, he would betake himself to the synagogue and become a Tehillim Yid—that is, throw himself on the bene-

volence of the community. Here were the same
characters that abounded in the pages of Zalman
Schneour's "Noah Pandra". For one reason or
another, the Jews totally monopolised the wagoner's
trade.

The carriers, who dragged heavy loads on their backs,
found it even harder to make ends meet. Thirty of
them, all Jews, would congregate near the wagoners.
They ranged from youths of twenty to the aged of about
sixty. It is true that the wagoner's lot was not an easy
one. But once he was on his wagon, and the road was
level, he was like a king as the horse drew the wagon-
load towards its destination. But the carrier had to tie
a sack or box to his back with a rope, and with twisted
body would deliver the load to the customer. He
would strain himself to the limit in order to earn twenty
kopkes from the small storekeeper who mainly
employed them.

The more prosperous among them equipped themselves with a barrow, which they would load with
something like six sacks of goods, inspan themselves
in the barrow, and drag it along. Jews are well-
known for their compassion, and when they saw one
of these carriers pulling his load up an incline, they
would invariably give him a hand. When the Sabbath
brought a day of rest, the older ones used to
spend the day reciting psalms in the synagogue, while
the younger ones slept all day to recuperate their
strength for the coming week. Quite a number of
them, despairing of ever making ends meet, drifted
into the underworld.

The third category I propose to deal with are the cab-
drivers. There were Jews and Christians in this particular calling, and they were also sub-divided into those
who operated by day, and those who operated by night.
Later in life, when I lived in big Russian cities, I noticed
that there were two classes of cab-drivers—"vankas"
and "lihachis".

The "vanka" was an old peasant who owned a horse

with one foot in the grave. His cab or sledge showed a number on a glossy tin-plate, but everything else about it was old and decrepit. The "lihach", on the other hand, was a vigorous looking Christian youth who wore a blue coat and red girdle, and red braid bordered his sleeve-ends and pockets. Their "shtivel" shone with their high polish, and their peaked caps gave them a swaggering look. Their horses, too, were in the pink of condition, well-groomed and well-shod. The harness and everything about them sparkled.

In Dvinsk, the Jewish cab-drivers resembled the "vankas" in their lowly status. They were old, bearded Jews. And their horses were so limp and listless, that they could have been inspanned into the cart of "Tevya der Milchiker". They lived at Pletzer, where they hired a cheap hovel for themselves, and a stable about to collapse for their horse. Droning away in their high seats, they would wait for the train to come in and hope to obtain a fare. And when the train departed, they would spread themselves through the main trading centre of the town. Competition among the cab-drivers was keen. The call "isvoschik" drew them in a rush to the prospective client. The cab-driver, like the wagoner, had his position, which he would take up and cling to so that his regular clientele knew where to find him when they wanted him. They had to fight hard not to fall below the bread-line. Those who had built up a regular clientele were even able to save a few kopeks.

After eight o'clock in the evening, many of the Dvinsker betook themselves to the lurid part of the town, with its plenty of goings-on. The night cab-drivers were the true "lihachi". They started out shortly after eight, and took up their positions at the railway stations, hotels, officers' clubs, but mostly on Podoloski Avenue where the leading brothels of the town were located. Their clients were made up of those who were spending an evening on the rampage. Two lovers would hire a cab for as long as an hour to

drive in exhilaration about the town. Many were
taken to a destination of vice. And they also took
parties to theatres and dance halls. All paid well for
service. There was no change from a rouble. What
the cab-driver desired above all, was a rich drunk client
who would soon fall into a deep sleep with the swaying
of the cab. That was the time when he rifled his
pockets, left him at the roadside, and drove off as
quickly as he could. When the passenger awoke in the
early hours of the morning, he crossed himself and
thanked the good Lord that nothing worse had befallen
him. He was sensible about it all. But the fool made
for the police station, where they promised him to detect
the thief— an unkept promise.

The last category of wagoners were the "kayetchniks"
—that is, those who conveyed sand, stones and bricks
for the building trade. They were made up of four
families. They must have regarded themselves as a
kind of aristocracy, for they intermarried and allowed
no interlopers into their closed family circle. Actually,
they were of the lowest order of humans who belonged
to the underworld. They earned a fair living in summer, but in winter the women earned a living for the
men in less reputable ways. They lived on the Peshki,
the lowest part of the town built on the sands.

The restaurants were not allowed to sell liquor, for
the Government had a complete monopoly of the
liquor trade. If the Government had got to know how
much liquor was really being sold in Jewish-owned
restaurants, they would no doubt have handed the
monopoly over to the Jews, for it corresponded more
to the situation as it existed. But the Police Chief was
not worried about the doings of these liquor-selling
restaurants, for reasons that were all too obvious, and
it was assumed that everything was kosher on the
liquor front.

There were dozens of such liquor-selling restaurants

in Dvinsk, but I was acquainted with only a few. Very prominent was the one known as Chaike Tanz, which I have already mentioned. To this day I do not know how it came to its name. But it was not as disreputable as the name sounded. For Chaike Tanz was actually a respectable middle-aged woman who had married Mendel der Melamed. It was situated near the market Talkoets. It was not one of the high-class restaurants. Apart from liquor, one could get there the more coarse Jewish dishes like "kishke" and potato pudding. But it had a reputation for not adulterating its liquor. With its good name, it drew a large clientele. It was not easy for the lower classes to pass by Chaike Tanz without dropping in. Even the horse could scent when he had reached Chaike Tanz, and he automatically drew up and allowed his owner to descend. All day long, you could see quite a number of cabs and wagons outside Chaike Tanz, the horses drowsing away through the hours. Inside there was a spirit of hilarity and abandon.

You would have expected from the class of person who frequented Chaike Tanz, that scuffles and fisticuffs would be a regular feature of the place. But actually peace and quiet reigned there for most of the time. For even the habitues of the underworld had a certain regard for Chaike Tanz. On Friday after midday, with the Sabbath approaching, Chaike used to shepherd the drinkers out of the place with her impressive manner—and they would quietly depart for their homes. The place was closed for the whole of the Sabbath, as also during the Yom Tovim.

The Chassid Zalman Kohn owned the other liquor-selling restaurant in that part of the town. For some reason or another, the husband of Chaike Tanz had never set foot in the pub and neither had the wife ever made her appearance in the pub owned by Zalman. Zalman's pub drew a more refined clientele than Chaike Tanz—market auctioneers, traders and the better type of working man. A feature of Zalman's pub were the five rooms that formed part of it, where customers could discuss their private affairs without any interference. Zalman wore his "yarmulke" all day long, and from his unbuttoned frock coat could be seen his long "tsitses". He prospered, and with his new-found wealth was able to buy for his sons an exemption from military service. Eventually, he became the part-owner of a big textile concern.

Frume Beila plied her illicit liquor trade in the pub near the meat-market. She personally served the butchers, and provided a higher class of fare than that served up in Chaike Tanz's and Zalman's establishments. The most reputable pubs were situated in the centre of the commercial area, where the customers were the merchant classes, who conducted their negotiations in the pub. The best-known amongst the pubs in this area was the one owned by Moome Etke. It was a household word in the whole of Dvinsk, and her excellent dishes made the Dvinsker smack their lips. The shop assistants displayed their presence in this upper-class pub, in an attempt to aggrandise themselves. It was a status symbol.

As Friday afternoons came, all commercial activity steadily drew to a standstill. The butcheries put up their shutters. Here and there a wagoner or a carrier was still busy with his final assignment. Those who had laboured and schemed all week how to amass larger profits, made preparations to welcome the Holy Sabbath. A new mood came over everyone. Hesitant customers were being edged out of the shops. "It is time for lighting the candles!" called out the shopowner. "What lighting candles!" a customer examining some goods protests. The shop-owner begins to bridle. "Who cares if you buy, or you don't buy," he snarls. Everybody is making preparation to go to the "bod". The Sabbath is on its way.

It is said that when a Jew has nothing more to write about, he writes about the "bod". Now what is there to write about a "bod"? One can have a bigger or smaller backside. But whatever the physical differences, there is total equality in the "bod."

Dovid's "bod" had a long and ancient history, ranging over three generations. When Dovid died, he bequeathed the "bod" to his son, Berl. And when Berl died, it was inherited by the grandson, Hirschl. But it continued to own the name of the grandfather, who had first built it. When Benyomin der Geller, who was approaching one hundred years, was asked when the "bod" was built, he replied that it had always been in existence. I, myself, recall when the "bod" had to be reinforced with strong underpinnings, for fear that it might otherwise collapse. And I can also remember when the owner replaced some of the old wooden buckets by new ones. From time to time taps were repaired. But, in general, the "bod" had remained more or less as it was for the last three generations. It can in truth be said that it was a monument. It was the first "bod" in Dvinsk, situated near the fish-market and Talkoets, in the heart of the Jewish commercial centre.

Hirschl was an honest Jew. Testimony for this, is that he heated up the "bod" only on Thursdays and Fridays, in preparation for the Sabbath. Thursdays were set aside for the old Dvinsker merchants. There is no need to catalogue in detail the wealthy ones who graced the "bod" with their presence on Thursdays. It is enough to say that when the banker Wittenberg returned from a distant journey on a Thursday, he immediately betook himself to the "bod". Many a Jew would have been happy to earn in a week, what the "bod" cost Wittenberg on one Thursday. To be sure he was very generous to the owner, the masseur Zusse who lashed him with the broom, and the beggars who had taken up their positions at the exit the moment the news reached them that Wittenberg was inside. The rich timber merchant, Moishe Kaplan, used to tell that he had travelled up and down the whole of Russia, and had visited any number of "bedder"—but nowhere had he encountered one to match the steam from the stone-oven of Dovid's "bod", or a beater with the broom, like Zusse. These words fell sweetly on Zusse's ears.

Let me confess that I have never experienced the inimitable pleasure of seeing how the very wealthy look on Thursdays in the "bod". The "bod" was divided into two sections—in the one you paid three kopkes, and in the other five kopkes. Children were given a reduction. And here I must add that I never had the pleasure of seeing those poor who frequented the section at a charge of three kopkes. By "bod" standards, I was a middle-man. I attended the "bod" on Friday afternoons, in the company of the average Jew who is already known to you.

When it came to value for money, I have to concede that the Christian "bod" outshone Dovid's "bod". The Jew took to the "bod" a change of clean underwear and shirt. The Christian "bod" provided lockers where you could hang your clothes—one place for the clean apparel and the other for the dirty. Then there was a special place for the "shtivel". But in Dovid's "bod" only a box was provided, where everything was packed in—the clean underwear and the "shtivel" covered with pitch; and where the louse or bug enjoyed full freedom to move from the dirty clothing to the clean. Then, again, in the Christian "bod" the vestibule where everybody undressed was clean and hygienic. It was furnished with soft couches, where you could stretch yourself out as if you were in your father's vineyard. You could take things at your leisure, and nobody interfered with you.

Let me now proceed to give you some detail of the doings in Dovid's "bod". From the vestibule you entered the main washing chamber through a door. The people came there to cleanse themselves of the dirt and grime their bodies had accumulated during a week of labour and toil. It was in the nature of a purification for the approaching Sabbath. Benches were placed all around the walls. There were any number of wooden buckets and a plentiful supply of hot or cold water. The Jew soaped and washed himself, as if his life depended on it. They scrubbed each other's backs. And when they had finally washed themselves down, they went into the adjoining chamber where they could steam themselves. There they sprawled on six wooden tiers before the steam oven, inside of which were placed huge stones that had been heated for a considerable time and looked fiery. As you ascended the tiers, the hotter was the steam that came from the oven as buckets of water were thrown onto the stones. There were benches on the top tier, on which you could stretch yourself and get a friend to beat you with a broom made from linden twigs, which could be acquired in the "bod" at a kopke a time.

The steam was almost unendurable on the top tier. But the Jew there would keep exclaiming: "Davai parre!"—"More steam!" When it happened that Yoshe the old blacksmith, lying stretched out to the full, passed out they carried him down and took him into the washing chamber. The "bod" was always full to capacity. Every place was occupied. There were no superior ones in the "bod". Full equality reigned, and nobody would dream of giving up a seat. But here was an emergency. "Make room for Yoshe the blacksmith!" they would call out. A few would immediately rise from their seats, along which Yoshe was stretched, and they resuscitated him with the buckets of cold water that were poured over him.

I have said that there was no preferential treatment for anyone in the "bod". That is not quite the case. There was some deference paid to the wagoners, carriers, butchers—all those who had strained themselves lifting heavy loads and had ruptured. "Hey, there, make room for Yerachmiel! Can't you see his treasure hanging from him, which he will take with him to the next world!" Immediately room was made for

Yerachmiel to sit down.   There were any number such as Yerachmiel who sat on the benches with their "killes" as big as a full moon.   They received every attention. Buckets of water were brought to them. Everything was done to make them comfortable. Finally, they were led into the steam chamber and placed on the bottom tier where they could steam themselves at the lower temperature.

The superintendent of the "bod" was Zusse der parschik—also known as Zusse der Gubernator. Though approaching 70, he still had a powerful body. He had been in the service of Dovid, and now he was Hirschl's right-hand man. When Zusse lashed your back with the birch broom, you could hear the bones crackle. If a dispute arose over the ownership of a wooden bucket, Zusse would intervene and immediately restore peace. He was respected by all and sundry. It was one of his duties to watch the temperature of the steam, in an effort to keep down to reasonable proportions the number who were passing out. And he also looked after the clothes. On top of it all, he sold white bread and "kvass" to refresh those who had just passed through the purgatory of the "bod". He was popular all round.

In the vestibule could also be found Berl Lazer the barber—a corpulent Jew who wore a "yarmulke". His black over-sized trouser-legs were let into his soldierly "shtivel".   His shirt, from which a number of buttons were missing, was invariably wide open. From his waist-coat, adorned with a silver chain, there emerged his "Arbe Kanfoth" with the "tsitses" reaching down to his "shtivel". As he finished cutting the hair of one client, the next one took his place. He had the reputation of being an honest God-fearing Jew. Not for a whole rouble would he take off a beard or a hair from a "paye", for it was a contravention of religious precept.

One day someone asked Berl Lazer how he had acquired such skill as a barber. His answer was — "What! do you call it a skill—it's like plucking the feathers from a chicken. All you need is a light hand and a good head." "Why a good head, Berl?" "So as to remember who had paid and who had not paid, before leaving." In one corner was to be seen Nochum Izak, der Feldscher. Around him were gathered a dozen naked Jews, and he was giving them a treatment of "bankes". It was painful to see the blood streaming down their backs.

All good things come to an end—even the "bod". "Tru! ru! ru!" It is the first siren call. The Sabbath is quickly approaching. Talkoets has now ground to a standstill. The shops are locked, bolted and barred. Hurry up, Jews! The "bod" begins to empty out. Berl Lazer has still a head of hair to cut. Zusse der Gubernator calls out—"Enough, Berke. The Sabbath is upon us. Thirty three heads—I've counted them. How many more do you want?" Replying to him, Berl says politely: "May so many teeth fall out of your mouth, as I am short of thirty heads! And what of the three who did a bunk without paying? Am I going to go in search of them? You're swollen with your profits. Do I count the number who came here today, and filled your pockets?" "Tru! ru! ru!" the second whistle sounds. They hasten home, like firemen running to put a fire out. Hirschl runs into the "bod" and shuts off the water. A single Jew, who has soaped himself from head to foot, begs Hirschl for one bucket-full of water. "Nothing doing," Hirschl tells him.

The last Jew has now left the "bod". Jews, hurrying along the streets, call out to a cab-driver or a wagoner. This is the time when no fee is charged. The streets soon empty. Trade has come to a standstill. The town is as if sinking into sleep. Even the Christians are aware that the Sabbath has arrived. "Tru! ru! ru!" It is the last call to the Jews. In the windows can be seen candles being lit. It is Sabbath!

Chapter Six

THE RELIGIOUS WORLD

I have so far described to you Dvinsk as it appeared in its more profane garb—commerce as it is conducted by the prosperous, and also by those who are struggling against total submergence; the fraudulence of Talkoets, the pubs, the lurid colours of the underworld—and much else. After all the clatter and din, we have arrived at the Sabbath—with everybody cleaned up physically in the "bod". But in all fairness to Dvinsk and its tradition, I feel I should turn to what is more positive and sacred in its life. There is much to tell here.

Dvinsk was famous for its Rabbinical Gaonim—Reb Meir Simcha Kahana and Reb Yosef Rosin, also known as the Ragachover Gaon. Their memories are hallowed to this day. They were both so pre-eminent in their own spheres, that it is difficult for me to decide which one to give precedence. Since Reb Meir Simcha was a "Cohen", it seems that he should receive pride of place. I was actually acquainted with Reb Meir Simcha, from time to time when my father had celebrated a "bris" in our home and had asked Reb Meir Simcha to act as "Sandig".

Reb Meir Simcha was a Misnagid who prayed in the Kahalse Minyan, situated near his house. He could be seen going to the Shul for prayers three times a day. He was of medium height, on the portly side, with a high forehead, long "payes", but not with a long beard. His total appearance was patriarchal. There was a magic glow in his eyes, that captivated all who gazed on his countenance. The eloquence of his talk charmed all his listeners. Visitors came to his home all day long to be in communion with the holiness of his presence. All kinds and types came to him—holy

Jews, merchants, but mainly women, the presentable and the lowly.

He dwelt on the second storey of an old house, situated in Officer Street. It was not exactly a fitting abode for one so celebrated. But he eschewed that affluence and comfort, which was associated with some of the Rabbis of other towns. As far as I can remember, his home had three rooms. One of them was assigned to the reception of visitors. The walls were blotted out by rows upon rows of Judaica and Talmudical literature of the highest value.

There were always more visitors than chairs on which they could be seated. The room in which he discussed matters with his visitors had a table and three chairs.

Unlike so many other Rabbis, he had no Gabboim to collect donations for him. Neither could it be said of him that he deferred to the rich. All classes, from the highest to the lowest, were convinced that a blessing from the Rabbi would bring them fortune. Strangely enough, his wife was a "yente", and his only daughter suffered a mental breakdown and was confined to an institution all her life.

The Rabbi had a world reputation, and Dvinsker from many lands sent him donations. But, as I have indicated, nothing was so removed from his whole being as luxurious living, and any money he had over was given to charity. A poor bride would receive not only his blessing, but some material help to see her on her way in life. And it was known that he would, one way or another, replace the horse of a wagoner which had perished from toil and age. He had asked all synagogues to have in supply a stock of firewood for the poor, and to make sure that the peasant who had brought it had received his fee. His virtue and probity were a byword both among Jews and Christians. Officers would salute him as they saw him in the street. Even Christians would seek his judicial wisdom in a dispute. Let me now relate two episodes from his life to indicate the stature of the man.

In the First World War, the German Army was held up for months at the Dvina, where the fortress proved impregnable. The Germans terrorised the town with intermittent shelling that proved destructive of life and property. Apart from the Germans, the Cossacks who had blood ties with the pogromschik Khmelnicki of the seventeeth century, were stationed inside Dvinsk and constituted a constant menace to the Jews. Jews made off to the interior of Russia whenever the possibility offered.

"Shomer Nafshechah"—"Guard your life!" was the slogan of the Ragachover Gaon. He himself packed his chattels and property, and made off with the wealthy Dovid Potash for Petrograd. Although part of his home was destroyed by a random shell, Reb Meir Simcha refused to budge. His friends and the community at large urged him to leave Dvinsk. "As long as there are nine Jews in Dvinsk, I shall be the tenth," the Rabbi answered them. "Does your life mean nothing to you?" they pleaded with him. "The fate of the last Jew in Dvinsk will be my fate," he replied.

And now let me relate another incident surrounding Reb Meir Simcha, where the Christians played a part.

The end of the First World War saw the whole region round Dvinsk fall into a state of chaos. Armies from different nationalities—Russian, German, Polish, Lettish—fought for mastery. Then came the Bolsheviks with the Red Army. Each conquering army brought with it a new kind of suffering for the inhabitants. All kinds of tribute were imposed on the people who were being bled white—all this apart from the pillage and robbery that is inseparable from a semi-disorganised soldiery let loose on a population.

For a time the Lettish Bolsheviks were in control, under the leadership of the Lett, Dutza. He took drastic action to enforce discipline. Executions went on night and day, among them the rich Movshonson and 16 other Jews. The total number of executions on one certain day reached 107, including some clergy.

All of a sudden a pall of sorrow descended on the Jewish quarter of Dvinsk. Fear stalked everywhere, and rumours were rampant. Then the news broke that Dutza's Letts had arrested Reb Meir Simcha in the dead of night, and had placed him in solitary confinement in a prison cell. This was confirmed by the Rebbetzin, who told that he had taken with him to the prison his "tallis", "tefillin", a few volumes, and a piece of bread. The women sent up howls, and the men raised their voices in prayer to the Almighty. The hearts of Dvinsk Jewry were filled with anguish. The Rabbi was under arrest!

The proposal was made that the community should collect a sum of money, which would be taken to Dutza and offered in return for the release of Reb Meir Simcha. But who was going to take the money to Dutza? Who was going to bell the cat, as it were? Some of the bolder spirits among the youth suggested that the prison warder should be bribed to let Reb Meir Simcha escape from the prison. But there were more suggestions than volunteers for this hazardous undertaking—as so often happened with the Jews. The religious Jews did their part by offering up endless prayers, and the endless reciting of psalms. They even fasted. Four days passed, and there was no sign of salvation.

It is recorded in the Talmud, that a place will be found in the world to come for those Christians who have behaved humanely towards the Jews. Some of them, I feel sure, will be selected from the Christians of Dvinsk of that time. Who could have suggested that two young "skotzim" would bring about the freeing of Reb Meir Simcha?

Both were members of the Revolutionary Committee. The one was Lyovka Kishatznik who, as his name suggested, worked in the slaughterhouse, with its "kishkes" and offal. He had been gaoled by the Tsar, and eventually banished to Siberia. The revolution had brought him freedom. The other one was Ignati

Kravchenko, the son of a washerwoman. He was a carpenter by trade. He had participated in the slaying of two police provocateurs and been sentenced to twenty years banishment to Siberia. He, too, gained his freedom with the Revolution. Both told Dutza that it was an error to have arrested Reb Meir Simcha, who was revered by all sections of the population. They argued that the Rabbi was not unsympathetic to the Bolsheviks, and that he had always helped those who were in need, both Jewish and Christian.

It was no easy matter to get Dutza to change his mind. Kravchenko then urged that the Rabbi should be released, until such time as a charge was preferred against him. He himself would bring 100 witnesses, both Jews and non-Jews, to prove that the Rabbi was no counter-revolutionary. Dutza refused as he was afraid that, once the Rabbi was free, the Jews would whisk him away from Dvinsk. But Lyovka and Ignati were prepared to guarantee that he would stand trial. There was a third guarantor, Dora Herring, the daughter of Yankel Yoshe the baker. She, too, was in the Revolutionary Committee in the capacity of secretary. When the Jews took the Sabbath "tallis" and Sabbath kaftan to Reb Meir Simcha, they nearly fell over backward with surprise when they met him in front of the gaol—a free man. It is hard to describe the rejoicing that swept through the whole of Dvinsk.

Reb Meir Simcha Kahana was the Rav in Dvinsk for 54 years. When he died on the operating table in Riga, he was 83 years old. Before his death, he had made the request to be buried in Dvinsk. The funeral took place on the 4th day of Ellul, 1928. Not in all my life have I witnessed such a huge funeral. They came from all over to pay their last respects to this saintly figure. The General of the garrison provided guards at the funeral, both to control the massive crowd of mourners, and also as a sign of respect. An endless stream of people, both Jews and Christians, followed the bier to its last resting place.

Let me now write about the Ragachover Gaon, Yosef Rosin, who was different in every way from Reb Meir Simcha. He had a big reputation as a scholar throughout the whole of the world. I cannot speak of his Talmudical erudition, which was beyond my capacity to understand or assess. But all were agreed that he was endowed with divine attributes.

He was of medium height, with long flowing hair and a prominent beard. He had a clear complexion. But it was difficult to tell what vision his mystery-laden eyes were concentrating on. He never walked, but ran. Three times a day he could be seen hastening to the Chassidic Planover Minyan. He was so immersed in esoteric studies, that he would hardly acknowledge a greeting— or simply nod his head, and hasten onward. The Christians called him the mad Rabbi. As he entered the Planover Minyan, he would with a gesture brush aside those Jews who had come to offer their respects to him, hasten to his seat next to the "Oren Kodesh", don his "tallis" and "tefillin", and commence the morning prayer, oblivious of the people in the Shul. If the Cantor was too slow in moving through the service, he would be reproved by the Ragachover for wasting the time of the congregants. The service completed, he would take off his "tallis" and "tefillin", and hasten out of the synagogue with the sense of urgency with which he had entered it.

When as a child I came to Dvinsk, the Ragachover Rov was already installed; and when I left Dvinsk in 1928, he was still there. There was no end of stories about the Rav. At eighteen he was ordained as a Rabbi. His parents were determined to marry him off quickly. And he did not even have time to notice that his bride was both a hunchback and of a sickly disposition. And she also conformed to the adage that every cripple is bad tempered. A few years after the wedding she died, and left no children behind. The second wife of the Rav was born in Dvinsk. But this time he took the trouble to have a good look at the prospective bride.

She was pretty, hailed from a rich family and was both well brought up and cultivated, being fairly acquainted with Jewish and world literature. She conducted herself as becomes a person with a modern outlook. She lived in a home that was gracious and sumptuous. And she also wore her dresses becomingly.

The Dvinsker Chassidim would never have accepted the Ragachover because of his youth. But his reputation had spread far and wide. He moved about in his home with that same restless energy that he moved through the streets. He was constantly at his studies, and he delved deeply in the labyrinth of the Talmud, that massive and majestic collection of the wisdom of the Jewish nation and its rich experiences. He had a phenomenal memory, and it was said that if by some mischance the Talmud were to disappear from the face of the earth, the Ragachover would be able to reconstruct its contents from memory.

He was rather brusque with those who came to question him on certain legalities. And he would tell them to go to Reb Meir Simcha, as he had not the time for these matters. "I Have Not the Time" became the cognomen of this impatient Rav who appeared to be dwelling in a different domain. How his community fared, or anything of earthly interest, was outside his concern. His whole life and intellect were concentrated on the Talmudic tomes. He was more a Rav for angels than for ordinary mortals, it was said. The Jews of Dvinsk never came close to him. On top of it all, he was a hot-tempered man and stubborn.

As a man of intellect and knowledge, he was more eminent than Reb Meir Simcha. I have been told by someone intimately bound up with religious affairs in Israel, that while the name of Reb Meir Simcha is mentioned now and again, the Ragachover is constantly referred to as an authority on all matters Talmudical.

I have described the two chief Rabbinical figures in Dvinsk. But there were also outstanding teachers and

Talmudists in that part of the world, who would have been an ornament to any community.

Half the Jews of Dvinsk were Hassidim, the other half were Misnagdim. Their services differed in many important respects. The Misnagid supplicated the Lord with laments and tears. The Hassid, on the other hand, served Him with dance and song. Even after a Kaddish Yarhrzeit was recited, the Shamos used to spread out a velvet cloth over a table, place a bottle of brandy on it, and a feast followed. And after Mincha, when the Misnagdim recited a "kapittel Tehilim" with mournful voice, the Hassidim made merry as they farewelled the Sabbath with a "Melavi Malka".

The "Melavi Malka" was in the nature of a feast, comprising a few bottles of brandy, a half-dozen herring, "kichel" and "kitke".They washed their hands, and the Rabbi offered a blessing, after which they ate and drank in praise of the Lord. With every "Lechaim" the mood became more exhilarating. Merriment was followed by a feeling of ecstasy. And then they broke into song accompanied by the clapping of hands. Hands were joined, and they danced and stamped their feet in a quickening rhythm. And suddenly, the Shamos told the Rav that the time for Maariv had arrived. Rich or poor, they had all rejoiced in the glory of the Lord on high, and the human beings on this earth.

The Planover was the biggest of the Hassidic Minyanim. It was open all day and all night, both summer and winter. Before dawn Jews had already arrived with their "taleisim" and "tefillin". The moment a streak of light could be descried in the eastern sky, the first Minyan began. And then it was followed by a second Minyan, a third and a fourth. According to the "Schulchan Aruch", the "Mincha" service can be held from one in the afternoon till dark sets in. Throughout the afternoon these Mincha services were held.

A cab-driver, a wagoner would draw up with his horse outside the Beth Hamedrash, and nip in for a Mincha. He had not to wait long, for a Minyan of ten Jews was always on hand. The Maariv service could be held any time till midnight.

In the Planover Minyan there were several long tables, at which a Rebbe discoursed with a number of Jews on the problems raised by the Sedra of the week. Another Rebbe was busy with the intricacies of the "Mishnayes" or the Shulchan Aruch. Other Jews came to study the Gemarra. And in another part, removed from the rest, were the Yeshiva Bocherim, unravelling the mysteries of the Talmud, till sleep overtook them.

On Friday nights the town fell into a peaceful silence. Beyond the curtains draping the windows of Jewish homes could be seen the Sabbath candle illuminations. And then, after the necessary preparation had been made, the fathers and their children, attired in their Sabbath best, made their appearance on the streets. They were on the way to Shul to greet the Sabbath bride, the women and girls remaining at home. The table was decked with a white table-cloth. Two white loaves were covered with a silken cloth, edged with fringes of blue or red. The candle-sticks of silver or brass were highly polished, and the decanter of red wine threw off all colours in the glow of the candle-lights. Clad in their best, the women busied themselves with laying out the cutlery. The young girls looked like princesses.

In the poorer quarters, the hardworking Jew came from the "bod" and changed into the Sabbath best. If he was fairly well to do, he would have an extra pair of "shtivel" to change into for the Sabbath. But otherwise he used a liquid polish called "varvel" to give a shine to the ones he had been wearing all week. The trouser legs were drawn over the "shtivel". They changed into the Sabbath frock-coat, donned their best hat, and made for the Shul. The woman of the home could not always afford the five kopkes for the "bod", but she had spent some time washing herself at home. And when she had finished, you could hardly recognise her as the same woman, that a few hours ago was covered with grime and smut from performing her many chores in the kitchen and elsewhere. She had found the time to cook the "tsolent", wash and plait the hair of the children, and tie a red ribbon around their heads.

And so they awaited the return of the King of the family from Shul. This King was just not the same person who was immersed in his toil and dirt during the week. He had been spiritually transformed, and he discussed all kinds of problems with the learned ones about him as they walked home from Shul.

The Shul was brightly illumined for the Sabbath. The floor had been cleaned and was spotless. Everything was spick and span. In winter the ovens were heated to provide protection from the elements. It was bright and comforting. The first ones to arrive in the Shul were the small traders who had returned early from the villages. They had not "davined" in a "minyan" the whole week, and it was like slaking a thirst. Before going to Shul, their wives had prepared a "tsimes", which they also did not have all week while going from the village to the next.

When the service was over, the Jew made his way home, where he was greeted by his wife who bore herself like a queen. The children had an angelic expression on their faces. The resourcefulness and good taste of the woman of the house was visible in every corner of the dwelling. Everyone was seated at the table, the head of the family stood up, and with a voice loud and clear recited the "Yom Hashishi . . ."—a proclamation of the holiness of the Sabbath. The "Kiddush" completed, the meal proper began. The quality of the dishes prepared naturally depended upon the financial means. The rich man was envied. But the poor man did not do badly with a well-prepared "tsimes" made from grated carrots. It was, oh, so sweet and fragrant. And then there was the stuffed "kishke" to bring more delights to the palate. Everything was eaten with relish. It was good to be a Jew! And when he had had his fill, and more, there issued a sweet melody from the King at the head of the table. His eyes began to be laden with sleep. From the kitchen there was wafted the smell of the "pootsa", to be eaten the next day. He finally sank into a deep slumber.

There were any number of synagogues in Dvinsk. There was not a street in the centre of the town, but it had two synagogues. In Officers' Street, there were six. The biggest amongst them were the Choir Shul, the Kahalse Beth Hamedrash, and the Planover Minyan. The Minyanim were named after the celebrities of the town—Wittenberg's, Kadishe's, Dobkin's and many others. Then there were Minyanim carrying the names of trades—carpenters, tailors, butchers, cab-drivers and others.

On Saturday the women accompanied the men to Shul. There was no shortage of worshippers. When they poured out of the synagogues, the streets became packed with Jews. The men tied their "taleisim" around their necks; the women wore their most handsome clothes, and their heads were covered with many-coloured shawls. They walked home leisurely, despite the fact that they were hungry—for no food was to be eaten before the service. They ambled along and spoke, not about business and all that but of matters of more spiritual import—the performance of the Cantor, the choice of an Aliyah. They waited expectantly for the Sabbath midday. Even the poorest could afford some fish dish, a pickled herring, "pootsa", even a portion of meat. Certainly a "kugel". There was enough to satisfy the appetite.

It would be incomplete not to say something about the "Magidim", who were an institution in that part of the world. The "Magid" used to arrive in the town on Fridays. The material for his oratory was drawn from all manner of sources, both from this mortal world and from the world to come. It was mostly very emotional, and tears flowed copiously from the women listeners in particular. And many a man's eye, too, became moist. Notices of the arrival of the "Magid" were pasted by the "Shamos" on the doors of the synagogues. There were two classes of "Magidim"—the infantry, or lower ranks, who were simple people without much of a reputation. Then there were the top echelons among the "Magidim", who were given a place of honour in the Shul, greeted by the "Gabai" himself as they entered the Shul, and led to their seats. They would on occasions be asked to officiate, and the "Gabai" invited them to his home, where they partook of the best.

When the midday was completed, the "Magid" and the leading people of the town betook themselves to the synagogues. After the congregants had seated themselves, the "Magid" began his sermon. The first part of his address dealt with the awesome punishments that awaited sinners in the world to come, where they would burn in hell and be dipped in burning pitch. His words were like fire and brimstone hurled into the congregants, and he struck fear into their souls. The women in particular could not endure the terrifying descriptions and the lengthy catalogue of punishments that awaited the sinner. Their cheeks were drenched in tears.

He would pause for a few seconds, and then tell of Paradise with the magnificent marble halls and candelabra of the finest splendour, where the righteous will dwell for ever enveloped in the "Shechinah", and where viands of incomparable delicacy will be served at a repast, at which the guests will include Abraham, Isaac, Jacob, Moses, Aaron, King David and King Solomon. He was so graphic in his description, that you could think he had just come from there.

When the "Magid" had completed his oration, the Jews "davened Mincha", after which the poorer among the congregants recited psalms. Twilight soon descended, and with it a pall of sorrow enveloped the Shul. Their laments were indicative of the hard, tragic life that was their lot. Yes—their lives were bitter with sorrow. The Sabbath had brought them a measure of comfort and consolation. If only they could hold on to it, and not let it slide into the tumult and toil of the week ahead. And so they delayed with the "Maariv", which brought the Sabbath to a close. But darkness now descended in ever deepening hues. The "Shamos" slapped the table, and "Maariv" commenced—"God will have mercy on you, and forgive you, you sinful ones!" this prayer says.

But why are you sinful Jews? The whole week you toil and sweat to earn a morsel of bread. And the whole Sabbath you offer up your prayers in Shul. What are your sins?

The Sabbath afternoons were always very lively in the Planover Minyan. Jews from all over Dvinsk—Pletzer, Gayok, Griva — all came to hear what was going on the world over. There were amongst them the politicos, known as "Chachmai Lisanka". They knew everything that was happening on this planet of ours, and also what was going to happen, to make things more interesting. A vast variety of subjects was on the order of the day—Moshe Montefiore, Baron Hirsch, and other notables in Jewish life. But subjects from the remote past often engaged their attention—such as the number of bricks King Nimrod used to build the tower with which he was going to ascend to heaven. And they also talked about the black Jews who dwelt on the other side of the mythical Sambation River. They talked and talked, till the Shamos announced that Maariv time had come.

When they came out of the Shul, they blessed the moon. They shook hands over a "Sholem Aleichem" as if they had not seen each other in months. The

"Sholem Aleichem" was actually intended for the moon.
But since the Jew could not hope to reach the moon,
however high he may jump into the air, he bestowed
the "Sholem Aleichem" symbolically on the Jews standing next to him. The Sabbath has ended. As he
arrives home he finds his wife in her weekday clothes,
engaged in her regular chores. He, too, changes into
his old clothes. The week, with its toil and sweat,
begins once again.

As the summer wanes, a melancholy settles on the
heart of every Jew. It is the month of Ellul. The
"Baal Tekiah" is preparing himself in the handling of
the "Shofar", for Rosh Hashanah is approaching. The
Talmudists are practising with the "Shofar" diligently,
so as to qualify as "Baal Tekiahs" and earn a few extra
kopkes. Everyone has a keener look in his eye as the
Day of Judgement is nearing. The "Tehillim Jews"
fear it more than anyone else. And this fear drives
them to say the whole "Tehillim" every day as a penance
for their sins, and the judgement that awaits them.
With the approach of Rosh Hashanah, there was
much more doing on the Friday market. The women
looked everywhere for the head of a pike to present to
the husband, as a symbol of his primacy in the family.
It is the season of apples, pears and plums, in which
trade is brisk. The booksellers make their appearance
in bulk on the market, for with the awesome days
approaching they do quite a trade in "Machzorim",
"Tehillims", "Tsitsis", "Sidurim." The women make
for the "Techinas."
And then came Rosh Hashanah. After the service,
Jews wished each other long life and happiness for the
coming year. The midday meal completed, everybody
hastened off to perform the ritual of "Tashlich", the
discarding of the year's load of sins into the fast and
broad-flowing Dvina. They all headed for the Dvina
in an unending procession—men, women, children,

young, old, believers, non-believers. They numbered
more than 20,000, and the total load of sins being got
rid of was immense. There they stood on the banks of
the Dvina, clutching "Sidurim" and "Machzerim". They
prayed, shook their pockets in an effort to unload their
sins. And when they had succeeded, they started once
again on the sinful road that is inseparable from human
existence. A peasant in his boat beholds this mass of
Jewry, and curses them at the way they are polluting
this great Russian river with their Jewish sins.

The return from "Tashlich" is much easier. They
have discarded their sins, and they walk more nimbly.
They wend their way to the Shul, and read their "Tehillim". And then follow the days of penance between
Rosh Hashanah and Yom Kippur. On the afternoon
of the Eve of Yom Kippur, they go through the
ceremonial of "shloggen kapores". At "Mincha" the
Jews entered the Shul with trepidation, for they were
about to receive the 40 symbolic lashes in expiation of
their sins. There I can see them, kneeling on the straw,
their frock-coats raised. And then the Shamos who
administered the lashes began his assignment, counting
—"Achad, shtaim, sholosh . . ." till he reached the
figure of 40. Having done penance, the penitent raised
himself, offered a donation to the Shul, went home and
began his fast. And then he returned to the Shul for
the most momentous occasion of all—the Kol Neidre.

That whole of Yom Kippur was a day filled with
laments and heartbeatings, and supplications to the
Almighty for forgiveness and long life. There was
Shlaime with the wooden leg, who confessed to the
Lord in cries of anguish that he had broken his leg
while running to do evil. With Neilah, and the sounding on the Shofar of a "Tekiah Gedolah", Yom Kippur
has ended. The fate of every Jew is sealed. After the
mourning and mortification of Yom Kippur comes the
release with the festive Yom Tov of Succas. A note of
rejoicing has once again entered into Jewish life. Merry
songs are sung to the glory of life and being.

All businesses were closed on the Sabbath and Yom Tovim except the pharmacy. There were small sinners about. On the quiet, a shopkeeper sold some odds and ends. Surreptitiously, a youth smoked a cigarette behind a stable. A greedy merchant would walk over to a distant part of the city, hire a cab and make for the fortress. But even they felt the pull of the Sabbaths and Holy Days. All in all, Dvinsk was as pure as you could expect any aggregate of human beings to be. The Messiah could without embarrassment have landed in Dvinsk. But for some reason or other, he did not land in Dvinsk.

Chapter Seven

THE SECULAR WORLD

Every Jew was prepared to give his right hand to have his child educated. Even the most indigent one would scrape and scrounge to ensure that his child could learn to "daven". Following the Oriental custom of relegating womanhood to a lower status, the young girls were not given any kind of Judaistic education. As the Talmud has it—"He who teaches his daughter Torah, it is as if he were blaspheming the Lord." But it was different with the young male child. At the early age of five he was sent to cheder.

There were as many of these chedorim as "Botei Midroshim". In most streets, as you walked along, you would see above the window sill the little heads of the children studying from the Aleph-Beth to the Gemarra. With the sweetness of their childhood voices, they were absorbing the treasured heritage of Judaism. There was no shortage either of Rebbes or children. To the rich another child was no problem. As for the impecunious one, his reckoning was that one day there might be born to him a wonder child who would solve all his problems. If no wonder child appeared in the first eight of his progeny, who knows but the ninth would be the lucky one! The Jew must never stop hoping.

The rich and not so rich paid fees for their children to be enrolled in the chedorim. Those who could not afford to pay sent their children to the Talmud Torahs, where there was no fee. There were a few such Talmud Torahs in Dvinsk and also one in Altstadt. The Community paid the salaries of the teachers. The chedorim were better kept than the Talmud Torahs, which were mostly in a neglected condition, and the teachers were not fully qualified. The children there, even at the advanced age of eleven, scarcely knew how to read Hebrew. When a child in these Talmud Torahs showed promise, he was aided by the Community to proceed to the Yeshiva to pursue his studies.

There were two Yeshivas in Dvinsk, and they greatly helped to promote religious scholarship. Quite a number who emerged from these Yeshivas, took their knowledge with them to different parts of the world as they emigrated. At the Wittenberg Yeshiva the enrolment of students stood at 120, ranging from 12-18 years. Two-thirds of them had come from Lithuania. The rest came from Dvinsk and its suburbs. The majority of the Yeshiva students were too poor to pay their way, and they relied on the generosity of the wealthy ones to see them through. The Yeshiva was totally financed by Moishe Wittenberg, the eldest of the richest family in Dvinsk. The Head of the Yeshiva was Yehosua Arsh, a Rabbi and a noted scholar.

Here I would like to pause in order to tell the reader about the Wittenberg family. The Wittenbergs were hardware and steel merchants, whose name and fame had spread as far as St. Petersburg and Riga. Merchants from far afield came to make their purchases from the Wittenbergs, largely because of their high reputation for honest dealing. Moishe Wittenberg "davened" three times a day in the Shul, and often visited the Yeshiva where he would enquire about the wellbeing of the students. He was a learned man himself and when, on examining a student he found a fine talent, he would pay for his transfer to the famous Slabodka Yeshiva. His wife Dinah was as communally minded as he was. She founded the Wittenberg benevolent society, where loans were advanced without interest. She had also founded a "Hachnoset Kalah" for assisting girls to get married. When Moishe Wittenberg died, the family continued to pay for the running of the Yeshiva.

Satze's Yeshiva was situated in Pletzer. When I was 12 years old I was enrolled in this Yeshiva. I was friendly with another student. As religious studies were not exactly our metier, we found after a time that swimming in the Dvina was preferable to delving into the ancient tomes of learning. After a year and a few months, they advised us that we could do much better by leaving the Yeshiva. That was when I became a shop assistant. This Yeshiva was maintained by Yisroel Hurvich, of whose many financial interests I have already spoken. This Yeshiva was bigger than Wittenberg's, with an enrolment of over 300. A kitchen had been installed for the provision of meals for the poor students, and also a dormitory where they could sleep. Reb Meir Simcha visited the Yeshiva twice a week. When Yisroel Hurvich died the Yeshiva disintegrated, as his sons squandered his fortune.

Then there was another category of student around the age of 20, who had qualified at a Yeshiva but could find no gainful employment. They spent their day, and much of the night, in the Botei Midroshim. They mostly stood at a lectern on which an open Gemarra rested. Their bodies swayed backward and forward as they wended their way through the mysteries of the Talmud. When a wealthy man entered the Shul, they would raise their voices in the hope that his attention would be attracted and he would invite them home for a meal. Those who were lucky would be invited seven days in succession for a meal. And there were others whose teeth might have been considered redundant because they had nothing to eat for days on end. Theirs was a sad lot.

These students were known by all kinds of nicknames " Umziste Togesser", " Gan Aden Fihrer", and "Patronnes". Their aspiration was to gain entry into the Slabodka Yeshiva, from where they were certain to qualify as Rabonim and Shochtim. They were regarded as the unfortunates among the students, as they were too old to learn a trade. Neither did they have enough of a secular education or a knowledge of the Russian language to be able to become assistants in shops and warehouses. In the end they married elderly spinsters or girls with physical defects. A number became "lamdonim", "shadchonim", "badchonim", collectors, "shamoshim" and such like. A small number were, with the assistance of a benefactor, able to pursue secular studies and even distinguish themselves professionally and academically.

An interest in general culture and education became perceptible in Dvinsk around the turn of the century. There had always been schools, where Jewish children could attend. But few had availed themselves of this opportunity to gain a secular education. And then, again, parents given over to a religious way of life were reluctant to have their children mingle with the non-Jews. But a change came about at the beginning of the century, when parents made every effort to enrol their children in the Government schools. It became a status symbol.

The father was proud to see his son in the handsome uniform of a student, with polished silver buttons and a cockaded cap. But with the passage of the years, it became increasingly difficult for Jews to gain entry into the schools on account of the ten per cent **numerus clausus.** The Jews, as was their wont in the face of difficulties, resorted to various artifices, such as bribes. When the child gained admission, the mother would accompany him to the school in his fine uniform, as if to let the whole world know of her achievement. In one year, for which I looked up the statistics, the number of Jewish children in the schools was 360, as against 1210 non-Jews.

In the Town School the children were taught the whole day, and also on Saturdays. It goes without saying that Jews did not send their children there. From the two hundred Jewish families in Altstadt, only two Jewish families enrolled their children in the Town School. Private Jewish teachers gave tuition to child-

ren of school-going age, and they were largely responsible for their educational advancement. There was
Sholem Radus, in Altstadt, a private teacher who taught
twenty children, among whom were a few girls. He
was much looked-up to. This was all very well for the
rich, who could afford it. But the poor did not have
enough to buy pens and ink, let alone find money for
the tutor.

There was one Jewish school with an enrolment of
one hundred and fifty scholars, where Yiddish and
Russian were taught. It was a non-religious institution, and for that reason it received no financial support
from the Kehillah.

The Jewish trades school was situated in Pletzer,
near the railway-line. They taught there cabinet-
making and fitting and turning. In addition, the pupils
were given some grounding in general education. The
Principal was a qualified engineer, and the instructors
were qualified tradesmen. It was a three-year course,
and regular examinations were held to test the pupils.
The main purpose of the school was to train Jewish
children to become productive workers. In all, there
were only ninety pupils at the trades school at one time.
Most of them came from workingclass families or from
the poor, the majority from the provinces. This was
the period in Jewish life when productive work was
frowned upon. But after a time a few recruits joined
from amongst the holy ones in Dvinsk, who realised
that only a productive trade would give them that sense
of stability which was lacking in the Jewish "luft-
mensch" existence. At the turn of the century, the
trades school underwent a big improvement. What
was not more than a big shed, was rebuilt into a splendid structure of two storeys, of which any big town
could be proud.

A commercial school, recognised by the Government,
came into existence in 1900. The pupils had to have
a certain amount of education before they were allowed
to enter the school. My sister and brother were the

only ones from Altstadt to attend this school. But its span of life was very short, for it closed after being in existence for one year.

There were also two schools for the daughters of the rich—a Government and a private school. It was an expensive matter to keep a child at these institutions. The enrolment stood at around one hundred and fifty. These were the fortunate ones with rich parents. But the majority of girls received no education whatsoever. As they grew up, they mostly sat at home waiting for a suitor to turn up, or went to work as shop assistants.

Until the year 1900 there was not a single Jewish theatre in the whole of Dvinsk. The Jews never got beyond organising a "Purimschpiel". A Jew would affix a beard to his face—and this made him Mordechai Hatzadik. Someone else did nothing at all for a disguise. But he behaved like a drunkard—and this made a Haman of him. The role of Esther Hamalke was also taken by a man, who donned a dress, wore a wig, and coloured his cheeks with rouge.

But the first time I witnessed real theatre was in the year 1900. It was in the Mishke Fishsohn Theatre and, considering the times, the repertoire made available was sufficiently enlightened to gain the interest of the progressive elements among the youth. The older and middle-aged Jews kept away, and also prohibited their children from going there. The males among the youth ignored the prejudices of their parents, but the young girls obeyed them. The bulk of the theatregoers were drawn from the young workers, young girls who had come from the villages to work in the town, and the older pupils from the cheder who saved a kopke to be able to enjoy what the stage had to offer. Children who secretly visited the theatre would be severely spanked by the fathers if they were caught.

Seats in the stalls were 50 kopkes, and it was not often that every seat was taken. But there was never an empty seat in the gallery, where admission was ten kopkes. The season lasted six months in the year. Then the famous theatre of Julius Adler came to Dvinsk. And others followed. Julius Adler specialised in plays by Goldfaden and Yaacov Gordin. Every Saturday afternoon my friends and I hastened to the theatre. From the gallery, we could often see a middle-aged Jew, ordinarily amongst the boycotters of the stage, who had surreptitiously slipped into the stalls to see some theatrical attraction that had tempted him. Their numbers continued to increase. They were drawn by such dramas in Jewish history as— "Churban Yerusholaim", "Dos Pintele Yid", and "Uriel Acosta", which were the big attractions of those times. Julius Adler brought new spiritual life to the Jews of Dvinsk.

The Russian theatre was in Padolski Street, adjoining the railway line. Plays were staged there the whole year round, and the patrons included the Christian intelligentsia of the town. When the Jews had a foretaste of drama on the Jewish stage, they felt they had qualified for the Russian theatre. The actors were drawn from towns in Russia. The fare offered was of a good standard—Ostrovski, Gogol, Pushkin, Chekov. Most of the plays written by Tolstoy and Gorki were forbidden by the censor.

Durov's circus was also a feature of the town's entertainment. It drew its audiences mainly from the peasants and the non-Jews.

From 1900 onwards, there was a perceptible advance in the outlook of the youth. Young couples, not yet affianced, could be seen promenading down the streets. On the Sabbath, youths would make their purchases in the sweet and chocolate shops. A new spiritual world was dawning in Dvinsk.

"God alone can perform miracles!" says the Talmud. But this miracle, about which I am now going to speak did not descend from heaven. One day in 1901, the people of Dvinsk could not believe their eyes when they beheld Colonel Zoranowitz driving down Riga Street in the horseless carriage. Berl swore to his wife Yentel that, if it was true that he wanted to see his daughter Dvoshke under the "Chuppah", then it was also true that he had seen the Colonel driving in a carriage without the aid of horses.

Jews and non-Jews, women, shopkeepers, youngsters — all massed on Riga Street, near Gastchina Rad. They had come running as if to a fire or a burglary. They stood on tiptoe and on the window sills, craning their necks to get a sight of this wonder of wonders. One peasant scratched his head and mumbled—"Without a horse! Impossible! By Jesus, this is a wonder of wonders!" And he crossed himself. The police chief came along and told them to disperse. They moved away a little, but their curiosity drew them to the spot from where they could view the miracle more clearly. The Colonel turned a crank. The engine began to make a chug-chugging noise. He got into the car and pulling a lever it edged slowly forward. A thousand pairs of eyes, as if mesmerised, followed the automobile till it disappeared from sight.

But this was not the only technical invasion that had stirred the people of Dvinsk to their depths. Round about the same time, rumours were making the rounds that living people could be seen on a silver screen in a certain hall, which they called by the imposing name of Grandelektra. And what a melange could be seen there—murderers, weddings, markets, horses, cattle. It was the new wonder that had descended on Dvinsk round about 1904. Admission to the Grandelektra was 20 kopkes for adults, and 10 kopkes for children. How my heart palpitated as I entered this strange emporium for the first time. And one Jew who had witnessed this miracle, said to his friend that you could no longer doubt that even the dead could rise from their graves.

This was all climaxed by the new wonder invading Dvinsk: candles and kerosene were being exchanged for electric globes. The shops were now brilliantly lit up. They gathered at homes to talk over this latest miracle. Everyone wanted to press the "poopikel", which was what they called the switch. "God said let there be light—and there was light!" They even knew that Thomas Edison had invented electricity. And they also knew that Thomas Edison was a Jew. For did not his name end with **son**, exactly the same as Jacobson and Chaimson—both of them well-known Jews in Dvinsk. It was the wealthy ones who at first had benefited from the introduction of electricity. A number of years had to pass before the average householder began to use it in his home.

There were two big parks in Dvinsk—the Old Park, about which I shall write at a later stage, and the New Park, which was also known as the Dubrovinski Park. In autumn, the parks became orphaned in their desolation. The falling leaves were driven in every direction and covered the streets. The trees looked like skeletons. The snow took over everywhere in the winter, and not a living being passed through the park gate. It was not till Pesach that the snow began to melt and the warm sun dried out the puddles and the quagmires. That was the time also when the convicts from the gaol were led to the park under escort, and began to clean up the debris that had accumulated over the months.

It did not take long before the young couples, Jews and Christians, came there once again, to spend many and enjoyable hours. In the Dubrovinski Park there was a dairy, where you could drink fresh milk. Peasants erected their little kiosks and sold cream, fresh cucumbers, spring onions, and raddishes. On the quiet, they sold a bottle of vodka. When the couples got tired of promenading they betook themselves to the kiosks, where they could rest and regain their energies.

On Sunday afternoons, the Dvinsker Volunteer Fire Brigade organised dances and amusement. Two uniformed firemen, who sold admission tickets, were posted at the gates. Quite a number evaded them by climbing over the redoubtable fences. Inside the Park, the Firemen's Orchestra played tuneful music, to which the couples whirled in a dance. Others lay on the lawns and talked of many things—but one theme.

Talking of the Fire Brigade, I must stop to say something about the dwellings in the poorer part of Dvinsk, which were built with such a disregard of all architectural principles that they were headaches for the firemen. A house was built so that it leant lamentably against its neighbour. Not a thought was given to the erection of a wall that could act as a fire-break. Houses in a state of decay were turned into little workshops. Stables for horses, goats and cattle also made their appearance at random. Sheds were erected to store the firewood; dustbins, waterclosets were made from creaking boards. Ramshackle houses were to be found in Pletzer, Gayok and Esplanade. The houses were so ancient for the most part, that the wood was like dried-out cinder, and highly inflammable. The roofs were covered with shingles and wooden boards of the cheapest quality.

Was it any wonder that things went up in flames when a chimney caught fire? And the fire would spread to the neighbouring houses, and in no time the flames were devouring a whole block. But it must be conceded that another factor that was not unhelpful in the spread of fires, was the fact that insurance companies, with romantic names such as Salamandra and Yakir, had come into being in that part of the world. One advantage resulting from the destruction of the old hovels by fire, was that some fine modern houses were built in their place. Not a week passed in summer, but a sizeable fire broke out in some suburb of Dvinsk.

The headquarters of the Fire Brigade was near the centre of the town. Every variety of machine or artifice for the extinguishing of fires could be found there. The Brigade consisted of nine professional fire-

men. There were two other Fire Brigades, one at
Pletzer and one at Altstadt. What such miniature
Brigades could accomplish in the face of a raging fire—
and sometimes there were two fires raging simulta-
neously—can well be imagined. And that was the
reason why a Volunteer Fire Commando had come
into being. Hundreds joined it.

These volunteers came mostly from wealthy homes.
It was not easy for a worker or a trader to gain membership for two reasons. The one was that it entailed
quite a sizeable personal expenditure. Membership fee
was five roubles. Then one had to provide his own
uniform and metal helmet. There was also the consi-
deration of the time spent, which a workingman could
not spare. Every volunteer had to spend time in
training, and he could be called upon any time, night
or day, to help in bringing a fire under control. There
were also parades, manoeuvres, and a whole lot else.
Discipline was enforced. There were a few Jewish
volunteers from the lower social strata. I, myself, was
a volunteer for many years.

The duties of the volunteers were manifold. They
not only helped extinguish fires, and rescue people from
the flames, but guarded chattels and property from
burning homes against marauding thieves. A special
section was deputed for this purpose. They wore green
caps and green armbands. It was a high honour to
belong to the volunteers. The head of the Volunteer
Commando was Robert Wittenberg, of the well-known
Wittenberg family.

As in other countries, Saturday afternoons were
devoted to sport—mostly ball games. But it was not
a ball game, such as is popular in the Western world.
For it was with snowballs that time was passed in recreation, and it was on the icebound Dvina where it
took place. The contest was usually between the
Russians from Griva and the Jews from Dvinsk. Those

who indulged in this pastime were mostly from the underworld, or the "kayechnikes" who were resting from transporting their loads of sand and stone. The children prepared heaps of snowballs which served as ammunition. At the outset, only snowballs were used in the combat. But, as is the case in all warfare, weapons and ammunition with time begin to improve in effectiveness. And on the Dvina, too, they decided that if a piece of jagged ice was inserted into the snowball, it would add greatly to the fun. Those who participated in the actual contest were not so many. But the number of spectators was not much less than that at a football cup-tie in Britain.

Both sides had experts at this particular form of sport. The most celebrated figure among the Jews was Avremke Katok, who worked in a brush factory. He would remain in the background for a time, and only join in when the Jews were faring badly. His snow trajectories were hurled with uncanny accuracy, and they landed on the target with such force that many a Russian had to withdraw momentarily under the devastating fusillade. Any number of the participants came away from this sporting tourney with bloody heads and faces.

On those days that the Jews emerged victorious, they went home singing songs of triumph. But when they were defeated then, as is the fate of the defeated, the spectators jeered at them to add salt to the wounds. "Go and make tefillin and mezuzahs—or sew tsitsis!" was an insult that was commonly hurled at the defeated. When the contest ended after "Havdolah", they made for Chaike Tanz, where they heavily indulged. And as their spirits rose with the consumption of more alcohol, they vowed to vanquish the enemy on the next Saturday.

One day rumours were current in Dvinsk that a famous Jew, Dr. Herzl by name, was negotiating with the Turkish Sultan for the purchasing of Eretz Yisroel

as a homeland for the Jews.   It was said by one of the
experts in this field of international diplomacy, that
Herzl was a few thousand rendels short.   But what
were a few thousand rendels between Jews!   The
necessary amount would one way or another be made
up, and the Jews would once again have a homeland of
their own.   We all wanted to know just exactly how
much it was that the Sultan wanted.   But it was impossible to gain the exact figure.   The Zionists were
inclined to diminish the amount, and the Bundists to
increase it.

In the meantime, every Jew was called upon to buy
a Shekel, and the price was by no means excessive—40
kopeks in all.   Could the price of a Shekel be high
when it would gain you admission into Eretz Yisroel,
which was about to become our own?   Herzl was the
Moses of this age.   And just as Moses took the Israe-
lites out of Egyptian bondage, so would Herzl lead
them out of the Golah.

And when all this speculative talk, and wilder dreams,
had begun to subside, an organisation was founded and
the Jewish intelligentsia, men and women, began to
flock to it.   There were idlers amongst them who had
nothing else to do with their time.   But, on the other
hand, there were a number of idealists who strove night
and day to draw new recruits from the youth for the
Zionist movement.

Round about this time, an event of some occasion
took place in Dvinsk—a library was inaugurated.
There was a membership fee of one rouble, and a charge
of three kopkes for every book borrowed.   Russian
and Yiddish books were made available at this library.
Among the Yiddish books to be found there, were
those by the sentimentalist Dinensohn—"Even Negev"
and "Yossele" being the most popular.   All the works
of Mendele were obtainable, except "Die Klatze",
which was banned by the censor.   Jules Verne's works

were heavily borrowed. The Russian classics—Pushkin, Gogol, Turgenev—were popular, as were translations from the famous writers of other countries. From the outset almost, the library was too small to cope with the demand for its too numerous subscribers—for the most part tailors, carpenters, locksmiths and also maidservants, to whom romantic novels made a great appeal.

In Altstadt the library arrived late on the scene, as happened with most things that started out in town. But this shortcoming was made good by Zusse the carrier who would arrive from time to time carrying a load of booklets by Shomer Blaustein with such lurid and exciting names as—"Der Meshumed", "Der Tzvei Weibernik", "Der Treifenik". But he also balanced them out with booklets by Tannenbaum, that carried such romantic titles as—"Die Gan Aden Feigele", "Der Prinz un die Prinzessen", "Der Pastech in Wald". Complaints were lodged by parents that this literature was demoralising the young. The Rabbi ordained that all Zusse's books should be burnt, and Zusse himself was driven from Altstadt.

Chapter Eight

THE WORKING CLASSES

The workers of Dvinsk could be divided into a number of categories. Here they differed from conditions in the small villages, where only bootmakers and tailors were to be found. And there were usually twice as many of them as the village had need of. If the truth may be told, they stood on a rather low moral and cultural level. And it was well known that they had an unbridled appetite for alcoholic beverages. This was in a way quite understandable. The boy who became apprenticed to a bootmaker or tailor was usually about eleven years old and hailed from a very poor home, torn with domestic strife. "If only he could have learnt his prayers," the father would lament. "And if he knew how to pray, would it be of any use to me?" the mother would answer him. "Can you ever get him to do anything, except to play 'lapta' with the shkotzim? And what of the complaints about broken windows?"

The father wanted to know from her if the bootmaker, who had not food for himself, would even be able to provide food for their son. But for all that, there was little for him to do except take his child to become apprenticed to the bootmaker. The arrangement was that the bootmaker had to teach him the trade in three years, and provide board and lodging for him. No contracts were drawn up, to be stamped or sealed. The word was given with a handshake. The father told his son to be obedient and intelligent, kissed the "Mezuzah" and departed.

The first assignments given to this bootmaker apprentice lay well outside the trade itself. It was to take the rubbish-bin out of the house, wash napkins, do the washing at the riverside, and look after the goat in the grazing fields. And if it should happen, as it all too often did, that the bootmaker was without work and feeling bitter about it, he would land his apprentice a few sharp slaps on the cheek to relieve the tension. And in addition, the woman of the house would join in the pastime of making life a misery for the apprentice. Like Oliver Twist, it often happened that the apprentice resorted to flight.

The life of the tailor's apprentice was as trying. Apart from his many other chores, it was his duty to blow the cinders in the press-iron to maintain the heat. The soot would blow back in his face, and you would think that he was a coal-miner. For some reason or other, the tailoring trade was monopolised by the Jews. From early morning till late at night they sat on the table and stitched, stitched, stitched with their needles, their heads growing dizzy with the fumes of the kerosene lamps. When there was a dearth of work in Dvinsk, the tailors would betake themselves to other centres like Vilna, Riga, Kovno, in search of employment. In Dvinsk, the tailors stood on a higher cultural and intellectual level than in the small villages. They could read a newspaper, and even a book. During the Revolution they played quite an important part. A fair number in the tailoring trade were women. They were prominent in the workshops where uniforms and other clothing were manufactured for the army. The girls apprenticed to the tailoring trade were often under ten years. They were in demand, for when they were not engaged in tailoring they could tend the child of the house. And they were more handy at it than a boy. Everything was expected of them in this regard—everything, except to suckle the child.

When they qualified as tailoresses, their troubles commenced. Pay was at a minimum. And on top of it all, there was the extra aggravation a dressmaker had from her feminine clientele. "Do you call it a dress?" a woman complained at a fitting. "Why, I look like a mountain. And my breasts are like seven pots of milk." "But you are nicely filled out, my dear madam," the dressmaker pleaded with her. And then there was another client who complained she looked like a wooden board, and insisted on being "filled out."

The workers of Dvinsk, though poorly paid, were not without dignity. On Saturday nights they ambled up and down the park, neatly attired and self-confident. They had not yet developed any kind of literary taste, for there was no time to read.

There were any number of sub-divisions within the building trade. The Russians did most of the heavy work, such as excavating the foundation. They also formed the bulk of the bricklayers, and could build the framework of a house or building right up to the roof. Now and again a Jew strayed into this sector of the building trade. If the Russian building worker kept away from drink, he could earn enough to live fairly comfortably. There were five thousand building workers of the Christian faith. After Pesach, with spring setting in, many of them took on jobs in other parts of the country.

The technique employed was still of a primitive order. Thirty bricks were placed in a wooden crate, which was carried on the shoulders as high as the fifth floor. It must be remembered that the walls built were three times the thickness of walls in countries with a warm climate. Wooden houses were constructed from heavy beams. Building operations were seasonal. Everything closed down in the winter, but when the summer came there was plenty doing. A large number of unskilled workers were employed in the trade. The contractors had to guard against desertions and drunkenness, and for that reason employed a greater complement of workers than they actually required.

If the Christian building workers were responsible for the erection of the skeleton, the inside work was completed almost entirely by Jews. They were carpenters, plasterers, oven builders, glazers, painters—and, in later years, plumbers and electricians. Contractors employed sub-contractors.

There were one hundred Jewish carpenters and joiners in Dvinsk. They were physically of a stamp entirely different from the stoop-shouldered, weedy-looking tailors. They were well-built and broad-shouldered. Apprentices to the trade were past their Barmitzvah, and there were no women to lord it over them. The work required physical strength, for mechanical aids were very sparse. Beams were sawed into planks, and boards were made into stiles, rails and panels. The doors and window frames were solidly made. Only a youth with a good physique could enter the trade.

The carpenters and joiners worked in the open. They moved about a great deal in search of work, often finding themselves in towns where Jews were forbidden to live. Their pay was by no manner of means excessive, and they worked from dawn till dusk. In winter, with everything grinding to a standstill, a number switched to the furniture trade. The old carpenters were hard put to it to make ends meet. They could not compete with the younger ones, and they were reduced to earning a rouble here and there on such casual jobs as repairing a broken door or table. They ended their days, the way all workers did—they betook themselves to the Beth Hamedrash, said their "Tehillim" from morning till night, and relied on the mercy of the other Jews. The building workers were amongst the most prominent supporters of the Russian Revolution.

And now for a few words about my own trade—I was a painter. In our family we were all workers. Search as you will, you could not find a single holy one who made his living from promoting religion. We were mainly building workers. My father, formerly a house-painter, became a building contractor, and conducted himself like a civilised capitalist. There were three hundred Jewish painters in Dvinsk. Few of them were real craftsmen. A large number of painters

were employed for work on the railways. Huge contracts were issued for the painting of railway stations,
bridges, the living-quarters of the railwaymen, telegraph
poles, and much else. According to law, railway
property had to be repainted once in four years.

The biggest contractor was Voyin, and he held contracts covering a huge area. My own father, Mordecai
Flior, was given the contracts for the Dvinsker Fortress,
the huge State Hospital, and the railway line from
Kovno to Wersbulova, near Germany. The day after
Pesach he sent out 25 workers to complete jobs on the
railway line in his charge. About 200 painters in all
spread themselves out in the environs of Dvinsk, doing
various jobs. And there was also plenty doing in town,
where hospitals, post offices, schools, and residences of
the rich had to be renovated. By the time Shvuas
came, the only unemployed were those who were drunkards or lazy. The painters stood on a higher intellectual level than the tailors and bootmakers. The
apprentice received a rouble a week. In the autumn,
some painters and carpenters carried crates of glass and
repaired windows, or put in extra window-frames for
the winter.

Quite a number of sizeable factories had made their
appearance in Dvinsk about this time. I have made
mention in a previous chapter of Zacks' match factory.
But I propose to deal with it in greater detail, as it con-
veys to us a graphic picture of the industrial conditions
of that period.

It was situated in Pletzer, next to the cemetery. It
used to be said that when you entered into the employ
of Zacks, you were on the way to the cemetery. Of the
800 hands employed, 400 were girls from the age of ten
years and upward. The children packed the matches
into the box, pasted on the labels and the excise paper
bands. It was an art that they had to acquire, and
during the period of their apprenticeship they were

paid 50 kopkes a week working 14 hours a day. There were no laws protecting the health of the worker. The factories were dilapidated, and the machines were out-dated. Frequently, a worker left a finger or even a hand in the machine. And there was no provision made for compensation. When the worker was too old to be of any use, he was discarded like a squeezed-out lemon.

At six in the morning, the factory siren summoned the workers to duty. And they had to work till eight in the evening, according to the regulations. But who worried about regulations? When you once started work, you kept on working. Parents had to endure the searing spectacle of their ill-clad children going out in winter in the snow and sleet, and head for the factory. But what alternative had they? Above the workers stood the foremen. They were the only ones who earned a proper living. It was their business to be on guard all day, detect the slightest sign of slackness on the part of a workman, and in this way ensure a profitable output for the owner. Slackers were dealt with mercilessly. There was no appeal against the decision of the overseer, and no redress. His word was law. But whether they were dismissed or not, their days in the factory were never of a long span for, sooner or later, they fell victims to phosphorus consumption.

Most factories had the same regime as Zacks'. But there was one exception—Natanson's button factory. Natanson was a progressive capitalist. He employed 300 men and women. The hours of the working day were fewer, and wages were higher. Neither were workers summarily dismissed.

The white-collar shop assistants regarded themselves as being superior to the factory worker. Their hands were clean and manicured. And they wore elegant collars and bow-ties. And the women, too, dressed appropriately, and moved about gracefully. They spoke with a measure of refinement. But it was not altogether plain sailing for them. They had to acquire

the art of wheedling the customer into buying, and
fawn on the owner, especially on his wife.   There were
300 of these shop assistants.   And it often happened
that an irate owner would hurl ribald remarks at them,
if they failed to entice a customer into making a purchase.   If an assistant was dismissed, he had less
chance of getting another job than a worker.

In the year 1900, the news made the rounds in Dvinsk
that in Vilna there had come into being a league, known
as the promotion of modern thought (Haskalah), and
they made it their programme to bring progressive
thought and learning to the mass of the people.   Nobody knew how this Haskalah started.   But before long
this plant had reared itself to sizeable proportions.
The word itself derives from the Hebrew, but the
movement conducted its campaign in Yiddish.

The worker toiled too long and hard to join a movement, and when his day in the factory was done he took
to his bed in an effort to recuperate his strength for the
next day.   What leisure did he have for study purposes?
But things began to change, and with his will he over-
came his fatigue and his ears found the new movement
alluring.   This was also the time the Botei Midroshim
asked themselves what had happened to the youth.
Here was the Sabbath, and there was no youth to be
seen.

The reason was that on the Sabbath the young men
and girls awoke early, dressed themselves in their best,
and took to the park instead of the synagogue.   In this
park they sat themselves on benches in a row, and a
better-read person let them come into contact for the
first time with the treasures of the literary world. Among
the literary guides were the middle-class elements—
schoolteachers, nurses, intelligent workingmen, and
sons and daughters of the rich.   On Saturday afternoons, groups met at various remote points in Pletzer,
and there taught the uneducated workingmen the rudi-

ments of grammar, reading and writing. There was a tremendous appetite to absorb every kind of learning. It was so irresistible, that workers often absented themselves from work to pursue their studies.

Everybody derived enormous satisfaction—both teachers and pupils. In a short time, quite a number acquired a working knowledge of Yiddish and Russian. But there was one commodity in short supply—books. The library had too few books to cope with the demand, and interest in the old type of books began to flag. They were now getting more interested in works with social content—works by Tolstoy, Gorki and Zola. The more advanced sector of the working classes studied political economy, of which Marx's Capital formed an important feature. Many of the books were banned by the censor. But, as the saying goes—forbidden fruit tastes sweetly. A secret library came into existence, with translations from different languages. The masses read and read. They attended lectures on every subject.

The Haskalah movement in Altstadt made a big step forward through a strange incident. One day, the news spread through the whole of Altstadt that the police sergeant had taken a Jewish girl from the train, and had lodged her with the non-Jew Archip, the carpenter, just beyond Altstadt, near the village Liksna. You can imagine the wild talk that started everywhere about the reason for her coming to live with Archip. "Anyone can tell that she's pregnant, and is going to have a child there to cover her family's shame," was the explanation that one woman offered. "Then what has that go to do with the sergeant?" her friend enquired. A third one gave the explanation that she was pregnant by the sergeant himself.

It was a cold November day, but knots of Jews stood around trying to find an explanation for the girl's arrival. Someone put up the suggestion that a bribe of three roubles would soon elicit from the sergeant the identity of the girl. A Jew who went to the sergeant to investigate the matter, returned with the news that the girl was a political prisoner. She had fought both against the Tsar and God—"even our own God." She had been a whole year in prison in St. Petersburg, and she was banished for a further two years to the district of Liksna. She was forbidden entry into Dvinsk, and nobody was allowed to visit her. The Jews were all incensed with her, and they cursed her uphill and down dale. For they feared that she would bring only misfortune to the Jewish people.

For all that, we were all curious enough to have a look at her. And she obliged us by appearing in public the next day. Her name was Beilke. She was dressed like a Russian student girl, in high boots, a short fur-coat, and wearing a round hat on her head. She was tall and dignified in her appearance, and a typical Jewess. "Good morning, Jews, I am sure you're discussing me," she said half-playfully. They were astonished at her forward manner. They answered her good morning and started chatting to her. After all, she had robbed nobody and she was a freedom fighter. She was actually on the way to report to the sergeant.

It was in the home of Archip the carpenter that the Haskalah first began to take root. Although he had been deputed by the law to guard over the girl, young Jews and Jewesses met in his house to help spread the new spirit of Haskalah. It goes without saying that Archip was rewarded for his helpfulness. Students from Dvinsk and other towns forgathered there regularly, and often slept over. It was a central venue for study groups, lectures, readings, and much else. There were a number of Altstadt people who made a name for themselves in the Haskalah movement—a schoolteacher, a carpenter who had been to a number of big towns in Russia, Hirschele a painter and a one-time Yeshiva bocher from Satz's Yeshiva.

It was Christmas. For three days celebrations were held everywhere. Everything was closed. But in

Altstadt, the Jews were eagerly awaiting the first Zionist meeting. A number of Zionist emissaries were due to arrive from Israel. The Zionists called themselves Herzlisten. Jews were expectant, hoping to get news of the Wailing Wall, Rachel's grave, Jacob's ladder, and also about the Black Jews who lived on the other side of the Sambation. As the Christians were busy celebrating, and would not give up their time, the Jews and Jewesses themselves cleaned up the Beth Hamedrash, in preparation for the Zionist meeting that was due to be held there. Shortly after midday, the Jews began to forgather in the Beth Hamedrash. Women and girls also came, in violation of the law that prohibited their presence there.

At last the delegates arrived by cab. They were well-dressed in fur-coats and karakul caps. Two of the delegates were well-known to the people who had assembled. One was Dobrin, a teacher from the Yiddish school. The second was Kaplan, who had been a bank-teller. There was a third one with them, middle-aged, and wearing heavy spectacles with golden rims. They were well-received. A chairman was chosen—Chatzkel, the son-in-law of the Shochet. Dobrin was the first speaker. He made a powerful appeal for funds, and also for workers who would be prepared to dredge marshes, construct roads, and build a Homeland for the Jews of the world. Kaplan more or less repeated Dobrin's words. He urged Jews to join the Zionist organization and buy Shekolim.

The third speaker, who was supposed to have come from Israel, did not prove as acceptable as the other two. Apart from other considerations, he spoke with a sharp Polish accent that drew repeated laughter from the listeners. In the audience was also to be found Beilke.

She mounted the platform, together with two workers. As she started to speak, the religious Jews who regarded the voice of a woman as profane made for the door. But they were forestalled by a number of work-

men, who urged them to return to their places.   Silence
followed.   Beilke, in a voice that was clear and loud,
said that she supported the Zionist ideal.   It was right
that Jews should have their own land.   And she added
in Hebrew that the Jews were scattered to the four
corners of the earth.   It was like balm to a wound.
"A country, however, cannot be bought," she said—"it
can only be fought for."   Again, she quoted from
Tanach—"They took the land from the Amorite with
the sword."   And she started attacking the delegates.
"If money is needed," she declared, "let the rich give.
They have more than they need.   The poor cannot
afford to give.   Remember we have to fight for our
freedom here as well."

At this, there was a loud uproar, and they would not
allow her to continue.   They cursed and threatened
her.   For the police had forbidden her to speak.   At
this, Hirschke, the strong man of Altstadt, mounted the
platform and warned that if anyone informed on
Beilke, he would not only shake the money out of him
but also his lung and liver.   He was followed by
Hirschele, the son of Yosse Itze, the wagoner.   He was
a one-time Yeshiva bocher who had turned to the
Socialist movement.   "If the rich would be prepared
to make sacrifices, Yisroel would soon belong to the
Jews," he declared.   "The poor have nothing to give
away.   You want us to go to Eretz Yisroel to work.
Good!   Let Zacks and Grilliches and others transfer
their factorie to Eretz Yisroel, and we'll go and work
there."   He ended by calling on everyone present to
join the Bund.   Right or wrong, I there and then
decided to become a member of the Bund.

Chapter Nine

THE RED YEARS

One swallow doesn't make a summer. Beilke, the banned one, was, however, the one swallow that did make a summer in Altstadt. And if one person could accomplish so much, you can imagine what a number of active workers could achieve in Dvinsk, and specially in Pletzer where the most advanced workers were to be found. A new spirit descended on Dvinsk. The youths stopped drinking and gambling. The girls gave up dancing and such pastimes. Everybody tried to improve himself intellectually. The Russian Minister of Education Porbedonovtzev had summed up the situation accurately, when he issued the warning that Russia had to guard against enlightenment.

This was the time when the Russian revolutionary movement was beginning to show its head. Ministers, generals, and governors feared for their lives. And Tsar Nicholas was terrified that the fate which had befallen his grandfather Alexander II, who was assassinated, would also befall him. In Dvinsk, the political education of those days related to the peasant uprisings of Stenka Razin and Emilyan Pugachev. They studied the history of the Dekabrists and the Nihilists, and were uplifted by the reckless courage of the terrorists. There was little that the Government had to offer, except to encourage drunkenness among the workers and peasants, so as to take their minds off the political agitation that began to sweep through Russia at the time.

In 1901 Easter Monday fell on April 18th. It was for the Russian people an awesome week, comparable to the Yomim Naroim. This was the week when the worshippers went to the priest to make their confessions, and ask to be absolved from their sins. Pregnant

young girls confessed who their lovers were. The
priest received his stipend, the way the Jew pays his
due when he sells his "chomutz." The ceremony of
confessing was followed by a tremendous procession in
which priests, Archimandrites and other clergy participated. Banners, with Jesus and Mary, were unfurled
to the heavens. The church bells pealed incessantly.
A choir of young boys dressed in white chanted hymns.
The mass of worshippers made up the body of the
procession which now stretched four blocks.

April the 18th, was May the 1st, by the Gregorian
Calendar in use in the West. And this was the day
that the workers of the world, including Russia, celebrated workers' day. Four merchants stood in the
doorways of their businesses, overcome by a sense of
agitation. They were worried as to what was going to
happen that day. Radus, who had a poetic way of
expressing himself, said that he sensed new winds
blowing. "I hope I am wrong," he said, shaking his
head. "But I have an uncanny feeling that there is
going to be trouble to-day." His friend Magidson
jeered at him: "Trouble, did you say? What trouble?
Are the little bootmakers and tailors going to overthrow
Tsar Nikolai? Let them try to demonstrate with their
banners, and Police Chief Kourlandski will whip them
into submission." "Where do they think they are,
these plebeians—Paris?" asked the one-time Yeshiva
bocher Averbuch. My own employer Yawitz wanted
to know if there was no day left in the calendar to stage
a May Day procession, other than on Good Friday
when the church holds a procession of its own. "It's
the first of May, and they want to imitate the French,"
Averbuch explained. "Noch tohn die Franzaisen,
wellen zai laifen mit fulle haizen," was Magidson's
ribald comment in couplets.

Just then there came into sight Benzion Odes.

"Where are you running to?" enquired Radus.
"Can't you see Jews talking? Tell us—what's new?
What's new?"

"It looks to me that there's going to be a demonstration to express full solidarity with the world proletariat," Benzion answered him.

"What kind of 'proletariataler'? What kind of language is this?" my employer Yawitz asked.

"The workers of the world are uniting," said Benzion.

"Uniting today, uniting tomorrow—are you going to overthrow the Tsar?"

"You'll get what's coming to you," added Magidson. "He laughs best, who laughs last."

"And if you will go out with your flags and banners, will you bring down the little plate from heaven?" Yawitz asked mockingly.

And then, as they stood there speaking, there could be seen in Riga Street, in the distance, a mass demonstration singing songs. They had soon reached the Gastchina Rad. Workers, six in a row, were marching down the street like soldiers on parade. Three Red Flags preceded the procession, with the inscription in flaming letters on the first—"Long Live the First of May!" On the second banner was inscribed the demand for an eight-hour day. And on the third banner a worker was depicted breaking his chains. There were any number of red banners in the body of the procession itself. Women were noticeably absent. They sang "Die Svua"—"Brieder und svester fun arbeid und noit . . ."

The pavements on both sides of the street were massed with spectators—men, women and children. They were pushing and shoving to get a better view. Those who were afraid as the demonstration drew nearer, hastily betook themselves elsewhere. But the ones with proletarian pride joined the demonstrators, who were chanting songs of freedom. At the Parade Square there was a moment of tenseness and drama as the workers' demonstration and the religious demonstrators met head-on. It was as if two ages were in collision. The Red Flag confronted the Icons and banners. A worker stepped on to a box, and started haranguing. The police were quickly on the scene, and they dispersed the workers' procession.

On this occasion, the police behaved with commendable discretion. They used no force and allowed the demonstrators to disperse. The reason may be that this was a situation they had not been confronted with before, and they looked for a peaceful way out. The demonstrators were not made up of workers only. There were also the sons of rich merchants, who through the Haskalah movement had begun to move leftward.

There were no further demonstrations until midsummer. But the workers were not idle. They arranged gatherings in the Stropper Forest, at Mayak, on the cemetery, and at Slabodke. They were well organised. Sentries were posted at strategic points. And when the police staged a raid, it was seldom that anyone was arrested.

I have already described the conditions prevalent in Zacks' factory. Thursday was in the nature of Judgement Day for the workers. As they were handed their pay, they were told if they were still required or not. One Thursday, shortly after Shevuath, three hands were sacked, after their pay had been given to them. They were very popular with the other workers. A good deal of grumbling and discontent followed. But Zacks stood firm, and the workers decided to go on strike. This did not worry him. In fact it suited him, for the shelves in the factory were overstocked with manufactures that could last him for months. "When they've had a few days of starvation, they'll come back with their tails between their legs," said Zacks. The storekeepers, the holy set, and the merchants resented the action of the strikers.

The factory was idle for three weeks. Then there appeared on the scene a number of strikebreakers among the better-paid workmen, and they received the protection of the police. In due course, the wheels in the factory began to move slowly. The workers remained confident that without them the factory would not go into anything like full-scale production. They cursed the strikebreakers, but as this helped very little it was decided to take more drastic steps. One morning, when a policeman was escorting a worker to the factory, they were set upon and beaten so fiercely with sticks that the policeman ran for his life and the strikebreaker had to be taken to hospital. And that was more or less the pattern for all strikebreakers.

The workers were put to a severe test when winter arrived. In summer, it was still possible for the strikers to earn some money working in the building trade, helping wagoners. The women helped in vegetable gardens. They were getting support and sympathy from the other workers. Some money even began to arrive from America. But it was not nearly enough for the hundreds of strikers who had to be fed, and also their families. And then one day, a number of strikers were arrested and taken into custody outside the town. So far from the workers being intimidated, they became more aggressive. They even stepped up their demands: In addition to asking for the reinstatement of the three workers, they demanded higher pay, and the abolition of child labour under the age of thirteen. They also demanded half-pay for the time they had been on strike. As was to be expected, Zacks refused to consider these demands.

The strike lasted six months. The factory stocks had been depleted. The strikebreakers were doing work they were not used to, and a number of machines were put out of order. Many of them were lumpen elements lacking in elementary discipline. More often than not, they were drunk. Zacks started negotiations with the strike leaders. After protracted discussions and disputes, he yielded almost on all counts. From that time onward, the militance of the Dvinsker workers gained them the cognomen of "statsnikes."

The workers from the other factories now saw what a powerful weapon a strike was, and there followed a whole series of them. They lasted from a few days to a few weeks. The only exception was Natanson's button factory. Natanson met the workers' delegates, and they ironed out all difficulties amicably. In a number of factories workers demanded that foremen who were inconsiderate should be sacked. Fights between foremen and workers became a common occurrence. Many arrests followed, and quite a few workers were sent to prison.

One Tisha B'Av, the workers staged a demonstration in the Old Park. They had not got very far, when the police charged them and they scattered. There were no immediate arrests. But when night fell, the police raided the homes of the workers' leaders and took them away.

The Dvinsker Gaol had three names—the Red Building, the Gaol, and the Dvinsker Bastille. It had been built many years ago at Gayok, adjacent to the highway which led across the railway line to Pletzer. The Gaol grew with every passing year. From one storey, it was built up into two. In 1904 it rose to four storeys. Later this was increased to six. It was built of red bricks. The highway was in line with the third storey of the Gaol. The Gaol served not only Dvinsk, but a big part of the Kovner Gubernaie. It was surrounded by a thick brick wall. You entered the Gaol through a heavy iron door that creaked noisily on its rusty hinges. A sentry stood on the highway at a point nearest the Gaol, and he saw to it that everybody moved on without stopping to gaze or make inspections.

Many have written on gaols and gaol conditions. No convict is ever short of pain and sweat. That much they all have in common. But their suffering is somewhat relieved when they find themselves in the company of friends and acquaintances. And woe unto him who finds himself in the company of strangers or enemies!

A worker from Zacks' factory told me of conditions inside the Gaol. He had been arrested during the strike. The first thing he resented was when his clothing was taken away, and he was given a convict's uniform to wear. This was contrary to regulations, which allowed political prisoners to wear their own clothes. As soon as the warder left him in his cell, a few criminals who were with him fell on him and took away his food. When he asked them for a piece of bread, they assured him that he would not peg out.

Among the convicts with him, was a merchant convicted of fraud, who quietly told him to control himself, as there were a number of them who were to be tried for murder. The next day, when the merchant was taken away, he knew what he meant by it. They had a game they called—"Slappings". One convict had to let down his trousers, and the others slapped him till he guessed the one who had given him the smack. They forced him to bend, and they started with their recreation. At the end of the fun he felt that his buttocks had swelled to twice their size. He did not know their names. And he did not even know when his agony had come to an end—he had been unconscious. When he recovered, he had to be their servant. If he had had to remain with them he would have gone insane, he told me. But luckily, the next morning he could hear footsteps. The cell door opened, and they led in six Jewish youths who could use themselves.

Let me now tell you about these six. There were a number of workshops in Beskin's courtyard. Amongst them was one for making brushes, also a bookbinder, a few bootmakers, a tailor, a maker of uppers, and a joiner's shop. The joiner made windows and doors in the summer, and in the winter he manufactured kitchen furniture. The owner, Yoshke Rosenberg, was considered a well-to-do man. He employed six workmen and three apprentices. And he worked himself.

It happened one day that an apprentice mucked up
his job, as often happens. The boss would usually let
it go by with a few curses. But on this occasion
Yoshke, who was holding the leg of a chair in his hand,
landed the youngster with it so that he fell to the
ground, his head a mass of blood. Another apprentice
ran into the uppermaker's shop next door and called
out: "Quickly, Chatzel! the boss has killed Mottele—
he's dead." Chatzke threw everything down and
rushed to his brother Mottele. He found that his
brother was not dead, and that they were washing the
blood away from his head and face. Yoshke Rosenberg
was lying prostrate on the floor, and Avremke Katok,
the brushmaker, was administering him so many kicks
that there was little left for Chatzke to do. In the
midst of all the tumult and screaming, the police captain arrived with a number of policemen. How they
got there, nobody knew. Avremke Katok, Chatzke
and four other carpenters were placed under arrest.
In the meantime, a doctor came on the scene and he
took the apprentice with him to hospital. Yoshke was
taken to hospital in a cab.

And now let me resume the story of the six of them
in gaol, as it was told to me by the striker. Of the six,
he knew Avremke Katok well. He had seen him quite
often shying snowballs at the Russians in a fight on the
frozen Dvina. Avremke did not give the impression
of being a very strong man. He was of medium height.
When he was lodged in the cell, he had with him a
packet of food a woman friend had managed to slip
him. The other convicts saw it, and they snatched it
from him. "Wait a minute, we'll share it out," one of
the carpenters said to the convict. "We're all arrested.
Why should we fight?" One of the convicts, Vanka
Kabiloff, called out: "Crack the bloody Jew on the
jaw!" A fight broke out. It did not take long before
Avremke had gripped Kabiloff's throat and was bang-
ing his head against the stone floor as if it was a rubber
ball. The warders came running in and separated

them. Blood was streaming down their faces. They had to carry Kabiloff out. He was barely breathing. But they did not bring him back to cell No. 24. After that incident, things were normal in that cell.

I became a member of the Bund before I turned sixteen. What had made it possible for me to join the Bund before I was of age, was that I had qualified as an assistant, and even had an apprentice under me whom I was teaching the trade. There were two reasons that had enabled me to qualify so early on. The one was that I had a good working knowledge of the Russian language. I had grown up amongst Russians. The other was that I was a favourite with the manager, Gedalia Hedekkel. His father was a painter, and my father had helped him to get painting jobs in town so that he did not have to walk miles from his home to railway stations and similar places.

Before I had joined the Bund, I had already read a number of books I had borrowed from the town library. I had actually set up a small library in Altstadt with the aid of two girl-friends. There were other Bundists at Yawitz's—Gershon der Vilner and Ida Abramovna, a personable girl, no longer young, but cultivated. Ida collected funds when the strike was staged at Zacks' factory. Shortly before Succas, the assistants at Yawitz's received their presents of money from the factory owners to induce them to push their goods to customers. My share was 8 roubles, 50 kopkes. When Ida asked me what portion I was contributing to the strike fund, I impulsively told her she could have the lot. The example I had set was followed by the others, and quite a considerable sum of money was collected. My action had impressed them, and they felt I was excellent material for the Bund. I was recommended by Gershon and Ida, and I was admitted.

My duties at first were to attend lectures and educate myself in the work of the Bund. The lectures com-

menced at 9 in the evening, and finished at 11. And
then I had to make my way to my home in Altstadt.
It was quite an undertaking, for I arrived home at one
in the morning. I did not have a key. Doors were
bolted and barred from inside. When I knocked on
my mother's window, she called out: "Where you have
been until now, there you can also go and sleep." When
after a while my father let me in, I had to find a good
excuse to explain my late-coming. It was either that I
had worked late at the business, or that I did not have
anyone to accompany me home. It often happened
that I slept over at my aunt's place in town.

When winter came all strikes were brought to an end,
and also the demonstrations. The movement, like
Nature itself, became dormant in winter. But after
Purim, with the arrival of spring, the tailors took counsel and decided to go on strike. As was usual in those
times, they demanded higher wages and fewer hours of
work. The bosses, some of them the politicians of the
Planover Minyan, called the workers every name under
the sun for going on strike just before Pesach. The
strike was long drawn-out. They decided to go to the
Beth Din, who were to arbitrate. The employers
argued that orders for suits taken had to be executed
at the old prices arranged, but they promised to raise
wages after Pesach. The workers, on the other hand,
were against waiting till after Pesach, when work fell
away and the bosses would be at an advantage. But
as neither the strikers nor the employers had much in
the way of resources for a drawn-out struggle, they
arrived at an agreement. When the tailoresses went
on strike, the women employing them begged for
mercy as a stoppage would ruin their businesses. "Do
you think I am Zacks, and can stand a strike for six
months?" one of them pleaded with them. The girls
relented.

An incident worth recalling, that caused quite a stir,
took place in a high-class women's fashion workshop
owned by Isak Gervis. He was considered a Don Juan

and he took great delight in measuring the women. It was said of him that he liked it so much that he would measure them over and over to ensure that he had not made an error. Fifteen girls worked in his place, and they resented the amount of unpaid overtime they had to do. One day, a girl refused when he ordered them to work through the night. He slapped her face sharply with the back of his hand, and told her that he would not stand any nonsense. This incensed the other girls, and they belaboured Isak to such good purpose that they had to remove him to hospital. This was typical of the rising temper of the times between employers and employees.

Chapter Ten

THE RISING STORM

By 1902, the workers' movement was growing and making itself felt throughout the whole of Russia. It was clear to us that a great deal was happening in St. Petersburg, Moscow and other big centres. News reached us, despite the censor's clamping down, that there were workers' demonstrations and strikes all over. Important officials and high-ranking police officers were being assassinated. The students were also stirring. A fire was beginning to smoulder, that eventually got out of control. But let us leave the happenings in Russia for the time being.

It was now on the eve of Pesach in Dvinsk. For a whole month everybody was making preparations for this important Festival. Many families did not eat or drink in order to have enough for a splendid Yom Tov. I can still recall that the Halamoed Pesach was very quiet in our home. My father had to send out a team of workers to renovate the stations for which he had contracted. By Halamoed, very many more than he required would put in an appearance asking to be taken on. His door hardly closed, as one workman came in and another went out. In this particular year, Pesach had gone by and not a single workman had sought employment from him. Even workmen from his own family, whom he always employed, were keeping away. It was known that a building workers trade union had come into being some while back. But my father, who was used to old times and fashions, could not believe it that they had gained such an influence over the workers in such a short time.

My father was getting worried at the state of affairs. He was to have sent a team to do the hospital and officers' club. But he had no one to send. The day after Pesach had ended, two painters from Pletzer who had never worked for my father came into the house. They were accompanied by a third bespectacled man, who was obviously not a worker. My father greeted them and asked them the purpose of their visit.

"The building workers have organised a trade union," the bespectacled man answered him. "They have gathered in the trade union hall in Miasnichki Street, near the market. An employer requiring workers must apply to the secretary of the union. Workers are forbidden to go to the houses of employers to seek work."

I was listening to what was going on, and I realised that a worker had to obey his union, or he would find it difficult to get employment. My father was further informed that the union had fixed the working day at nine hours, and that pay was to be raised by one rouble fifty kopkes a week.

"And if I don't go to the union?" my father asked.

"Then you'll not get a single worker," one of the painters answered him.

"No threats, please. If necessary, I'll do the work with members of my family." Three brothers and two uncles were in the employ of my father.

"We're not threatening you," said the other painter. "We're asking you to come to the union for workers. You, yourself, were once a working painter. Do you want your brothers to clash with their fellow workers?"

"We'll see what's what," my father said.

When the three of them left, I can recall that he started an argument with my mother. For her, they were rebellious "statsnikes", to whom there could be no yielding. But my father saw them as quite honest people who were demanding what was their due. The next day he went to the building workers' headquarters. My mother told me to accompany him, for fear that he might be assaulted. When we arrived there we found hundreds of workers milling around, and others standing in little groups talking animatedly. A couple of small building contractors came up to my father and urged him to employ non-Jewish building workers, and not to yield to the "statsnikes".

"I am not short of good advice," my father said sarcastically. "But I propose to do as I think fit."

All this time, a number of contractors had engaged carpenters. My father went into the office. There he had a talk with the chairman of the union, Mikhoel the carpenter, and he forthwith engaged fifteen workers and three apprentices, apart from the members of his own family who were in the building trade. Altogether, about fifty or sixty workers were signed on that day. The numbers were so few, that a clash between the workers and the contractors seemed inevitable. On top of it, some contractors discharged them before the end of the week was up, after hiring them on the Sunday. The union insisted on a full week's pay.

A few weeks passed and the union emerged on top. All carpenters and plasterers were in employment. But the biggest painting contractor, Voyin, refused point-blank to go to union headquarters and beg for workers whom he could employ.

"I am the boss here—and not they," he challenged them.

In the dead of night, a number of unemployed painters made for Voyin's house and offered their services. This leaked out, and the union placed pickets round the house to prevent it. Shevuas was approaching, and a large number of workers remained unemployed. The wives now took a hand in matters. They made for the union and cursed the officials, whom they held responsible for the plight in which they found themselves, without money to buy food for Shevuas. They threatened to put an end to the union. In the midst of all the excitement, there came to the fore Zuske Pesachowitz, otherwise known as Zuske One-eye. He was a tough from the underworld. In the nights, he was a cab-driver.

"Women—betake yourselves to your homes," he called out — "tomorrow all your husbands will be at work. I can give you my assurance for it."

That same evening, Zuske collected around him a band of thugs after his own heart, and he made for Voyin's house, which he unceremoniously entered.

"How long do you expect your workmen to go about without work?" he said to Voyin.

"Till they'll come and ask for it," Voyin answered him.

"Is that so?" called out Zuske, grasping him by his shirt. He looked at him menacingly with his one eye, and said: "If you don't take on the workers by tomorrow morning, you will no longer be in the land of the living."

He pushed him against the wall. His mates overturned the table and the samovar that was standing on it.

"Hooligans! murderers!" Voyin's wife kept shouting.

Jews came running from everywhere. She was told to send for the police captain. The next day, negotiations went on for several hours between Voyin and the trade unions. Finally, he agreed to sign on all his workers. This was a great victory for the union. They punished those workers who had tried to make up to the bosses on the quiet, and for informing against other workers. The union started a campaign against the prevalence of drunkenness among the workers. That summer, there was full employment in the building trade.

As the First of May was approaching, the whole town was pasted up with leaflets. Printed in Russian and Yiddish, they were plastered over windows, gates, doors and synagogues. For the first time, these leaflets took on a political character. The Tsar and his henchmen were accused of cruelty and oppression towards the people. They were charged with gaoling them, banishing them to Siberia and even shooting down a number who opposed them. Pogroms against the Jews and the ill-treatment of Russian workers were fiercely denounced.

Round about this time, there appeared the first number of the newspaper "The Proletariat". One copy passed through hundreds of hands, to be avidly read, so that the lettering was almost rubbed away. All news of workingclass activity in Dvinsk was printed in "The Proletariat". The workers' organisations continued to grow by leaps and bounds. One leaflet pasted up in the town called for a May Day demonstration. Both the workers and the police made full preparation for this day. Two days before the demonstration police reinforcements were brought into Dvinsk. At every corner in the centre of the city two soldiers and a policeman were posted. They had orders to shoot, if necessary. They even set up a cannon in the Parade Square to intimidate any troublemakers. By the time May Day arrived, the town was swarming with soldiers and police.

The chief of police Kourlandski had his way—there was no May Day demonstration. Instead, the workers congregated at prearranged spots in the surrounding forests, and held meetings there. When Kourlandski learnt that three hundred workers were meeting in the Tserepova Forest, he turned red with anger. Arrests were widespread. Both those innocent and guilty were drawn into the net. Amongst those arrested was the first Jewish girl—Rachel, a dressmaker. In a few days, leaflets were pasted up telling of the May Day demonstrations that had taken place throughout Russia: demonstrators had been shot in St. Petersburg, and there had been disturbances as far afield as the Caucausus. Students had erected barricades in Moscow. A provincial Governor had been assassinated. One of the most exciting events had taken place at the Bezdoni Station, two stops from Vilna, on the way to Dvinsk.

Bezdoni was a quiet place with a small station, where the train stopped for five minutes. This was the spot where twenty four members of the Polish Socialist Party, led by Pilsudski, raided a train and took away

150,000 roubles. Amongst the twenty four was a Jewish woman, Helfman, and her son. To add insult to injury, Pilsudski sent the Tsar a letter, not to thank him for his splendid gift but to tell him that the gallows awaited him. The envelope carried the stamp of the Polish Socialist Party.

Von Wahl was the Governor of the Province of Vilna. It became known in Dvinsk that after the strikes, demonstrations and Pilsudski's raid on the train, Von Wahl had ordered that political prisoners should be lashed with wet thongs. This punishment was administered in the Vilna Antikol Gaol. It created a great stir in Dvinsk—as if the inhabitants themselves had experienced the smart and pain of these brutal lashings. Women were not excluded from this savagery. They raised their fists as a vow to avenge these evil doings.

Hirsch Leckert lived in Vilna at the time. He was born in a small Lithuanian village near Dvinsk, called Kamaai. He was a bootmaker from his boyhood in Kamaai, where he had lived in dire poverty. Since it is as easy to endure poverty in a big city, as in a small village, he decided to go and live in Vilna. He became a member of the Bund, married, and set up a little boot-shop in the wealthier part of the town, on the Konstantinovski Prospect.

The bestiality of the Governor of Vilna had unsettled him. He managed to acquire a revolver, and one day when the Governor took a walk past his little work-shop, he plugged him with two bullets, crying out as the Governor collapsed—"These are your medals, you sadist." Hirsch Leckert was hanged. He conducted himself bravely as he went to the gallows. His last request was that he should not be blindfolded, so that he could see the hangman who would eventually share the fate of the Tsar on the gallows. That same week the student Karpovich was hanged in the Peter Paul Fortress for assassinating the Governor Bodganovich.

Leckert's death created a stir amongst the workers and intelligentsia throughout Russia. Songs and elegies were composed to commemorate his act of heroism. There were protest demonstrations in many parts of the country. Dvinsk, too, made preparations to honour the Jewish hero. One morning, four hundred young men and women gathered at the Old Park. They lined up in serried ranks, and unfurled red and black banners carrying the slogans—"Down with the Tsar! Avenge Leckert!" They marched down the street and the public joined in, swelling the ranks of the demonstrators. They continued some distance and dispersed. There was no interference from the police, who thought it more discreet to keep their distance in view of the angry mood of the demonstrators.

The craven behaviour of the police was a humiliation for Kourlandski. The revolutionaries had marched through the streets, and no one had dared to molest them. In a widespread night raid, over one hundred men and women were arrested and lodged in gaol. Mothers wept bitterly as misfortune swept on them and their homes. Amongst those who were detained, were Zionists who had been dreaming of going to Israel. Although they were innocent, they were not only thrown into gaol, but severely beaten up. Two days later the anti-Semitic "Novoya Vremya" of St. Petersburg carried the news that the gendarmes with the aid of the brave police chief Kourlandski had dispersed a demonstration of Jews in Dvinsk. A hundred had been arrested, including the leaders, without any shedding of blood. In an interview with this paper, Kourlandski said that the Jews were cowards, and that within three months he would sweep them out of existence. After a few weeks a number of those arrested were released, some were banished from Dvinsk by administrative decree, and others were handed over for trial. A fund was started to help Hirsch Leckert's widow and child, and the workers excelled themselves with their generous contributions.

The strike fever that had started at Zacks's factory continued to spread, as each category of workers also sought to improve their conditions of service. Even the conservative elements took a hand and made demands on their employers. The wagoners and carriers also demanded something better out of life. They won the strike, and shops began to close at six instead of nine.

In summer at six in the evening the sun is still high in the heavens. When the day's work was done, everybody made for the Old Park. It was not only a place where people gathered and promenaded up and down, but it was a centre of intellectual activity. The Haskalah movement flourished there. The Park was a huge square garden bordered by a wooden fence. At the sides were broad alleys, along which benches were placed at regular intervals. Six or seven people could comfortably seat themselves on them. On Sundays the tightly-corseted women in their finest garb paraded up and down like peacocks. They came there for possible encounters, amongst other things. The Russians from Griva came with their highly-polished "shtivel" and embroidered shirts. Their women wore their best velvet coats. It was noticeable that nearly all of them had pock-marked faces. The reason was that these Old Believers were not allowed to vaccinate themselves, and as a result small-pox wrought much havoc amongst them.

With the leisure time now at their disposal, the workers also began to frequent the Old Park. The subjects they discussed there ranged far and wide—world politics, religious problems, literature, the heavens and the world to come. The Park became congested with visitors, many of whom took to the streets leading off from it. It was the assembly point of the organised workers' movement. The moment a worker discarded his overalls, he betook himself to the Park. They walked and talked there till the early hours of the morning. And when they separated, they looked forward to the next day's meeting.

The workers' movement continued to grow in

influence and size. So much so that celebrated figures from St. Petersburg and other centres visited Dvinsk on important occasions and addressed gatherings there. Needless to say, these gatherings were held outside of the knowledge and the view of the police.

The arrests had so far taken place in Dvinsk and Pletzer. Not a single arrest had been made in Altstadt, although the membership in the various political organisations from this part was quite high. For this, the police sergeant and his two underlings were largely responsible. Sergeant Kharlapoff had an enormous paunch, and a red face with handle-bar moustache. He would show his face in the village at 9 in the morning. In the daytime he was accompanied by the policeman Ziermov, a Ukranian, who was thin as a rake and as lazy as you make them. When they entered a store, the owner knew that he had to place a glass of vodka before them, and a piece of gefilte fish. And when they left the premises, a rouble was quietly slipped into the sergeant's hand. Their final stopping-place, after making the rounds, was at Etke, the widow, where they continued with their carousal in earnest. It often happened that they slept over at Etke's, or the policeman would take the sergeant home much the worse for liquor.

The policeman who accompanied Kharlapoff on his rounds in the night was called Filelaiko. He was a 70-year old idiot, on whom the uniform hung raggedly as on a scarecrow. During the summer nights, when he was supposed to be on duty, he made a habit of stretching himself out in the fields. He had made arrangements with the shepherd to wake him if he overslept, which he usually did. Yermilo, the crippled shepherd, used his trumpet to good effect in an effort to awaken Filelaiko. And he would add a few wild screams to boot. "Filelaiko, wake up—the sun is already high in the heavens," he kept calling out. And then the shep-

herd went into the village itself and called on the milk-
maids to rise, as it was milking time. In winter, when
it was too cold to sleep in the open, Filelaiko found a
resting place from duty in the Jewish women's "bod."
The Russian Potophera, who was in charge of the
"bod", would allow him in and wake him in the morning. Such was the strong arm of the law in Altstadt.
And it may well be assumed that the political organisations had little to fear in going about their business.

On Friday nights a number of us walked over to the
Soonia Lake, where we hired a rowing boat from a
peasant. We rowed along singing revolutionary songs,
till we reached the island in the centre of the lake.
Lectures and debates on the movement were held there
till the early hours of the morning, when we would row
back under a night sky massed with stars. When
special large gatherings were held, several boats were
hired to take the people there. The boats would move
up and down till everyone was on the island. Celebrations and parties were also held there from time to
time.

After the Hirsch Leckert demonstration, the police
made an arrangement with the forest rangers to let
them know of political gatherings held in the forest.
When a ranger in the course of his duties found such
remnants as cigarette butts, match boxes, wrappings
from sweets, and other signs that people had foregathered on that spot, he would notify the police.
Kourlandski then instructed those under him to bring
the political criminals to justice at all costs.

One day, the political organisation decided to hold a
big gathering on a Saturday, a non-working day, at a
spot in the pine forest of Srednaya Pogulanka. As this
forest was on the outskirts of Altstadt, the members
from this part were asked to gather first at Bentze, the
tailor. I was there. We were sent out to act as
patrols, and were told the watchword. There were ten
ways of entering the forest. The patrols walked in
pairs, a youth and a girl together. At four in the morn-

ing, my girl and I were on the way to the fortress to take up our positions. We remained at our post till ten at night. Food was brought to us during the day. Two hundred people passed through our hands, and we directed them to the spot where the meeting was being held. Among them were workmen, middle-aged men and women, and also quite a number of the sons and daughters of the wealthy. It was the biggest mass gathering ever to have assembled in Dvinsk. Over one thousand had rolled up. It was a day of speeches, of singing, and also of feasting and merry-making.

As twilight was coming on the ranger Antonov, accompanied by his assistants, made his appearance. They were in civilian clothes. But they had metal emblems on their caps. A number, seeing the metal emblems, mistook them for police and they started to panic. They ran as fast as they could, as if their lives were at stake, and left all their belongings behind. But the leaders of the gathering retained their presence of mind. They invited Antonov and his men to join them in some drinks. They were kept there till nearly the whole gathering dispersed. The ranger and his men were fast asleep.

But the following morning, when Antonov awoke, he had a great deal to tell Kourlandski. He informed him that there must have been two thousand at the gathering. And he brought as evidence a raincoat and a number of ladies' garments. When Kourlandski visited the spot in person, he concluded from the amount of debris left over that there must have been three thousand present. He wanted to know what had happened to his police force and their intelligence, who were to have advised him in good time when a meeting was being held in the forest. He vented his anger on sergeant Kharlapoff, whom he summarily dismissed. Kourlandski set about paying peasants who lived in the neighbourhood of the forest for information about any political activity. But this did not prevent the movement from conducting its affairs. They transferred their meeting place to the Jewish cemetery.

After the huge meeting at the Srednaya Pogulanka, the police dispersed anything that looked like a gathering in the Old Park. The workers would regroup at some other spot. They cursed the police, and the police would in turn draw their swords from their scabbards and wave them menacingly. After a while, things took a serious turn as a rule. The workers would throw empty milk and beer bottles at the police, and the police would charge into them. One day the police fired at a hostile crowd in front of the trade union headquarters, and two workers were wounded. The anger of the mob rose to boiling point. And then, suddenly, a pistol-shot rang out, and Kourlandski was seen running wildly, waving his sword above his head. In hot pursuit of him were two workers, firing pistols at him as they ran. It was like a scene from a film. Kourlandski found shelter in the courtyard of the Ragachover Gaon.

This incident was followed by an ever-increasing number of arrests. Cavalry was posted at strategic points where the workers forgathered. They were generous with their beatings and arrests. Two storeys had to be added to the gaol, to accommodate those being detained. But it was to no purpose. The workers were intrepid in their dealings with the police, and they staged meetings in the face of arrests and beatings. It was quite a common sight now to see the mounted soldiers charge into the crowd at the Old Park, and use their knouts at random. The workers resorted to pelting them with stones and bottles. The horses neighed wildly. Often they reared in fear, and threw their mounts. It was remarkable how the workers stood their ground, while the soldiers, both those mounted and those who had been thrown, scattered in every direction and sought safety wherever they could find it.

The Christian workers were not as quick to get organised as the Jews. The workers in the railway depot belonged to the Railway Workers' Union, which extended to places well beyond Dvinsk. On the political front, they were tentatively joining the Social Democratic Party, to which the Bund was affiliated. It was this politically more advanced element that was on cordial terms with the Jewish workers. They even spoke Yiddish, as if it was their home language. There also came into being in Dvinsk the Social Revolutionary Party, the membership of which was mostly Lettish and Polish. The Jews began to join it at a later stage. They, too, worked in solidarity with the Bund and the Social Democrats.

Chapter Eleven

FLOOD TIDE

The political parties were beginning to stir. Not a day passed but arrests took place. A number of lecturers were detained, and also organisers, delegates to conferences, and couriers distributing illegal literature. About fifty of the top ranks were arrested, and they were banished by decree. As can well be imagined, the police sent agents provocateurs into the movement. They created a good deal of uncertainty, as suspicions became widespread and haphazard.

Kravchenko who, as already related, had saved Reb Meir Simcha when the Bolsheviks had arrested him, was in the beginning of the century a member of the Carpenters' Union. From his early days he distinguished himself by his courage and heroism. He was responsible for bringing a large number of non-Jews into the movement, and without being aware of it, two provocateurs, Putchilovski, a Pole, and Sobeleff, a Russian. These provocateurs were difficult to detect, for they were usually the most militant in the trade unions in the Party.

Putchilovski had a wife who was given to luxurious living, and she was inclined to be talkative. When people wanted to know how she could afford such luxury, she said that a rich uncle had been sending them regular amounts from Moscow. Kravchenko got to know about this, and he deputed a youngster to follow Putchilovski and watch his every movement. If Putchilovski had displayed more acumen, he would have been able to carry on undetected for years. But he was lacking in experience, and he underestimated the skill and resource of the counter-espionage. One day the youngster saw Putchilovski enter a church, and a few minutes later he was followed by a well-known detective. The evidence against him was beginning to accumulate. When Kravchenko got to know of it, he had more agents of his own tracking him down. And he soon discovered that not only Putchilovski, but also Sobeleff, were provocateurs. The rich uncle in Moscow who had been sending Putchilovski's wife money for her high living, was, in fact, the secret police organisation.

In Pletzer, away from the centre of things, there stood an old house in ruins and almost toppling over. Wooden planks had been nailed over the windows and doors. And so this house continued to rot. The Party decided to stage a trial there to investigate the doings of Putchilovski and Sobeleff. One Saturday night, Kravchenko deceived the two provocateurs into accompanying him to this house of ruins. They arrived in a cab. The driver was a member of the Party. As soon as they entered the house, and sat themselves on the rotted planks that was the floor, ten amongst the strongest of the Party seized the two provocateurs and bound them hand and foot. They were asked to give explanations of certain of their doings. It did not take long before they gave themselves away completely. And then, when they saw that the game was up, they started accusing each other. "I gave you life, and I will destroy you", said Kravchenko, quoting Gogol. He started beating them into pulp. Others followed, and sticks and iron bars rained down on them till they were like two slaughtered and skinned oxen.

When the two provocateurs did not show up, the police offered a reward of two thousand roubles to anyone who would discover their whereabouts. Kravchenko also disappeared. But he was later apprehended, tried, and sent to Siberia for twenty years. The two provocateurs who had been killed were discovered in the ruined house by a tramp who had come to take shelter there for the night. He ran to the police as fast as he could to report his grim discovery.

In this instance the provocateurs were Christians, but Jewish provocateurs were not unknown. The biggest provocateur in all Russia was a Jew, by the name of Azev. In Dvinsk the most notorious provocateur was a Jew named Kaplinski, a member of the Bund Presidium.

During all these stirring times, the Dvinsk underworld was not idle. They organised themselves into bands, who plied their profession of extracting money from people in whatever way they thought fit. They were real bloodsuckers. Their leader was Yokke Tzigan, whose doings in the company of Shenke with the Golden Hands on the Talkoets have already been recorded. His partner in crime now was Yisrolke Savinsky, the locksmith. And they had as colleagues the dregs from the underworld, boys and girls.

One of the girls would accost a provincial worker in the Old Park, who would congratulate himself on his good fortune. He first took her to Rublevski for a glass of tea. Then they would go to her room. Inside the room, he would suddenly receive a shower of blows that made him see stars. "What! molesting my fiancee, you son-of-a-bitch!" Yisrolke would call out. And Yisrolke's henchmen would join in chorus—"Kill him! Kill him!" The fellow was then cleaned out. The victim was so happy to have emerged alive, that he even forgot to complain to the police.

These thugs specialised in rounding up provincial workers. "Hey, yat, where do you work?" was Yokke Tzigan's greeting to a worker. The worker, shaking with fright, would tell him where he worked.

"If you want to earn a living in this town, you'll have to pay a rouble a week—or . . ." And here he drew a knife to make it clear that he meant business. When the worker told of this incident to a comrade, the chances were that this worker would in turn inform him that he, too, was paying tribute of one rouble a

week to Yokke. How the vampires Yokke and
Yisrolke came to a sticky end, has been told over and
over in Dvinsk. Leibl Katz, who was a cabinet-maker
in Dvinsk at the time, and is now the Life President of
the Dvinsker Society in Johannesburg, was a witness of
the incident I am going to relate.

Leibl was working at Pletzer on Mersansky Street in
a workshop with five or six workmen. One summer
day a worker from the provinces, by the name of
Mottel, was taken on. He was half-baked, but very
powerfully built. He could bend a 5-kopke piece with
his teeth, and twist a 5-inch nail out of shape. Of poor
breeding, he devoured a big loaf of bread, chewing it
like a machine. During the lunchbreak he stretched
himself out on the wood shavings and snored like an
animal. His trousers were made of coarse material,
and were held up by a rope tied round his waist. He
wore heavy and oversized military boots, and knew
exactly nothing about "davenen", Hebrew, or the
meaning of a joke. He could plane and saw all day
tirelessly, like a horse.

Mottel one day heard about Yokke and Yisrolke and
their doings. "Let them come," he said in his rasping
voice. "I'll break them in two." And he imitated the
breaking of a plank. They came, and after making
their exactions of a rouble from the other workers they
approached Mottel and told him to cough up. "Here
is your rouble!" And, grabbing the bow-legged Yokke,
he flung him away from himself. Seizing a tough
wooden railing, he proceeded to belabour Yisrolke,
blow upon blow. His eyes were bulging and aglow,
like a madman's, as he beat them into senselessness.
All the workers rejoiced quietly at the turn of events.

They brought Mottel to the trade union headquarters,
and took down all the details from him. The next day
a leaflet was pasted up on the walls, telling how Mottel
had dealt with Yokke and Yisrolke, and the workers
were warned not to pay any further tribute. Mottel
became a member of the movement, and they nick-

named him Captain. One day Mottel was sent to issue a warning to a strike-breaker to desist. Instead, he beat him up badly. "We told you only to warn him," a worker said. "Why should I go twice," Mottel pleaded, "when I can fix it in one trip?" Months later Mottel was arrested and sent out of Dvinsk.

In 1903 the flames of revolt were spreading throughout Russia, and particularly in the countryside. The peasants had no land of their own, and they were tenants of a count, a general, a landowner, or on church-lands. The landowners were living in luxury, while the peasants existed on the level of animals. Many a horse ate better, and had a finer place to sleep in than a peasant. The Social Revolutionaries turned their attention to the peasants from the villages. The wrath of the peasant rose with their agitation, and it was vented on the landowning nobility. There were a number of localised peasant uprisings. They burnt down forests, fields and the homes on the large estates. The Lettish peasantry played a vigorous part in all these doings. Outbreaks occurred round Libau, Riga and Dvinsk.

The Social Revolutionaries were determined to resist the onslaught of the Government forces. Throughout Russia there occurred acts of terrorism. Governors and police officials were removed by the assassin's hand.

The more impatient members of the Bund began to criticise their leadership with being too lackadaisical, in the face of these developing events. Were they waiting for the Messiah? was how they put it sarcastically. Some urged not only action, but terror. And when not enough was being done in response to their demands, they went over to the Social Revolutionaries. The Bund leadership declared strongly against individual terror, on the grounds that Ivan, who would replace Stepan, would act with greater severity—as had happened when Alexander II, who was assassinated by the terrorists, was replaced by Alexander III, who proved more ruthless. The Social Revolutionaries argued that

one successful act of terror would generate more
enthusiasm than ten numbers of the newspaper "The
Proletariat" isued by the Social Democrats. They
looked down on the Bundists as a women's social
circle.

And then there befell the Jews a disaster, which
rocked Russia and reverberated through the whole of
the civilised world. When after the Revolution the
archives of the Tsar were scrutinised, it was discovered
that the pogroms against the Jews had been organised
by the Black Hundreds and the police, who were being
instigated by Minister of Interior Plehve. Simulta-
neously, pogroms broke out in Kishinev, Homle, Bialystok, Zhitomir and Sedlitz. Preparations were being
made to spread pogrom activity to other larger centres.
Dvinsk was the first among the next ten on the list, the
archives revealed.

Dvinsk was stirred as never before by the brutal
slaughter of innocent Jews that had taken place in
Kishinev and other places. The liberal papers carrying protests against these unbridled brutalities, were
snatched up by avid readers. These pogroms hung like
a pall of doom above the heads of the people of Dvinsk
and elsewhere. Protest meetings and demonstrations
were staged against the inhumanity of the Tsar's regime.
Shortly after Pesach, a protest demonstration was
organised. As was the case with all such demonstrations, it began in the Old Park.

It was a stupendous gathering. Dozens of flags and
banners were paraded, calling for death to the Tsar and
to Minister Plehve. The demonstration moved forward for a few blocks, then turned back. They sang a
funeral march for the victims of the pogrom. The
police were lying in wait for them at the Park, and
fighting broke out everywhere between the demonstrators and the police. The demonstrators tore down
the fence of the Park, and with planks in hand met the

rifle butts of the police. But as the well-armed soldiers made their appearance, the demonstrators hastily dispersed. The soldiers and police hid in courtyards, and arrested passersby at random. Among those taken was none other than myself.

Let me relate briefly how it all happened. A friend Arke Gordon and I were making for our homes in Altstadt, after the demonstration had dispersed. As we passed Washbutsky's store, there sprang from a passage the well-known police sadist, Yeromov. He was armed with a rifle. "Don't move!" he called out. Every Bundist had more or less prepared himself for arrest. But it was a real stroke of misfortune to fall into the hands of the notorious Yeromov. He specialised in the brutal beating up of prisoners, even before he had brought them to the gaol. The Social Revolutionaries were determined to get rid of him, and in secret conclave sentenced him to death. Not long after Mendel Deutsch shot him in the head, but he did not succeed in dispatching him for good. But Dvinsk did get rid of him. He was transferred elsewhere.

Yeromov took us into a courtyard, where fourteen youths and four girls were lined up. He moved up and down the line slapping faces and cursing as he did so. His underlings assisted with their rifle-butts. My share of what was going was a bloody nose, a swollen face, and bruised sides. We were eager to be taken to a police station so as to escape his sadism.

When darkness came, they led us away to the police station under an escort. But Yeromov had not yet had his fill. He detained others walking about the streets and arrested them. They met the same fate as we did at his hands. We were twenty-four in all when we were brought to a police station. We found there another twenty who had been arrested. Then began the whole formality of taking our names, addresses and other details about us. They charged us with organising a demonstration, challenging state authority, and wounding a number of policemen. We refused to sign the statements they had placed in front of us. At one in the morning they transferred us to the political police.

The headquarters of the political police were in Officers Street, and they became congested with the arrests and trials—more especially during the last three months, as the Lettish and Russian peasants started setting fire to the landlord's estates. One of the most important sections of the headquarters was the basement. It was very big, and Gurevitch had once used it to store his vegetables, particularly potatoes, which were to be delivered on contract to the army.

The basement was divided into chambers. It had a glass roof to provide it with light, and it was heavily barred. There were tiny apertures near the top of the walls, to allow air to enter. Otherwise the vegetables would have decayed. But though the Gurevitch brothers had taken all precautions against human thieves, there was little they could do to keep the rats from their vegetables. The rats bred and multiplied on the excellent fare they were getting.

Those of us who were arrested were taken into this basement. Together with those who had preceded us, our numbers reached thirty two, including six girls. There was Shmoolke the carpenter, Moishke the upper-maker, one Gershon, and a student from a very rich family by the name of Menke Mankowitz. These were the leaders of our group. The basement became cramped. There was a wooden platform, where twelve could stretch themselves. The first thing we did was to discuss methods of establishing communications with the outside world. Paper was found, on which the names and addresses of the arrested were written down. A note was made indicating those who had illegal literature in their homes. Shmoolke was the master-mind behind all this, and I wondered how he was going to reach our comrades outside, as I had a few prohibited books at home.

The headquarters were guarded by soldiers and police. It did not seem possible that anybody from the outside world would be able to pierce this barrier. But no questions were asked, for the reason that no answer would have been forthcoming. Gershon ordered everyone to keep silent. The girls were told to rest for a while on the platform. The men stretched themselves out on the hard earthen floor. Nobody slept, for there was too much on their minds. It was a long and dreary night. It took a long time for the new day to dawn. We had no watches to tell the time by, for all our personal belongings, money, combs, handkerchiefs, and watches were taken from us.

When it was light in the basement, we heard a tapping noise near an aperture at the top. A few of us lifted Menke Mankowitz onto our shoulders, and he handed a note out through the aperture. From the outside they threw in cigarettes, matches, bread, herrings, polony, and even a bottle of vodka. The whole operation lasted no longer than a few minutes. The food supplies were distributed and hidden in every conceivable place — in pockets, bosoms, boots. The girls proved themselves very inventive. We sat ourselves on the floor, and each in turn related of the happenings in the demonstrations, of the beatings they had received, and much else. A number were fast asleep, stretched out on the floor, snoring loudly.

At around six in the morning, the Captain of the Police, accompanied by two policemen, entered the basement. They took a roll-call. The Captain called out the names from a sheet of paper, and each one answered that he was present. After the roll-call, two of those arrested were called by the police, and they went outside after them. They came back carrying tea and bread. The tea was no more than boiled water with a light tan, and the two pounds of bread each of us received was so soggy and tasteless that we could not eat it. Each one of us also received two pieces of sugar. One mug was provided for every eight prisoners. Whoever wanted tea could help himself liberally, for most of us found it too distasteful to touch.

But after a while we began to make preparations for a proper feast, from the largesse that had been handed down to us through the aperture. We ate and drank, and relieved the tension by smoking cigarettes. It was not the fare often on offer inside of a gaol. It was more like those feasts we used to arrange in the forests from time to time.

Round about nine that morning, each prisoner was called out, and asked to sign a paper admitting that he had participated in the procession, had disturbed the peace of the city, and had fought with the police. Everyone in turn refused to sign the admission of guilt. We were led back to the basement, and the same process was repeated for three days. The second day we were there, the girls were led from the basement. The following day twelve more were taken out, including Shmoolke and the other more prominent of the prisoners who were well known to the police. They were transferred to a gaol proper. The others, mostly the younger ones in whose homes no illegal literature was found, were left in the basement, and they were told that their cases would be fully investigated by a prosecutor. But since the prosecutor was overloaded with work, it looked as if we could take our time. So we sat back and rested, and tried to forget things.

The basement was now like the waiting-room of a railway station. Newly-arrested came every day. Some were allowed to go home, and others were banished from Dvinsk or placed in gaol. During the thirty days I spent there, there was an average of twenty to keep me company. The leaders had correctly assessed the position when they said that prison was the finest school for producing revolutionaries. While we were in the basement we organised lectures and study groups, ranging from political economy to scientific subjects. We discussed and debated with much zest. Everything proved of the greatest interest, with so much time on our hands.

There were two innocent Talmudical students among

those who had been arrested. The police accused them of being underhand revolutionaries. But they were as innocent as a new-born babe. They separated themselves from the rest of us, and spent all their time in a corner of the basement, clad in their "zoopitses". They swayed to and fro, as they offered up prayers without end. Now and again, one recited to the other a page of the Gemarra from memory. What bothered them above all else, was that they did not have with them either "taleisim" or "tefillin".

At first we tried to humour them, but we felt it best to leave them entirely to themselves. I noticed that they cocked an ear, so as to gather a few words from the lectures that were in progress. One day we were taken aback when Noah, the smaller of the two, entered into the discussion as to the origin of certain Hebrew words. And from that time onward a friendlier relationship existed between us. They participated more frequently in the discussions we held. When I left the basement, they were still there. A year passed, and I one day discovered little Noah working for my father as a painter. We recognised each other. He also informed me that his fellow student was employed in Vilna as a tanner. When they were released, the trade union had found employment for both of them.

Tsar Nicholas had not only provided me with thirty days free board and lodging, but I was actually paid seven kopkes for each day of my incarceration. That was a Government ruling. We gave this money to the guard, supposedly to buy provisions for us. But actually it was a bribe to get us parcels from outside. Visits to the arrested were strictly forbidden. But my father was acquainted with Colonel Grigorevitch, who arranged one visit for him. He told me that our house was raided and searched, but he had been forewarned in good time to remove certain books, and they had found nothing.

It was on a Friday midday that I was released. The reception I got from my mother when I entered the house, was very much the same that had awaited the others who had been released.

"Look, who is here", she called out. "Woe is me — what I have lived to behold! Here he is, my fine Talmudist of a son, who has been studying together in the Yeshiva of criminals and thieves! Woe is me. What his father and mother have taught him, means not a thing to him. What does matter to him, is what he has learned from his clever friends who know everything. A curse on their heads!"

I was happy at the thought that this was all she had to say. But a Jewish mother remains a Jewish mother. She told my sister to hand me clean undergarments, soap and towel, and she sent me to the "bod". The next day, on the Sabbath morning, I went to Shul. My comrades informed me that a large number had been detained, the merchants were sacking arrested assistants, left and right, and they were sure that my days at Yawitz's had come to an end. On Sunday, I went to work as if nothing had happened. Yawitz stood in the entrance, and I greeted him as usual. He turned away. If he is angry, let him be angry, I thought to myself, and I repeated my greeting. This time he answered me with—"Why did you come here?" Before I could say anything, he told me to betake myself where I had been all the time. I knew him well enough by now, and the blow was not unexpected. I told him that there was an unpaid amount of salary owing to me. At this, he turned red and cried out—"I tried to make something of you, you 'statsnik.' But for you, I suppose I am a bourgeois, a vampire and a bloodsucker!" He went into the store, and left me standing there.

In a moment or two, the manager Hedekkel came out and there was much that he told me. Grisha the Bundist, my very good friend, had been arrested. Ida had been sacked, and Yawitz had engaged a villager who did not know how to place a ladder against the shelves. Yawitz was in a fit of temper when I had come upon him. "Temper or no temper," I said, "he owes me three roubles for two weeks." He told me to call on Wednesday, after Yawitz had had a chance to cool off.

On Wednesday I met Hedekkel outside the store. He assured me that Yawitz would not take me back. "Very well", I said, entered the store, and approached Yawitz. He took out three roubles from his till and threw them on the counter, as to a dog. "Go and find yourself an easier way to earn your bread," he said to me. "Yawitz, I replied, "Remember, the time will come . . ." I did not conclude the sentence.

Time brought its vengeance. After the Revolution, fifteen years later, in Petrograd, when I was chosen as one of the heads of a factory where I worked as a mechanic, one day the same Yawitz came to my home and asked me to sell him some bread and potatoes. I wrapped some potatoes and bread in a newspaper, and I sent him away. I took no money from him. In any event, money had no value in those days. And here let it be added that many of the wealthy of Dvinsk shared the same miserable fate as Yawitz after the Revolution. The wealthy Leibe Zalkind could have been seen in Petrograd carrying a wooden tray and selling cigarettes and matches.

Chapter Twelve

THE REACTION

During the months that followed, the reaction dominated the town and made itself felt at every turn. Meetings were dispersed and forbidden. The building workers were allowed to meet till 10 o'clock in the morning, by which time they had to transact their affairs and then leave off. Strikes were forbidden. It was too dangerous to arrange meetings in the forests, as in the past. Occasionally, meetings of a few were held in private homes. But with time the political elements devised ways and means how to get going once again. On Friday nights, when fathers and mothers were in a deep and tranquil sleep, and the Shamos, after the steaming "bod", heavy repast, and a "shnepsel" to boot, was in an even deeper sleep—there used to forgather in the synagogue a score or so of the politicals. They had a double key to effect an entry into the synagogue. With the open Gemarras before them as a guise, they discussed and planned future activities. On Saturday mornings young boys and girls came to Shul, not to "daven" but to distribute illegal literature on the quiet.

That is how it continued for months. But things came to a head when the religious Jews noticed the goings-on and reported the matter to the "Gaboim". Others who took sides against the conspirators were the sportsmen of the Dvina, the sand-carriers, wagoners and, to be sure, Elke Tzigan and his coterie from the underworld. They would wait for them to forgather in the Beth Hamedrash, break in and not only bring the meeting to a close but beat them up as well. But it was not all one-sided. The revolutionaries gave as good as they got. But finally the underworld emerged the winners and they put an end to these secret gatherings.

A strange development, round about those times, was the number of workers who began to drift into the underworld. It worried the political parties no end. For it had resulted from the despair that overtook many at the difficulties which the movement was encountering. Our old friend, Avremke Katok, did not bother much as to what side he fought on, so long as he fought. He would put up a good showing in the demonstrations, and he could also use himself to advantage in the underworld. He was the toughest of fighters among the workers, and gave the police a good run for their money. He was arrested more than once for disorderly behaviour, and he would spend a few weeks in gaol. Avremke began taking an active part in the movement. Then one day he beat up a small shopowner on the market place, just by way of keeping fit, and he was arrested for his pains.

There were fears that he was too unstable a character, and that he might easily be seduced by the police into becoming a provocateur. One day he escaped from gaol with the help of some comrades. He hid with the lumpen of the underworld, and started up an affair with Shenke with the Golden Hands. Avremke's brother Yoshke was a member of the Bund. He urged his brother to leave the underworld. But Avremke was a spiritual schizophrenic—he was drawn both to the holy as well as to the profane. In this respect he was, in a way, symbolic of the Jews of that turbulent and unsteady part of the world. Efforts were made by the organisation to redeem the workers who had drifted into the underworld, and in most cases they were successful.

A new sergeant, Emilyan, was appointed to Pletzer. He was a cripple with one leg, and one of his avocations was pigeon-thieving. With his appointment, he naturally felt very important. He knew everyone, and he kept a watch on the rebellious elements like a lynx. He did not let up, night or day. Right in the middle of the street he would stop suspects, man or woman, and start searching them for illegal literature. One day someone fired a revolver at him, but missed. Under his draconian regime, it became impossible to hold a meeting in Pletzer. After a time he was transferred as a sergeant to Altstadt. With time he became, if anything, more ruthless. For during his stay in Altstadt he not only harassed members of the movement, but began to turn his attention to the Jews. He applied the laws against the Jewish shopowners with absolute strictness. Things that had been overlooked in the past as something that with usage had become part of custom—like the selling of liquor, or keeping open of a shop beyond the regular hours—became with him a matter for prosecution. Suddenly he would run into a Jewish store and start testing the accuracy of the weights being used for the scale. If a well was not covered, or refuse was thrown on to the street, he would lay a charge. The slightest offence was punishable by a fine of three to five roubles. He was night-and-day on the prowl, in an effort to detect offenders. Everyone received his attention, but it was the workers' organisations that he was determined to destroy. In turn, the movement was determined to destroy him.

There lived in Altstadt a Russian by the name of Papyan. He and his son were both hooligans and members of the Black Hundreds, a body given to promoting pogroms. They were bricklayers by trade. Papyan had a beautiful daughter, Anyuta, with whom the crippled sergeant fell in love. When Anyuta became pregnant, Papyan wanted him to marry his daughter. But the sergeant, who was given to philandering, had fallen in love with another girl. Papyan and his son would not let go of Emilyan. After a fierce quarrel they threatened to kill him. Members of the movement, who worked together with Papyan, incited him against the crippled sergeant. The curses and threats began to increase in fierceness.

One night three members of the movement came to Altstadt to assassinate Emilyan. They found him all alone on his nightly rounds. They grabbed spades, and doled him so many blows on his head and body that they left him dead. The police investigated the matter, and Papyan and his son were arrested. Everybody confirmed that they were responsible for Emilyan's slaying. After a long and exhausting trial they were acquitted. They arrived back in Altstadt pale and thin. It was never discovered who the guilty ones were.

The town was now full of spies and sleuths. No one felt safe, and the position had so deteriorated that many workmen began emigrating to America, where it was easy to gain entry. Engaged couples usually made off for the New World to start life afresh, for there was no future for them in Dvinsk. Raids and arrests became the order of the day. Homes were broken up. The engaged couples saved evey kopke they could to be able to have enough for their passage money. Before they set off for their new homes in far-off America, they usually arranged for their wedding celebration to take place in a spacious hall owned by one named Ratz. The celebration was also the occasion for taking leave of their comrades.

There were two aspects to a wedding celebration. On the one hand, the members of the family came to celebrate. There were the musicians and a cleric who used to deliver an address in praise of the newly-married couple, mostly in rhymes. This part of the celebration was hastily disposed of. But as soon as the members of the family and the oldsters went home, the next celebration would commence and last till well into the early hours of the morning. A large part of it was given to politicising, with addresses and discussions.

But the police had got to know of these antics, and it often happened that they threw a cordon round the hall and staged a raid. But these raids on wedding celebrations usually ended up with the police drinking themselves to a standstill. A bribe of a few roubles, slipped into the sergeant's hand, would bring the raid to a happy end. The comrade saw the wedding celebration as a good method of conducting political work, and for a time the ruse was resorted to of staging bogus weddings with a "Chuppah" and all the other paraphernalia. For a time the police were outwitted, but not for all time. And eventually Ratz was forced to close down his hall.

Shortly after Rosh Hashanah, those of age were called up for army service. There were three districts from which the selections were made. The first draft was for those from the Dvinsk boundary to Kreuzburg. Ninety per cent of them were Letts. There were also a few Jews who lived in Odetins and Livengoff. For the Letts army service was like going off to a celebration. They wore high boots, three-quarter coats lined with wadding or pelt, and stuck flowers into their fur caps. Occasionally, when they had a few drinks, they would in their high spirits molest a Jew. But it was more in fun than in earnest. Going off to the army was a time for some reckless pranks. The Letts were so keen on soldiering that they supplied more than their quota to the army. The Jews in these Lettish areas were less enchanted with life as a soldier, and they got exemptions through the necessary bribes.

The second draft was from the Vitebsk area. They were mostly Russians, but with quite a sprinkling of Jews from the towns of that region. The Russians were given to more turbulent behaviour when they were drafted. There were a number of drunkards and criminals in their ranks. People avoided them, but it was not always possible to escape from their molestations and crudeness. They wandered about the town in bands, and when they were drunk they made for the Jews.

One day, in 1904, a number of them came to the Gastchina Rad, played havoc with the goods stands, and began pillaging. Their pockets bulged with plunder. The women shop assistants became hysterical.

After overturning more tables and stands, they continued with their looting and rowdiness. The cries from the women brought carriers, cab-drivers, wagoners and assistants from the shops. With sticks in their hands they soon subdued the disorderly mob of draftees. But the friends of the recruits rallied to their aid, and an all-out fracas raged for a time. The Jewish storekeepers bolted and barred the doors and windows of their shops, and made off in a hurry for safety sake. But the Jewish workers, and some non-Jews from the factories, were not so timid. When they heard of the anti-Jewish outbreak they stopped work and joined in to protect their brethren. The Jews, who were the majority in the town, experienced little difficulty in gaining the upper-hand.

The third draft for the army was drawn from Dvinsk itself and its environs. A minimum of one hundred was the Jewish quota. The infantryman served four years in the army, and the cavalry five years. The soldier was sent far away from his home, so as not to be near his family. The authorities were concerned that nothing should distract him from his training. They often separated a man from his wife and child. The Jews were not so loyal to a regime that treated them shabbily, as to be keen on sending their sons away to the army, and they resorted to all sorts of stratagems to evade army service.

The sons of the rich had little difficulty in buying themselves out of the army. A lot of workers emigrated to America when their turn came to be called up. Parents would sell a house to obtain the necessary funds to send them off. The draftee often married a girl with some means, and they used the dowry to transfer to some new country. The first-born and main supporters of families were exempted, and also those with physical defects. If a youth failed to show up when called upon, heavy punishment was inflicted on the father, or even on a brother if the father was dead. A house could be confiscated, or a fine of three hundred roubles imposed.

But if the recruit had taken the oath, and ran away while in the army, nobody was penalised. Any number escaped while still on the train which was taking them to their destination. Only those who had no alternative went through with their army training. But they did so with heavy hearts.

The winter is now approaching, and with it the building workers are becoming unemployed. The cold winds blowing from the east chill the bodies and spirit, and bring the snowstorms with them. In the needle trade, there is the same grinding down to a standstill as the Yom Tovim are behind us. The workers and tradesmen have donned their warmest winter clothing—heavy coats lined with wadding, on top of heavy jerseys. The underclothing, too, is of the thickest and warmest material. They look bulky and shapeless. But more important than appearance is now the need to protect yourself from the elements that assail you mercilessly. Nobody leaves home, unless it is essential. They transact all their affairs inside the houses. Before the warm fire, girls sit and scandalise their friends. The men are busy playing a friendly poker game for cigarettes. In another house, a comrade has brought in some new political treatise. They read it, and then proceed to unravel the problems that it embodies—problems that, in one way or another, have been with mankind over the ages and still remain unresolved.

Friday night was the night for the Russian theatre, where the artist Mirsky was staging plays with a Socialistic tinge. A queue gathered hours before starting time. Money was not easily come by, and everybody was keen to obtain a good seat in the gallery or the loft, as it was also called. A number in the queue had no money, but in the crush they were somehow or another pushed through, without the lax doorman observing them. On other occasions, a coin had to be slipped into the hand of the doorman before the indigent one could get through. Below, in the stalls and the boxes, sat the wealthy of the town, with their wives splendidly bedizened in silks, furs and jewels. From time to time they turned haughty heads to the gallery, which was seething and bubbling with excitement. In the gallery itself, friends and comrades greeted each other. Packets of baked beans and sunflower seeds were passed up and down the rows, and each one helped himself. Frozen apples were also a favourite with the gallery.

Mirsky was a great attraction. Without coming into conflict with the censor, he was able to convey surreptitiously a message of protest against the social order, its fraudulence and inhumanity. His repertoire included Cain and also Hamlet, to which he gave a social twist. Theatre was a great source of inspiration for those who were active in the movement. It was also the venue for the exchange of illegal literature.

I have previously related how the terrorist Mendel Deutsch had avenged himself on Sergeant Yeromov. He was caught, and after a trial he was sentenced to death. The liberal Press throughout Russia protested at the sentence, for Yeromov had recovered from his wounds. The death sentence was commuted to a sentence of hard labour for life. Mendel escaped from prison and finally landed up in America. But Russia was calling him, and after the Revolution he returned from America. While in Saratov, he recognised the agent provocateur Kaplinski. He was handed over to the authorities who executed him. As a child, Mendel was more interested in the apple market than cheder. His Rebbe, Nechemia Shapiro, expelled him as a worthless truant. Then as he grew up he went to work on a land settlement. Finally, his explosive temperament brought him into the ranks of the terrorists among the Social Revolutionaries. From the first moment, he displayed heroism of an unusual order.

Before the excitement of Mendel's shooting of

Yeromov had died down, Meishke Blecher shot and killed the assistant Chief of Police, Buligen, in Riga Street, in the heart of Dvinsk. It was in the middle of the day. Meishke succeeded in eluding the police net that was cast far and wide. But they arrested his colleague, on whom they found a revolver. The acts of terror became a regular feature of those days. Hirschke Yankel, a carpenter, and Hirshele Borochowitz, a painter, with revolver bullets despatched the police-sergeant Ovshanikov. They both succeeded in escaping.

The organisation was jubilant at the successes it was having. But their rejoicing came to a sudden end when, through an accident, a catastrophe overtook them. They were holding a meeting in the circus. Armed sentries were guarding against a possible attack from the Black Hundreds. At the end of the meeting, they were all making for their homes. The roads were slippery from the frost and snow. Motke Gever slipped and fell. The bomb he was carrying blew up and killed both him and Borochowitz. Six others were wounded. Shmuel, the barber, remained with one leg for the rest of his life. Hirshele Borochowitz had worked for my father. He was a refined and keen-minded student, beloved by everyone. The affection in which he was held, may be gathered from the fact that everyone called him Hirshele.

It was a most difficult winter that we lived through. Winds and snowstorms followed each other in regular succession. On top of it, the police were on the rampage and added to our trials and troubles. Arrests were on the increase, and many a family was deprived of the breadwinner. The movement was in dire need of funds. Money was required for a printing-plant, for illegal literature, for aiding the arrested and their dependants. Prison guards had to be bribed to enable those arrested or sentenced to escape. Much of the money came from the sons and daughters of the rich, who were in the movement or sympathetic towards it. But as the situation grew more difficult, those who were not arrested drifted away. The movement was determined to acquire funds essential for its activities—by hook, if possible, and by crook, if necessary.

A plan was formulated to obtain contributions from storekeepers and the rich. It was a fight to the death. Many were imprisoned or sent to Siberia. And here were these merchants and the wealthy, living on the fat of the land and gloating into the bargain. A list of names was drawn up, and they were called upon to make their contribution. Apart from a limited number, nobody knew who was visited, those who had given, and those who had refused. Everything was conducted in strict secrecy. The business people begged to be left alone, bargained and ended up by giving their donation. If there was a straight refusal from anyone, they were warned that severe measures would be taken against them and their families. It was a desperate time, when desperate remedies had to be resorted to. The warnings helped. Nobody informed the police, and everything proceeded apace. But however much was collected, there was never enough to meet all the commitments.

There was in Dvinsk a Jewish usurer, by the name of Bachrach. He was a hunchback, and rich as Korah. He loaned out money on usurious interest, apart from which he owned a haberdashery store. He lived frugally in a tiny dwelling, without a servant. The movement decided to tax him. Four members were assigned to go and chat to him. Bachrach received them politely. He assured them that his sympathies had always been with the movement, and that if they did not make it too willing he would do his share. He conceded that all Jews were in danger from the Black Hundreds, and that it was only right that a Jew should help those who had sacrificed themselves so heroically, and some of whom were now rotting in gaol or in

Siberia. They listened to him intently, and assessed his contribution. Shmuel Ravdin nominated a figure. Bachrach bargained and pleaded. But he said that, all in all, it was not unduly excessive. He asked them to return the following day, when he would make over to them the amount fixed. They went away. But one of them remained unobtrusively behind to watch over Bachrach's movements.

To this day, nobody knows whether he left the house or not that night. But when Shmuel Ravdin, Abrasha Starovin, his sister Rosa, and Itzik the locksmith entered the home of Bachrach, they were surrounded by police, their revolvers at the ready. It was impossible to resist. Bachrach kept shouting at the top of his voice—"Here are the robbers! Arrest them!" They were hand-cuffed, and led away to the police station. There they found their four colleagues, to whom Ravdin was to have handed over the money.

When the Party discovered that eight members had been arrested through Bachrach's treachery, they met in secret and sentenced him to death. Even those who were not in any way connected with the movement agreed that he should not go scot free for what he had perpetrated. The religious elements, who always frowned on all revolutionary activity, also felt that what Bachrach had done was an outrage. Bachrach began to sense that his life was not worth a burnt-out straw. But he was no fool. For three days he never went anywhere, but in the company of a policeman. He disposed of part of his stock, packed some goods into suit-cases, and on the fourth day he disappeared into thin air. Ravdin, Starovin and Itzik were sentenced to fifteen years in Siberia. Rosa got off with five years imprisonment, and the other four got four years. Bachrach was cursed by all and sundry—"the hunch-back, the usurer, the informer." Women would make an oath—"May Bachrach be alive, if your fish is not stale!"

Four years went by. Two of those sentenced were

freed. The other two had escaped to America. Rosa was released, after a large sum of money had been made over.

As the saying has it—"the thief's fate is to end on the gallows." Bachrach met his end through a strange incident. It was five years since he had fled Dvinsk. Two Jewish working lads, Zamke and Motke, were drafted into the army for service in Mohilev. Motke was fifteen years old when Bachrach left Dvinsk, but he knew him very well. As they were both mechanics, they were assigned to the working brigade. They were on good terms with the officers, whom they often presented with little gadgets they made in the workshop. The officers used to give them a day off now and again. They made friends with some girls in the town of Mohilev, who one Friday invited them to spend a week-end with them.

It was quite a distance. They first travelled forty miles by train. A wagon took them for another eight miles, and they found themselves in a remote village. They were accepted almost as suitors by the parents. On the Saturday morning, they had to attend the service at the Beth Hamedrash. They were shown to their seats, and handed "Sidurim".

"Look who's there!" Motke called out as if he had beheld a spirit from some other world.

"Who's standing where?" Zamke asked.

"Look, for God's sake! It's Bachrach!"

Zamke did not know Bachrach, although he had heard of him.

"You're dreaming", he said to his friend.

"There's the hunchback—it's Bachrach as sure as I'm alive," Motke insisted.

It can well be imagined that they concentrated very little on the service. When they came home from the Beth Hamedrash they enquired about the man. He was definitely Bachrach.

They made the girls promise not to say a word, and to watch him. Then they went back to Mohilev. Ten days elapsed, and a number of youths from Dvinsk quietly made their way to the village where Bachrach had taken refuge. One early morning Bachrach was found hanging from a tree, just beyond the outskirts of the village.   When his home was searched, it was found that the floor-boards had been torn up and the mattress was ripped open. It can be assumed that they took a lot of Bachrach's money back to Dvinsk, to be handed to the organisation.

Chapter Thirteen

WAR AND REVOLUTION

I have already written of the loss of my job with Yawitz, following my arrest. It was almost impossible for a shop-assistant to get employment once he was dismissed. An assistant was scrutinised closely before he was taken on. He was measured and weighed, interrogated as to his character. His hands were examined for length, and if the fingers were sticky. And even then, he was often told that he did not qualify. For if he was any good, what reason was there for his dismissal? In my own case, all doors were closed to me. For I was a "statsnik"—and that was damnation enough. I had sullied myself for ever through my having spent time inside a prison. What would the other storekeepers say if it got around that a "statsnik" had been taken on? A storekeeper from Resitze had actually agreed to let me work for him. I came to the station with my suit-case. But he told me that something had intervened, and that I would have to postpone my journey for six months.

I was now a man of leisure—drinking, sleeping, and still conscious of my sense of dignity. My father was tolerant towards me—"It's only a matter of time, and you'll get fixed up," he said to me. But my mother took a poor view of my plight—"If only he had listened," she lamented. That "If" actually meant—if only he had been born into another generation. After a month had passed, I felt I was becoming a burden. The whole of Altstadt began to talk about me—I was a no-goodnik and lazy. I was feeling decidedly uncomfortable at the thought that, while others were in employment and earning their keep, I was spending my time doing nothing. I asked my father to let me accompany him to the Fortress. But he had previously made it clear that under no circumstances would he allow me to become a painter. "Wait till autumn," he said to me. "And if nothing turns up, I'll open a shop for you." The trouble was that, while in Dvinsk there were many like me, here in Altstadt I was the only one—the only sinner, I.

On top of all my misfortunes, our house abutted on the Beth Hamedrash. A fence separated us. Every morning the "Shamos" stood at the head of my bed, shaking me into wakefulness. "Come, Yudel," he nagged, "we're short of a tenth for a 'minyan'. It's a yahrzeit." At the beginning I yielded to him. But he never knew when to call it a day. His presence in the morning so irritated me that I chased him. But what was the use? The yahrzeit himself would come and plead with me. And can one turn his back on a mourner, who is pleading for the departed one to be elevated to Paradise? However much I resented it, I, the atheist, was the one who helped quite a number into Paradise.

Naturally, I sought refuge in Dvinsk as quickly as I could. The out-of-works met regularly in the two parks. We pooled our kopkes, and made our purchases on a communal basis. My mother refused to give me spending money, guarding the till of her shop as from a thief. My father now and again handed me fifty kopkes on the quiet, outside the knowledge of my mother. But I had a guardian angel, in the form of an assistant of my father's who lent me some money from time to time, which I shared with my commune of unemployed.

One month followed on the heels of another month. One day, when I was standing with some friends outside the trade union headquarters, I could see a posse of policeman, led by a sergeant, making their way towards us. They told us to disperse. Suddenly a pistol shot rang out, followed by more shots at regular intervals. The sergeant fell to the ground, with blood pouring out of him. In a moment he was dead. His colleagues shrugged their shoulders. Another police-man was wounded. The workers scattered. I ran into Bentze Stekel's courtyard where Avrom Itze, an old painter, lived on the third floor. He was a devoted friend of our family. His wife Gittel took me in, as if I was her own child. She made me comfortable, and brought me tea and jam. I, myself, was terrified, but she was almost in a state of collapse.

Avrom Itze came home at six o'clock. He was white as a sheet, at what he had heard. The sergeant's body had been removed, and the police were busy searching every house. They would not allow me out. Avrom Itze made his way to my parents to inform them that I was safe. As he was inclined to be talkative, he also told them that, if it had not been that I had found refuge in his home, there was no knowing but that I would have been arrested, with the possibility that prison would not have been my punishment. He returned to his home in a wagon. The next day when he went to work he asked me to accompany him, after I had changed into his old and tattered trousers, and a shirt splashed with paint. And so it happened that I became a painter from that day onward.

My father straight away sent me together with three other workers, with Avrom Itze in charge of us, to Verzbhulova, near the German border. I was happy to be earning a living once again. When I returned to Altstadt, I found that arrests had been a feature of daily life. In the Wallerstein chair factory most of the work-men, members of the organisation, had been lodged in gaol.

Despite the blows the organisation was receiving from the police, meetings of all sorts were held in secret. It was Pesach in 1904, when a fairly large gathering of about one hundred members of the organisation was held at the house of Henoch Sorkin, in Pletzer. The speeches and discussions were followed by festivities

and merrymaking, and the singing of revolutionary
songs.   This time, there was no interference whatsoever
from the police sleuths.   The songs came to a sudden
end when a young man, a member of the organisation,
came rushing in breathless and announced that news
had reached Dvinsk that war had broken out between
Russia and Japan.

At the start, the war was not at all felt in Dvinsk, for
it was mainly the Siberian garrisons that were mobi-
lised for action.   The soldiers and officers in Dvinsk
were all cock-a-hoop.   They regarded the Japanese
with scorn, promising to swamp them with Russian caps
that would be showered at them.   And they forecast
that one month would see the rout of the enemy.   Over
their drinks, they spoke of travelling to Tokio to pass
pleasant nights in the arms of the Geisha girls, and they
swore to bring the Mikado to St. Petersburg bound
hand and foot in chains.

One squadron of the Russian fleet, under the celebrated Admiral Rozdesvensky, sailed up the Yalu River
in preparation for action.   A second squadron followed
him, under Admiral Makarov.   But they got a hot
reception from the Japanese.   Both squadrons were
sent to the bottom by the heavy and accurate gunfire
of the Japanese.

The hero of the Russian Army, General Kuropatkin,
who was the Commander-in-Chief, himself took charge
of the fighting on land.   His past victories were praised
in song and story.   With the outbreak of the war
against the Japanese, his photographs were everywhere
displayed in the cities, towns and villages.   At Port
Arthur, the defeats of the Russian Army matched
those of the Navy, and Kuropatkin had to beat a hasty
retreat from there as he suffered one reverse after
another, barely escaping with his life.   He left behind
a large part of his army and masses of equipment.   The
war did not end with victory in one month, but dragged
on for a year.   And there was no end in sight.

The Russians now began to mobilise their reserves.

For the first time the war made itself felt in Dvinsk, where the 8th Division stationed in the town was issued with mobilisation orders. For a time this Division did not move off to the front, for there were behind-the-scenes negotiations to bring the war to a speedy conclusion. The Russians had been tamed by their unending series of defeats, and they were feeling more subdued than at the outbreak of hostilities.

There was much rejoicing among the workers and intelligentsia at the defeats the Russian Army had suffered, and particularly among the Jews who were still smarting from the wounds of the Kishinev and other pogroms, instigated by the Tsarist police. These defeats were celebrated in song. On the Island of Sakhalin, not many miles from the fighting front, there were thousands of political exiles, sent there by the Tsar. During the years of the Tsarist oppression, the workers had dreamed of revenge. The day was approaching as the Tsar's army was reeling under the heavy blows inflicted on them. The people lamented the fate of the soldier who had been sent out to fight and die in the remoteness of Manchuria. But they could not resist the alluring whiff of freedom that seemed to be in the air as the Tsar's difficulties kept mounting with the defeats.

Let me now relate the final disaster. The Russian Fleet in the Black Sea sailed into the Mediterranean and through the Straits of Gibraltar into the Atlantic. Then they headed south till they reached Cape Town, where they anchored for a few days. There are still people in Cape Town who remember the Russian ships as they lay outside Table Bay. From Table Bay they sailed east and then north, heading for Japan. It was in all a voyage of many months. When the Russian ships reached Japan, they were engaged by the Japanese fleet in the Battle of Tsushima, which proved one of the most disastrous naval battles of all time. Nearly the whole Russian Fleet went to the bottom.

Again Russia sued for peace. The country was

sinking into a doleful stupor, as the fighting forces were being humiliated in battle by a foe whom nobody had considered seriously. As the Prophet Jeremiah has it —"In the streets they were fighting with naked swords, and in the homes there was terror and uncertainty."

These fears not only derived from defeat in battle, but from the growing unrest among the various layers of society. The agitation against the Tsar and his incompetence grew. The unrest was not confined just to the towns but spread to the villages, that had been supplying the soldiers for the Army. For a time anarchy reigned in the villages. Manors and estates were burnt down. This inevitably followed in the wake of peasant discontent. The Tsar saw the full implications of these disturbances, and he took the strongest measures to bring them under control. Punitive expeditions were sent to every inflammable region, and a heavy vengeance was visited on the rebellious elements. Lashes and whippings became the order of the day.

But the peasants in their anger fought back with a fury that was drawn from centuries of suffering and oppression at the hands of the landed gentry. They continued with pillage, fire and slaughter of livestock. In the cities, the Social Revolutionaries were maintaining the tempo of revolt. There was a succession of assassinations of leading figures of the Russian ruling class —the Tsar's uncle, the Grand Duke Sergei Alexandrovich was killed; and the Minister of Interior Durnov was seriously wounded.

The year 1904 slid painfully into 1905—the bloody year, as it has gone down in Russian history. And January 9, has gone down as Bloody Sunday. The Russian middle classes, who were also dissatisfied with the Tsar, began to show their sympathies with the peasantry. The tax exactions made by the Tsar from the peasantry had for some time aroused their wrath. The war had brought with it defeat and poverty and suffering, which the peasants could no longer endure. A petition was drawn up by a gathering representing the whole of Russia, setting out the discontents of the peasantry, and they journeyed to St. Petersburg to present it to the Tsar.

At the head of the procession was the Priest Gapon, who was to deliver the petition to the Tsar. The procession had swelled to forty thousand. As they moved towards the Tsar's palace, carrying Icons and holy banners, they sang "God save the Tsar!" The procession was made up of peasants, workers, students and the liberals. As they reached the precincts of the palace, they noticed that it was being guarded by heavily-armed soldiers. Delegates asked to present the petition to the Tsar personally. The Tsar appeared on the balcony, and by way of reply to the petitioners gave the order to the soldiers to fire. The guns went off, and in a trice hundreds of dead and wounded were lying stretched out on the square before the palace. The snow shrouding the ground was splashed flamboyantly with red. Gapon himself was slightly wounded.

The holy banners and Icons were torn and trampled underfoot in the chaos and terror that swept the mass of the people. Amongst those in the procession was the Jewish engineer Ruthenberg, who had distinguished himself in the fighting with the Japanese and had become the first Jewish officer. He later settled in Palestine. It was Ruthenberg who led Gapon to safety. But it was not for long. For it was discovered that the Priest had acted as an agent provocateur, and he was killed by a terrorist for his treachery.

Following Bloody Sunday, the masses of the people who had hitherto relied on the goodness of the Tsar, and even called him Little Father, now saw him for what he was—a cruel weakling, who on that one day was responsible for the slaying of over two hundred innocent people. The streets were cleansed of the blood that had bespattered it on that Sunday. But a residue remained in the memories that nothing could wash away. For twelve years that day burned in the hearts of the Russian nation, and it was on January 9, twelve years later in 1917, that the Tsar paid for his misdeeds, as he was swept from his throne into oblivion.

The Tsar's bullets failed to subdue the growing discontent of the Russian nation with its inefficient rulers, who gave every sign of having outlived their historical usefulness. The discontent even spread to the middle and upper classes—students, industrialists and merchants. The terror organisation of the Social Revolutionaries once more swung into action and, following the assassination of the Grand Duke Sergius and Minister of Interior Durnov, they despatched the Minister of Education, Muraviev. The Governor Trepov lost both his legs as a result of a terrorist bomb outrage.

In the countryside the unrest was getting even more out of control. The situation became very dangerous in Latvia, where the Lettish peasants were particularly militant, and they vented their wrath on the Teuton barons. The Tsar and his advisors did not know what to do. They appointed Sviatopolsky Mirsky as Minister of Interior. But he proved too moderate and he was dismissed, to make way for someone who would not hesitate to use every means to restore normalcy. They found him in Count Stolypin, who became the Prime Minister.

The dramatic events in St. Petersburg, where the 1905 Revolution broke out and Workers' Councils were set up, had tremendous repercussions throughout Russia, including Dvinsk. The celebrated terrorist, Boris Savinkov, relates in his memoirs that Dvinsk was one of the strong-points of the revolutionaries. It was also noted as a town where revolutionaries and terrorists being sought by the police could find refuge, as the inhabitants were very sympathetic to their cause.

On Saturday, the 15th January, there took place a tremendous demonstration outside the Old Park. The people were in no mood to be molested by the police.

On one or two occasions they did essay to interfere. But they were met with the boards from the benches, and the planks ripped from the fence surrounding the park. The Yurovski Regiment, which had its quarters near the parks, was not called upon by the police to take action, as it was not sure how they would react. It was revealed at a later stage that they would have disobeyed any orders to act against the people, as they had been incensed by the happenings of Bloody Sunday.

Never had Dvinsk seen such a mass demonstration, or the enthusiasm that was evinced. It was such a heady atmosphere that had been generated, that the workers thought that the Socialist era had dawned. But they misjudged the situation. Tsar Nicholas was as yet very far from having shot his bolt. He still had plenty of resources — mainly the Cossacks who had been used since Ivan the Terrible to suppress the slightest symptom of revolt or subversion. In addition, he could still call on the Black Hundreds, who were becoming more active and ready to use draconian methods against the people. The Press was also a powerful weapon in the hands of the rulers, and they incited the lumpen elements against the workers and national minorities. The pogrom was the outcome of this agitation, which was also being fomented by the police on the quiet. In Kreuzburg the Cossacks under Colonel Esaville Krilov and Lieutenant Treschenko behaved with the utmost brutality towards the peasants.

A few hundred Cossacks were posted in Dvinsk to maintain order and guard against outbreaks. The whole town was placed under martial law. Meetings of more than three were forbidden. A curfew was imposed, and nobody could leave his home from 9 in the evening till 6 in the morning. The Cossack on his horse, armed with sabre, knout and revolver, became the master of the town. They used their knouts and whips very liberally. Those who received the attention of a Cossack, made sure that they did not get within striking distance again.

In Pletzer, two Cossacks were thrown from their horses, and beaten to death. This was answered by more terror from the military and the police. For a few days, everything in the town ground to a standstill, as if it had been overtaken by paralysis. The police terror soon began to show its insidious effects. Quite a number of youth, male and female, sought the quieter shores of America. For some reason or other, the authorities regarded every young person, boy or girl, as a revolutionary even if they had never been anywhere near the movement, and they were viewed with suspicion.

The biggest event that shook Russia was the mutiny of the Battleship Potemkin. The sailors killed the Admiral and his officers, and took command of the ship. There were also several mutinies in the Army, the most notable being in the Bobroisk Battalion, where the soldiers whipped the officers and took over. Even children played their part in the struggle. A band of children actually helped a number of political prisoners to escape as they were being transferred from one gaol to another in Vologda. The seething tempo was maintained by strikes, demonstrations and protest meetings.

The country could not survive such a period of convulsion. Stolypin announced a plan for the pacification of the populace. One day the papers came out with the news that the Tsar had agreed to grant a Constitution. Russia was to be a constitutional monarchy. The workers were asked to terminate their strike action, which had brought havoc to industry. The word Constitution acted like magic. A more tranquil period followed. The Liberals accepted the Constitution, and they urged the people to bring all unrest to an end with this new development. According to the Constitution the Tsar would remain as the absolute power, but the Constitution was to guarantee certain rights to the people. Men and women over twenty-one would be given the vote, and members for the Duma were to be elected by them by a democratic ballot. Laws were to be enacted by the Duma.

According to the Constitution, as interpreted by the Liberals, freedom of assembly and freedom of speech were to be guaranteed. "Constitution means Freedom!" became a popular Liberal slogan. All minorities were to be free and equal. The Jews for a time believed that the Messiah had arrived. There would be no restrictions on their movements outside the Pale. They could reside wherever they worked. And they could work wherever they chose. The **numerus clausus** would disappear from the schools and universities. A new life had dawned for them with the Constitution.

The Constitution was proclaimed on Tuesday, October 15th, 1905. It was a further excellent augury that it was a Tuesday, which Jews considered their lucky day. The contents of the Constitution were real enough, and the signature of the Tsar was appended. In Dvinsk the occasion was celebrated with a mass gathering on the Parade Square. The young boys and girls wore red ribbons in their lapels. Platforms were quickly erected. Speeches followed each other in an endless succession. They embraced and kissed each other, and rejoiced. Shouts rang out — "Long live Liberty, Equality and Fraternity!" It was even prophesied in certain quarters that the days of Tsar Nicholas were drawing to an end.

But on one platform, a workman was delivering a speech that seemed out of accord with the others. "Don't put your trust in Stolypin!" he declared. "Our freedom is not yet won. Nicholas will give you a proper Constitution, and not this fake one, when he will taste the ten plagues as Pharaoh of old did. Nicholas is in power, because of the support he is receiving from the ignorant soldier, Cossack, Black Hundred and every variety of hooligan and policeman. Be on guard!"

But the number of those with the necessary vision and foresight was small. They remained speaking. Nobody listened to them. Everybody was carried away by the one overriding fact that the Tsar had granted them a Constitution. Nobody noticed that the police had changed into mufti, that police reinforcements had arrived from the other towns, and that they were busy taking down the names of those who had spoken against the Constitution. In the mood of jubilation that had swept the town, nobody gave a thought to such details. They celebrated till the early hours of the morning.

The proper celebration was held on the following day. Workmen came to the Parade Square in their best Sunday wear, wearing red ties or a red ribbon in the lapel. The girls wore red blouses and red kerchiefs. All factories and shops were closed for the day. Red flags were aflutter and there was no dearth of oratory. The revolutionary spirit had seized everyone, even the shopkeepers. A demonstration was staged for two in the afternoon. The venue was Pletzer. The demonstration had to pass through the town, stop on the highway at the point closest to the Gaol and greet the political prisoners who were to be promised freedom the next day.

The calculations were all in order. They all went forward as to a dance. The demonstrators marched through Officers Street, turned into Miasnitski Street, and they found themselves eventually in Zeloni Street. Suddenly, shots rang out from the garrets. The demonstrators, panic-stricken, scattered in every direction. The wounded were carried out of danger by their comrades. Nine were shot dead, and sixteen were seriously wounded. They were taken to the Jewish Hospital. Someone came running along, bringing the news that the highway near the Gaol was being guarded by large numbers of soldiers. Within a few hours the whole town was under the control of the military.

The funeral for the victims was arranged for Friday

of that week. The police let it be known that only members of bereaved families would be allowed to participate. About three hundred accompanied the dead to their last resting place. It was a very mournful funeral, and with no disorders of any kind, for the police marched along all the three miles to the cemetery, flanking the procession. As the c o r t e g e approached the cemetery, some Russian hooligans who had taken up positions at the fence of the slaughterhouse jeered: "There is your Jewish freedom!" And they began shying mud, manure and stones. It took an enormous amount of self-control to prevent a fight. But the order had been given to maintain discipline in the face of every provocation. After the funeral orations, which were deeply moving, the members of the movement went into hiding. When the police raided their homes shortly after, there were very few who fell into their hands.

And this is the story of the Constitution that was lost.

Chapter Fourteen

THE FIRST WORLD WAR

There lived in Dvinsk a veterinary surgeon by the
name of Struckoff, who was an active member of the
Black Hundreds. His profession often took Struckoff
to the Dvinsk abbatoirs, where he came in contact with
Jews, and mingled freely with them. But in his heart
of hearts he was an incorrigible anti-Semite. He had
even travelled to St. Petersburg to take counsel with the
national heads of the Black Hundreds.

With the travesty of the Constitution, and the ugly
atmosphere that settled on the country, Struckoff began
to foment trouble. The Jewish workers were determined not to take things lying down, and they made
preparations to meet any eventuality. A number of
Russian workers volunteered their services with the
Jewish defence corps. Very prominent among these
were the employees of Grilliches factory. The Jews
called a secret meeting in a private house to decide on a
course of action. Uninvited, the wagoner Yankel
Yoshe and the carrier Beinas put in an appearance. They
were both in the sixties. They said they had come to
give a hand in dealing with the "pogromschikes". A
worker told them how much they appreciated their
splendid gesture, but it would have been much more
valuable if they had been a little younger. "My hero,"
said Beinas—"perhaps you would care to match my
strength!" The Jews were not idle during the days that
followed.

The news reached Struckoff that the Jews were
mustering their strength. On the surface, there was
scarcely a ripple. Nobody knew that Struckoff had
altered his tactics. He called together the rough
elements, with the pig-slaughterers predominating.
They decided to launch an attack on the Jews of

Altstadt.   As I have already pointed out,   Jews and Christians in Altstadt lived in complete accord with each other.

One day a Christian woman came into my mother's shop, and with tears rolling down her cheeks told her that on the following day all the Jews of Altstadt would be massacred.   She advised my mother to put up her shutters and make for Dvinsk before it was too late. When my father came home for his midday meal, he brushed the warnings aside as a figment of an old peasant woman's imagination.   But he felt less assured when he had discussed the matter with other Jews, and he took the precaution of sending my mother and the children into Dvinsk.   He and I remained behind to look after the home and shop.   My father reasoned that nothing would befall him, since the ten Christian workmen in his employ all held him in high regard. He was born in Altstadt, and he had been brought up there.   A spirit of friendship had always bound him to the non-Jews of Altstadt.   He was not singular in his optimism;   nearly all the Jews of Altstadt felt that it was inconceivable that the Christians of Altstadt would ever stage a pogrom.

For all that, when the Jews returned from the "Mincha" service, they felt something sinister in the air — either the Jews were keeping apart from the Christians, or vice versa.   But there was a clear deterioration in the relationship between the two.   Even so, nobody for one moment believed that a pogrom was imminent.   There was even a dispute among them as to whether the Jews of Dvinsk should be notified of the fears assailing them.   It was decided to inform them. But so as not to spread panic, the town Jews decided quietly to hide themselves on the fringe of Altstadt, in the houses and on the farms.   Thus they awaited developments.

The following morning, as soon as the shops were opened, the pogromists made an attack on two Jewish stores.   They shattered the windows with a fusillade of missiles, and began pillaging. The anguished cries of the women rent the air. Before we could put the shutters up in our own shop, there rushed in no other than Vanka Agapov, a carpenter employed by my father. With him were three hooligans obviously bent on mischief. "Hey, Fliorka! Hand over the revolvers!" he shouted at my father. My father displayed more courage than I would have ever credited him with. "What's the matter with you, Vanka, looking for revolvers on my premises—are you mad?" "Every dirty Jew is armed with one," he answered back. And he ordered his mates to search the place for weapons. There was nothing for us to do, but to stand there subdued like convicted criminals. They cleared the shelves of all goods, filled their pockets to the brim, and then packed all they could into an empty cask they had found under the counter. "More! More!" Vanka exhorted them. The last thing he did, was personally to remove my father's watch and chain. And what happened in our store was typical, except that from all accounts the pillaging was on a more massive scale elsewhere.

Before the "pogromschikes" had completed their work, the town Jewish butchers, wagoners and carriers came running from every direction and took a rough hand in matters. The hooligans realised the peril in which they found themselves and they ran for their lives, pursued by the Jews. The streets became one mass of flour, soap, candles, cigarettes, sugar. My father recognised his watch, which had been trampled upon. More anti-pogromists came running from Dvinsk, when the news of the pogrom reached them. Altstadt was congested with people. The Jews easily gained the ascendancy, and were making the most of it. So much so, that Christians ran to them for protection. That evening, a captain at the head of a company was despatched to guard the Christians from the anger of the Jews, that was now getting out of control. There were casualties, including two dead on both sides. But this was largely due to the active intervention of the Jewish defence corps or there might have been a disaster that day. As things turned out, Struckoff left Dvinsk in a hurry.

With the defeat of the 1905 Revolution, reaction was once again in the saddle. Tsarist sentiment was well conveyed in the slogan—"Destroy the Jews, and save Russia!" The members of the organisations were under fire, and they scattered wherever they could for safety. The trade union organisations were smashed. Those who remained, lost heart and gave up the struggle as hopeless. A mood of despair was gripping everyone. Those who continued with the fight, in the face of very heavy odds, were rounded up and sent to Siberia, and were seldom heard of again. More gaols were built, and the police force multiplied. Whippings of refractory peasants became a regular occurrence. Nominally, there was a democratically elected Duma in legislative control. But it had little real power, despite the strong representation of the Liberal elements. Two Jewish members of the Duma, Advocate Hertzensteig and the Editor Yalison, were one day found murdered. The Black Hundreds who were charged with their murder were acquitted, although they had been caught red-handed.

Stolypin was the victor. His reputation grew with his crushing of the 1905 Revolution. He was the Tsar's right-hand man, and he accompanied the monarch on all important occasions. A great military parade was being staged in Kiev, and the Tsar, Stolypin and their entourage were present. After the parade they attended a theatre performance. The city and the theatre had been specially decked out for the occasion. The dignitaries of the City, and some of the most eminent figures of Russia, were in the theatre. It was a gala night, such as has seldom been witnessed. Admission was for the select, and the strictest security measures were taken. At the first interval, as the light went on, a young man by the name of Dmitri Bogrov approached and fired two bullets into Stolypin, which proved fatal.

Bogrov was the son of an apostate Jew, a very wealthy Kiev advocate. Stolypin was a frequent visitor at the house. Bogrov was a respected revolutionary, and the organisation had entrusted him with considerable funds. Revolutionaries sought by the police found refuge in his house, which was never under suspicion. Then Bogrov developed a liaison with an actress, and he squandered the money belonging to the organisation. They asked him for an explanation, and he became involved with Stolypin who made large amounts available to him. Thus it was that he became a provocateur. But the organisation discovered his new affiliations and sentenced him to death. He begged of them that they should let him die like a comrade and not like a dog. It was arranged that he should kill Stolypin, to whom he had full access. "Even the Tsar—if you wish it!" Bogrov answered them. "Not the Tsar, but Stolypin!" they insisted. As Bogrov fired, he called out—"Death to you, you dog!"

The Russian generation that grew up after the 1905 defeat gave itself up to a mood of decline and decadence, and it reflected itself in the decadent literature that became a feature of that period. Most notable among these was Artzibasheff's "Sanin", in which sexual depravity and loose living is glorified.

One figure out of this black period is worth recalling—the Jew, Yevgeny Azev. He was the most notorious agent provocateur who served the Okhrana, the Tsar's secret police. He had succeeded in infiltrating into the highest councils of the Social Revolutionaries. It was only after the Revolution that his activities were uncovered. There was this singular about him—that he served both the Social Revolutionaries and the Tsar. He had actually participated in the assassination of important police officials.

In 1910, the name of Tsarist Russia became sullied throughout the world, with what has gone down in legal history as Beiles's Process. The whole of Russia was convulsed with this ritual murder trial which had clearly been instigated by the anti-Semitic elements. It turned into an important struggle between the liberals and the reactionaries. Beiles was acquitted after a trial lasting three years, in which the main witness was a prostitute. But the fact that such a trial could at all be staged, was proof of Russia's internal decay, which showed up all too glaringly in the war that was to follow in 1914.

The war broke out on the 27th of July, 1914, on the Eastern Front. The Jews were in the midst of the Nine Days of Av, mourning the loss of the Beth Hamigdash and their freedom. Proclamations were pasted on the walls of Dvinsk that all those under the age of 43 should report at the assembly points stated, within three days. On top of the "churban" out of ancient times, this was regarded as another disaster. There was no possibility of evading mobilisation for which the death penalty had been imposed. Fathers, sons, brothers, sweethearts all went to report. The Jews waited for the third day, which fell on Tisha B'Av. This was regarded as a bad omen. And it so happened that, from that day onward, the Jews had to endure unending trials and tribulations. There was a doctor at every mobilisation point. But he dealt summarily with the recruits, and both weak and strong, tall and short, were passed as fit for military service. They were moved to military headquarters, where they were given a uniform and sent to Vilna, which had become the main assembly point for that part of the country. Train-loads of soldiers kept passing through all the stations of Dvinsk. Their equipment of rifles, guns and cannons followed them. The Russian soldiers were swept by patriotism in those days, and they sang lustily as the trains headed for the front. As with the Japanese War, the Russian rulers were confident and declared that Germany would be brought to her knees within three months. They sang songs—"To Berlin! To Berlin!" and danced to the twanging balalaikas. The Commander-in-Chief of the Russian Army was a German by the name of Rennenkampf. Early on in the war, the Russian Army suffered a major defeat at the hands of Hindenburg at Tannenburg, when 80,000 of them were drowned in the Masurian lakes. A Jewish soldier from the Russian forces who escaped told of what he had seen in the battle.

As the Russians advanced from Etkunen to Innsburg, they did not encounter a single German. The corn had ripened in the fields. The fleeing Germans had left behind their houses and cattle. The progress of the Russians was so rapid, that for a time everybody believed that the end of the Germans was at hand. Then the Russian forces reached the Masurian marshes. The order was given that they had to move forward into the marshes—they were the orders from Rennenkampf. And so it was that they lost three-quarters of their army, as the Germans counter-attacked and their retreat was cut off. The rest were made prisoners, except for a few thousand who managed to escape.

Rennenkampf was not the only German at the head of affairs — there were many others in the highest ranks, close to the Tsar even, who were known for their pro-German sympathies. The head of the Dvinsk Garrison was the German Von der Osten Dresden. The Colonel of the Ostrovski Regiment was Von Fleischer. The Colonel who headed the Yurovski Regiment was Baron Getrovitch. And there were any number of Germans in the lower ranks. Dvinsk was no exception, and typical of all the major cities. In addition, there were any number of German young girls in Russia, who formed liaisons with the Russians and wheedled important military information from them. The Tsarina herself was a German Princess from Hesse.

After the Tannenburg debacle, the prestige of the Russian Army fell heavily. The German Army swept into Russia. The fortress of Kovno fell to them, and with it enormous stocks of armaments, ammunition and provisions. They next turned their attention to Vilna. Dvinsk became an important strategic point in the struggle, and a centre for the hospitalisation of wounded soldiers. The soldiers who had sung and danced as they made their way to the front, were now being carried from the battlefield on stretchers, moaning and screaming with pain.

The Dvinsk Hospital inside the Fortress, the Summer Hospital, and the Jewish Hospital, and other hospitals were brimful with wounded soldiers. Mattresses were placed on the floors of the corridors. And when things worsened, a number were even laid out on the bare earth in the courtyards. But it was not enough. Schools were turned into hospitals, and new structures went up to serve as hospitals. Apart from the sick and wounded, new contingents of soldiers — artillery, cavalry, infantry—were steadily moving into Dvinsk. Dvinsk became an important military centre. General Russky, head of the Fifth Army, was in control of Dvinsk. The influx of so many soldiers resulted in a great increase of trade, and large fortunes. Even the scribe of the Shofar Torah and the Shamos took to trade, and they did very well.

The Russian Army continued to suffer defeats. Those carrying blue identification cards, who had never been in the Army, were being called up. The Grand Duke Nikolai Nikolaievitch, a well-known anti-Semite with no ability whatsoever, succeeded Rennenkampf as Commander-in-Chief. The defeats this Grand Duke brought to Russia were even more disastrous than those of the past. Catherine the Great had once said that people are born, but earth is not born. And it would seem that the Grand Duke must have felt the same way about things, as he continued to sacrifice the manhood of Russia on the battlefields, with a prodigality seldom known before. One hundred thousand Russian soldiers laid down their lives in a short space of time on the battlefields of Kovno, Vilna and the approaches to Dvinsk. From the roads, for hundreds of miles, crosses could be seen in the fields in almost continuous sweeps, marking the graves of those who had perished. And scattered among them were not a few Magen Dovids. But nothing daunted, the Grand Duke called for more and more men. It would seem that he had decided to stem the enemy's advance with a massive wall of humans. But the enemy was not to be stopped.

As disaster followed disaster, and the masses of dead began to pile up into mountainous proportion, the Russian nation for the first time comprehended what a stark and forbidding future lay ahead of it. Discontent began to simmer at first, and then became more articulate. In the Duma the left elements and even the liberals wanted to know where the fault lay. Petitions of all sorts were sent to the highest in the land, in the hope that an improvement in the situation would supervene. The Commander-in-Chief had to find a scapegoat. And, as was customary in that part of the world, it fell to the Jew to assume this role. One fine day, a well-known newspaper, subsidised by the Palace, came out with an article, in startlingly bold type accusing the Jews of being responsible for Russia's defeats. They were charged with harbouring pro-German sympathies, and spying for the enemy. A cartoon even appeared showing a Jew and a German shaking hands, and the Jew filling his pockets with German marks. Every insult was heaped on the Jews.

In 1915, shortly after Shevuas, the Tsar issued a ukase ordering that all Jews should be evacuated from Lithuania. This uprooting of masses of people, and sending them thousands of miles away from their homes, must be accounted as one of the major calamities that had ever befallen the Jews. Homes and businesses were left behind in this sudden forced flight. And also valuable produce in the fields, which Jews owned in partnership with non-Jews secretly. Orders were given brusquely by the police, and they had to be obeyed forthwith. No concession of any kind was made—not even to afford one the opportunity of a last visit to the grave of a departed parent. Trains were provided free of charge for the refugees. Old and young, men, women, children, all carried as many bundles as they could. The more fortunate who owned a horse and cart offered help to neighbours and friends in every way possible. Peasants were paid to transport Jews from distant land settlements, to the trains waiting to take them into the interior of Russia. At 12 o'clock midday, on the eve of Shevuas, the Jews had all congregated on the railway stations of their villages and towns, in accordance with the Proclamation.

Among the departing refugees were sixteen members of my wife's family. In Dvinsk the Jews celebrated Shevuas, without being aware that across the border, in Lithuania, Jews by the thousands were crammed into freight-cars and every available means of transport, and being sent away from the battle-front. Neither could they hear the cries and lamentations from these Jews, rending the air and calling on God to protect them in their agony. The Jews of Dvinsk put their trust in the Dvina, which the Germans could try to cross only at their grave peril.

While I was in Shul attending the Shevuas service, I was called out by a youngster. In the vestibule stood my wife shivering like a leaf with fright. She handed me a note scribbled in pencil, which came from her sister who had lived in a Lithuanian village, by the name of Potsenell. It said that there were four thousand Jewish refugees on the Petersburg Station, heading for the interior of Russia, and that they were in need of tea, milk and a doctor. When I announced this to the worshippers, everyone took off their "taleisim", and before long many were streaming from their homes,

carrying bundles of food and everything they could lay
their hands on to bring some comfort to the refugees.
When I arrived at the station and saw the appalling
sight of this motley mass of humanity, I began to despair of the future of mankind. I did not know at the
time that greater tribulations and trials awaited us all.

Eighty freight-trucks stood on one of the railway
lines. They were without covering overhead. The
refugees on the move were begrimed and weary with
their journeying under such miserable conditions. My
wife managed to locate her brother, who led us to her
parents and the rest of their family. At one carriage,
I saw a Jew standing reading a "Tehillim". Tears
were streaming down his cheeks. In another carriage
the cry was heard—"Make way Jews! Show your
respect for the dead!" They were carrying a corpse.
In other carriages, Jews in "Taleisim" were in prayer.
The carriages were transporting loads of Jewish
misery.

An hour later, cab-drivers and wagoners from Dvinsk
came pouring onto the Petersburg Station, carrying
loads of food. Two doctors also arrived. A committee was formed to supervise the distribution of food.
Children were given chocolates. Oven-makers im-
provised an oven on which food was cooked. And
now wagon-loads of bread began arriving from the
Christian bakery owned by Mitrofanoff. There were
loads and loads of bread, bagels, and even delicacies.
Mitrafanoff was blessed by all for the compassion he
had displayed. Young Jewish girls from Dvinsk entered the carriages, and with sleeves rolled up proceeded
to clean up the debris and bring order out of the chaos.
The doctors vaccinated hundreds of children. Clothes
were washed; the heads of the children were being
lathered and scrubbed; and the Chevra Kadisha came
to take care of the dead. Some of us brought our
relations to our homes, after having obtained permission from the military authorities.

Reb Meir Simcha was, more than anyone else, responsible for this essay in human solidarity and compassion. He it was who, on hearing of the plight of the refugees, mounted the "Bimah" and urged his congregants to bring whatever succour they could. And although it was Yomtov, he gave permission to the wagoners and cab-drivers to inspan their horses and help in every way possible. It was hoped that the trains would halt there for several days. But at midnight that same day, they were once again on their way. Some members of the committee accompanied them as far as Kreslavka. There, too, the Jews received them with a great welcome and many gifts. They proceeded through Vitebsk, Polotsk, and finally most of them were settled in the Ukraine.

Now that the Jews, who were supposedly responsible for defeat, were evacuated from Lithuania and the battle-front, Russian victories should have followed. But it was not so. The Germans advanced on Dvinsk, and in the south were closing in on the Ukraine. The Germans took out of Russia anything that could help their war effort, even church bells. Vilna and the neighbourhood now fell to the Germans. Things had come to such a perilous pass, that the Grand Duke had to resign from his position at the head of the Army. With the approach of the Germans, Dvinsk began to take measures to defend itself. Reinforcements were brought up, trenches were dug and redoubts built up. Masses of artillery were placed in position to defend the Dvina at all costs. Many of the rich sold their belongings and sought safety in towns removed from the battle-front.

As the front drew nearer, the military hospitals in Dvinsk became more congested with the ailing and wounded. There was a big shortage of stretcher-bearers. The Volunteer Fire Brigade stepped into the breach. They took up their positions at the stations. where train-loads of wounded were due to arrive.

Service battalions were now organised from those on the home front to dig ditches and trenches.

When not enough volunteers were forthcoming, it was made compulsory to offer up a certain time for this work. Even houses were invaded. A large number bribed their way out. Bribery became a feature of life round about that time. The town was steadily sinking into a state of disquiet. On top of all its trouble, the Don Cossacks arrived. They created an atmosphere of fear, especially among the womenfolk. They helped themselves to goods from stores, without giving a thought to paying. Both trade and employment was fast coming to a standstill as the war progressed.

The German Army was halted at places well known to many South Africans who hail from that part— Rakeshik, Kamaai, Ponodel, Ponamunik and Traskun. From this point the Germans were gathering their forces to launch a final assault on Dvinsk. And then one day another new horror came to Dvinsk. Explosions were heard from above in the sky. Dvinsk was beholding the first aeroplane attack. It flew at a very high altitude, and circled overhead. A pall of fear descended on the town. Bombs dropped on the Petersburg Railway Station and the Fortress resulted in a number of casualties. People began to think in terms of flight. The poor who remained behind envied the Lithuanian Jews who had found safety in the interior of Russia. Jewish sorrow and suffering began to be recorded in song and verse.

On the eve of Rosh Hashanah, war became more intimately involved with the lives of the people of Dvinsk when a German aeroplane dropped a bomb that landed right in the middle of the market-place. The panic and screams that followed blasted the ears. The Christians crossed themselves, while the Jews tore the hair from their heads. Policemen, stretcher-bearers and doctors came running along. The toll was five dead and forty one wounded. There were countless who had fainted with fright.

When evening brought Rosh Hashanah, the Jews congregated in the Synagogue for prayer. The following morning they again packed the Synagogue, as if in search of salvation from a sense of doom. The girls even came to hear the sounding of the Shofar. And as they were making for their homes after the service, so that the streets were massed with people, an aeroplane flew overhead. The bomb it dropped took the lives of eight Jews, and a number were wounded. There was no respite from this plague from on high. The following day two aeroplanes dropped bombs, but this time it was on military objectives—the Fortress and the Pletzer. The casualties continued to mount.

These raids led to the partial evacuation of Dvinsk. The State Bank took out all its money. Important documents were removed from the municipal offices and the Fortress. The officers sent their families away. Then a miracle occurred—The Government provided trains to evacuate refugees. All who desired to leave could do so at Government expense. The Jews rejoiced. They packed their poverty and their sorrow into bundles. They gathered at different points along the railway line. Three-quarters of Dvinsk left home and hearth between Rosh Hashanah and Yom Kippur. The coaches, cattle-trucks and freight cars were jammed with fleeing humanity like barrels with herrings. The trains roared through night and day, as if in space, with no one knowing what his destination will be—or even caring.

Chapter Fifteen

REVOLUTION AND AFTER

I was twenty eight years old at the time. Militarily, I held a Blue Ticket, which meant that I was exempted from service. I also carried papers, stamped and sealed, certifying that as a painter of hospitals and other institutions of military service, I was not to be conscripted. I was now head supervisor of the contracts on which my father was engaged. But I was still assigned to the first reserve, and I could be called up with the next mobilisation of new recruits.

By 1915 Altstadt lost all civilian appearance, as it became one vast military encampment. There was such congestion that soldiers were quartered in tents. They dotted the fields. Before long, as was to be expected, the fields with their crops of corn, potatoes and beans were one mass of ruin. My parents and the rest of the family, except for myself, made their way to Petrograd, where my brother Joseph lived. My wife's family found refuge in Rudnia, a village near Smolensk. I then sent my wife and the two baby sons to her uncle in Dvinsk, Mendel Glickman. We were showered with letters from Rudnia, urging us to leave Dvinsk. With a great deal of reluctance, I sent my wife and the two children to Rudnia. A few days afterwards I followed them, as life in Dvinsk became more uncertain and hazardous. I arrived in Rudnia on the second day of Succas. After Simchas Torah we all took the train for Petrograd.

From the 20th September, 1915 until the 8th of October, 1918, I was in Petrograd, and I lived through some of the stormiest days in history, as the Revolution swept over Russia bringing a new social order with it. The days of the Revolution were so momentous and full of drama, that I could only do justice to it in a whole book. But I will attempt to give here some of my most salient impressions after returning to Dvinsk.

Although I was working in a food co-operative in Petrograd, and had enough to live on, considering the times, there was general starvation in the City, followed by an epidemic, and I decided to leave for Dvinsk with my family, to which there had been an addition of a male child. The train journey lasted a week. Dvinsk was still under German occupation. They had taken it over with the signing of the Brest Litovsk Treaty. The ravages of war could be seen in every street. Ruined houses with gaping holes met you wherever you looked. In parts of the town whole areas had been devastated, and potatoes and other vegetables were planted where people had once lived and thrived. Amongst the structures bound up with the life of the city that had disappeared was Dovid's "bod". Many wooden houses were ripped to pieces to provide fuel to keep at bay the unendurable cold of the winter of 1918. But despite all the heavy cannonading and air bombardment, the town though badly crippled remained alive. The will to live did not abate. Such is mankind!

There were now only twelve thousand Jews left of the forty five thousand that had been there before the war. There was an insufficiency of food, but nothing like the near-starvation of Petrograd. The Jews traded with the German occupation forces. But the trade had greatly shrunk. For all that, the theatre continued to keep its doors open and offer plays to the public. Life under the Germans was more or less normal.

With the end of the war, and the defeat of Germany, the German army began to move out. They sold whatever they could, and Jewish traders could buy commodities for next to nothing. On the 8th of January, 1919 the streets of Dvinsk, and particularly Riga Street, were decorated with red flags. The youth were celebrating as they prepared to welcome the Bolsheviks. The

Voluntary Fire Brigade had provided an orchestra for
the occasion. At eleven o'clock in the morning the
advance units of the Red Army entered the town. The
orchestra greeted them with a rousing Internationale
and Marseillaise, as thirty Red Army men stepped from
the incoming train. Their uniforms and boots were
bedraggled. Many of them wore short leather jackets
and buckles. Revolvers in holsters were a prominent
feature. One addressed those who had gathered to
welcome them and he promised freedom, equality and
bread. Led by the orchestra, everybody marched to
the Parade Square. They were singing songs of freedom and victory.

There were more speeches at the Parade Square, and
a promise that a Soviet would be set up for the town.
The youth were carried away with this new wave of
enthusiasm that was sweeping the whole of Russia.
The older ones were more hesitant about the turn of
events, and as a precaution against difficult days, they
bought up all provisions and commodities they could
lay their hands on, and hid them in places where they
would not be easily found.

From the following day, there was a shortage of food
in the town. The Bolsheviks were aware of what had
caused the shortage, but there was little they could do
about it. Things were getting out of control. Every
minute prices rose to inflationary levels. The peasant
was afraid to bring his produce to the town, for fear of
being expropriated, or even being robbed in a straight
way. With time he became arrogant, and told the
townspeople that they could come to him if they wanted
to buy his goods. With peasant cunning, he refused
to accept money which he knew to be valueless. This
was the beginning of barter. In short, hunger loomed
darkly over the populace. Prices soared, and finally
food became totally unobtainable. Unemployment
reared its head above the chaos. Precious possessions
were exchanged for bread. It was a state of affairs that
could not endure.

The new rulers opened a state store and bakery. Bread was exchanged for coupons. The rations were small, and usually late, as there was a shortage of flour. For some six weeks it was still possible to exist. During the first stage, the Russian Bolsheviks were in control. Among them were a number of Jews. But things took a turn for the worse when the more primitive Lettish Bolsheviks took over. Dutza, whom we have already mentioned, instigated a draconian regime aimed to destroy the bourgeoisie, as he called any little store-keeper or tradesman. The rich and clerics had a bad time of it, as execution followed execution. Speculators, small or big, suffered severely at his hands. Terror became the order of the day. Things worsened as epidemics spread with the misery. People died like flies. And I too, mourned the death of my youngest child.

I was at the time unemployed. One morning I went to the building workers' union to seek work. But there was nothing doing. I found a meeting in progress, and I thought I would hang around and listen to the wisdom of these men who seemed to know everything. There were about five hundred present. Two commissars in short leather jackets sat at a table on the platform. It was an orderly meeting, and there was a great deal of speech-making. The gathering decided to elect a committee to regularise the building trade. Eleven were chosen. As I had been employed in a big Petrograd ammunition factory, I was one of the eleven asked to serve on the committee. I became full-time paid secretary.

Much was written, and much was crossed out. But it was one thing to write on paper and another thing to get jobs for those who were seeking work. The unemployed became discontented and aggressive, as they failed to find work. "You're getting paid for nothing!" they kept accusing me. Weeping women took to coming to my home, begging that their husbands be found work so that their children should have bread.

Out of the eight hundred who had registered their names with the committee each day, thirty were found employment. I would gladly have resigned my post, but for the fact that the new regime would have regarded it as a counter-revolutionary act.

I had a stroke of luck. A number of Lettish Bolsheviks came to Dvinsk, and they had to be supplied with homes. There were a number of houses going, but mostly in a dilapidated state calling for heavy repairs. Windows were broken, roofs were leaking, doors were missing. As a result there was a shortage of dwellings. A committee was set up for the allocation of houses. Three were appointed to head the committee—the carpenter Kravchenko, Abba Chone Sawitz, and I. The dwellings committee on which I was serving was divided into four sections according to their duties : (1) Repairing houses; (2) allocating the bigger dwellings to a number of families; (3) the requisitioning of furniture for homes; and (4) to arbitrate disputes relating to dwellings and furniture.

I was in charge of the last of these. I had to give decisions in all manner of disputes, such as whether a bed and mattress could be expropriated; and whether an extra family could be lodged in a home in which others were living. A young, intelligent man was my assistant, and we had enough trouble on our hands. Hundreds of petty disputes came before me, and took up a great deal of my time. For all that, things were working out not too badly. But one day, an order was issued that all those working for the authorities had to join the Red Army, as the Poles were preparing to launch an attack. I had never handled a gun, and I sought a way out from joining up. I received a letter from my brother in Petrograd notifying me that my old job I had there was going. My wife was at the time pregnant. I had to leave her behind with our two children, and see what awaited me in Petrograd.

I found life in Petrograd had become more difficult during the six months I had been away from it. Civil war was stalking the land, and draining the life-blood of the nation. On top of it, Britain, France and America started a war of intervention against the Bolsheviks. The peasant kulaks, who were enemies to the death of the Bolsheviks, refused to send their produce into the towns and in this way hoped to starve the new regime out of existence. With the new levees, I, too, found myself with a rifle in my hand—for the first time. But I was released from military duty, as I was needed on the civilian front.

I lived in Petrograd until 1922, when I returned to my wife and children. Dvinsk was then under the Letts. Everybody was afraid that such a small country as Latvia would not be able to maintain order. Although there had been starvation in Petrograd, bread was plentiful in Dvinsk. Dvinsk had gone through a trying time during the three years I had been away from it. It had changed hands several times. First, it was occupied by the Poles and they worked together with General Haller who terrorised the town. Then came the Bermantsites. They were Germans from Latvia. Then came the Bolsheviks a second time, and the suffering of the population did not diminish. One regime was as bad as the other. Finally, the Letts took over, and theirs was a more stable regime. The President Chakste was a reasonable and intelligent man. All minorities were given full rights. Jews returned to the town and once again began to play an important part in industry and commerce.

But Latvia was a very tiny country, badly constricted within its borders. You had to have a passport to leave the country or enter it. Trade with Lithuania came to a standstill, and it was not easy to earn a living. During the first few years there was a certain amount of building activity. Buildings were being repaired and private residences were renovated. Building workers, tailors and bootmakers found a reasonable amount of employment. The workers began to organise themselves into unions, and they sympathised with the Bolsheviks.

A medical scheme was instituted, which brought many benefits to the workers. All kinds of clubs made their appearance — sporting clubs, political clubs, Zionist clubs. The clubs grew rapidly and attracted the youth. The Jewish children went to the regular secular schools. Those who wished to, sent their children to cheder in the afternoons. In this respect, things had changed completely from the situation before the war.

During the first years of Latvian independence the country made steady progress. With the aid from Britain, America and Poland, industry and farming went ahead, and the Riga University became an important technical and cultural institution. As the years passed, the Letts with the aid of the Government began to displace Jewish and other minorities in trade and industry. By 1927, Lettish nationalism tended towards chauvinism. Lettish became the only official language. Government co-operatives bought the produce from the peasants, where previously they had sent it to the market. The co-operatives were exempted from taxes, which increased yearly for those engaged in private trade. The contractors who in the Tsarist days had helped supply the army stationed in Dvinsk with its needs, suffered more than anybody else. The contractors were now all Lettish. The cry was—"Latvia for the Letts!"

A clandestine anti-Semitism was prevalent in Dvinsk. Jews were forced out of the economy. It was difficult to make ends meet, and they began to look for a way out. Immigration was the only hope. The Jews with foresight had left early on for America, which closed its doors in 1927. Quite a number sailed for Argentina and Brazil. Many of the youth settled in Palestine. The Jewish population of Dvinsk was dwindling fast. At the end of 1928 I left my beloved hometown of Dvinsk. Together with eighty three other Jews I sailed for South Africa. That was the last I saw of Dvinsk.

Translation of

In Memory of the Community of Dvinsk
(Daugavpils, Latvia)
55°53' / 26°32'

Translation of *Le zekher kehilat Dvinsk*

Originally Published in Haifa, 1975

Translation Project Coordinator: Ilana Lutman

Translated by Amy Samin

**Our sincere appreciation to Joel Gardner,
for kindly donating this translation.**

This book was published with the assistance of the Dov Aloni Memorial Fund

Kol Yisrael Haverim Junior High School, Haifa – 1974

The booklet was prepared by Grade 8A and Grade 8B

Under the guidance of teacher Tamar Amarant

Illustrated by Ganor Atzmon and Levy Zvi

[Page 1]

Remarks of the School Management

We continue with the holy work of memorializing the Jewish communities destroyed in the Holocaust.

This time, teacher Tamar Amarant and her students in the History of the Holocaust class chose to memorialize the Latvian community Dvinsk.

Dvinsk, which today is part of the Soviet Latvian Republic, was first settled by Jews in the first half of the 18th century. From a small Jewish settlement of a few hundred souls, the community grew until in 1913 it had reached 56,000 souls. The First World War brought about a reduction in the number of Jews in Dvinsk; by the end of the war they numbered about 13,000. In spite of that, the community flourished economically and was an important cultural center for the Jews of Russia.

The Nazis, who occupied Dvinsk on 28 June 1941, found the Latvian population to be faithful partners in their programs of destruction.

Within a short time almost the entire Jewish population of Dvinsk had been destroyed and another Jewish community had vanished.

You boys and girls, who were born in Israel and did not know the hand of the bitter enemy, recognize what a privilege you were granted, to be born in an independent country, to grow strong there and to protect the Jewish state, to ensure that never again would such a devil arise in the world to destroy the Jewish people.

Many thanks to the teacher Tamar Amarant and her pupils for their devoted work, which was carried out after school hours.

With blessings,

Esther Weiss
Supervisor, Junior High School

B Yaffe *
Principal, High School
Kol Yisrael Haverim

* Mr. Bezalel Yaffe passed away on 17 March 1975

May his memory be blessed!

[Page 2]

Yad Vashem, the Remembrance Authority of the Holocaust and its Heroes
The Committee for the Memorialization of Communities

To Mrs. Tamar Amarant and her pupils at the Kol Yisrael Haverim School

Greetings !

I feel I have a pleasant privilege to express my gratitude to you for your outstanding efforts in this project, which memorializes the community of Dvinsk.

The memory of the community of Dvinsk is very close to my heart, because I lived in that city for two years when I served as the emissary of the Education Department of the National Committee. This was forty years ago, and they were among the best years of my life. I found there a medium-sized community, but the Jewish cultural life there was a flourishing one. At that time, the Latvian government granted the Jews broad cultural autonomy. Schools operating in the Hebrew and Yiddish languages served the Jewish youth and they were paid for by the government. There were pioneering and Zionist youth movements from all the various streams and political parties. There were synagogues and houses of study. The cultural life of the Jews of Dvinsk was especially vigorous. Many other emissaries from Israel visited there in Dvinsk during those two years. The visits of Haim Nachmun Bialik and of Natan Bistritsky to the city left an indelible impression on the Jewish youth.

There was almost not a single young person who did not belong to some sort of movement. Hundreds of the pioneers who came to Eretz-Yisrael were students in the schools of the city. Many of them still live on the kibbutzim Giladi, Kinneret, Afikim and others, even today.

The booklet you have published, and your memorialization project, have awakened wonderful memories but also great sorrow that this splendid community was destroyed.

Congratulations on your excellent work!

Y. Arni

[Page 3]

Scroll of Remembrance

מגילת־הנצחה

בית־הספר "כל ישראל חברים" ב־ ח.ק.ב _____ במדינת ישראל

מצהיר בזה חגיגית, כי ביום ___ לחודש ___ תש"ג ___ קיבל עליו את המשימה הקדושה

להנציח את קהילת ____ דרבינסק ____ (באזור ____)

שנחרבה בשנות השואה על ידי קלגסי הנאצים הטמאים ועוזריהם.

תלמידי בית הספר, בשיתוף עם הרשויות החינוכיות ועם ארגוני
הקהילה בארץ ובתפוצות, ובעזרת הוועדה הארצית להנצחת הקהילות
שעל יד יד־ושם בירושלים, יעשו כמיטב יכולתם וימשיכו בפעולה
שהחלו בה להעלות לזכר עולם את הקהילה הכל בחייה ופעלה, עד
לשואה וכן בסבלה, מאבקה וכליונה בתקופת החורבן.

על החתום :

מנהל(ת) בית הספר _____ מחנך(ת) הכיתה _____

נציג התלמידים המספיחים: א) _____ ב) _____

רב ארגון הקהילה : א) _____ ב) _____ ג) _____

מגילה זו נתקבלה ביד ושם למשמרת עולם.

The Kol Yisrael Haverim school in the city of Haifa in the State of Israel affirms that on the 14th of Elul, 5734 (1974) it took upon itself the sacred mission of memorializing the community of Dvinsk (in Latvia) which was destroyed during the Holocaust at the hands of Nazi soldiers and their followers.

These school children, together with the educational authorities and community organizations in Israel and the Diaspora, and with the assistance of the National Committee for the Memorialization of Communities near Yad Vashem in Jerusalem, will work to the utmost of their ability, and will continue their activity which they began in order to bring to the world's awareness the aforementioned community, as it was during its peak and up until the Holocaust, and including its suffering, struggle and destruction during the period of annihilation.

This scroll was received at Yad Vashem to be preserved forever.

[Page 4]

Dear Pupils,

With awe and reverence, we continue the holy work of memorializing communities, a project which began in 1964.

This time, we have memorialized the community of Dvinsk, a vital and productive Latvian community before the Second World War which was plundered, anguished and extinguished after the war, whose fate it was to lose its sons. From the few remaining survivors, you attempted to glean information. The communities of Poland, Lithuania, and Latvia fell during the final plot of the Nazis to solve the problem of the Jews by completely destroying them.

The strength that drove the Nazis to carry out this unprecedented crime sprang from their ideology, according to which every Jew was an eternal and powerful enemy. German commandos were assisted by units of locals – Latvians, Estonians, Lithuanians, Poles and Ukrainians, and by the local police forces in the lands they had occupied. Their systemized camouflage and deceit succeeded in deceiving the Jews up until the last moment of their lives.

Thousands of communities of people, institutions, and culture were destroyed. Through our work in memorializing them, we are establishing a connection and contact between you, who did not experience the Holocaust and the content of Jewish life in the European Diaspora before its destruction. Through your work, you are erecting an eternal monument to the lost communities.

This project illustrates for you the fate of the Jews and provides you with the sensation of partnership and mutuality with them.

May you be blessed, and may this booklet serve as a memorial for those who are no longer with us.

Your teacher, Tamar Amarant

[Page 5]

Introduction

The Holocaust – what a word – monstrous. What a horrific phenomenon, a deep wound in the flesh of our people – and how depressing for humanity.

Children of Israel who were born and grew up on Israeli soil, in the state of Israel, are witnesses to the revival and resurrection and are, in their classes at school, trying to understand the meaning of that same Holocaust.

They are trying to decipher the diabolical mystery, to understand that which is inconceivable.

Occasionally one can reconstruct and revisit the past lives of the sacred communities, may their memories be blessed, which the Nazi ax cut down. Afterwards, the Soviets schemed to extract the roots of their memory.

Blessings and thanks to the pupils of the Kol Yisrael Haverim School in Haifa, who have kindled a memorial candle for the community of the town of our birth, the city of our youth, the city where we buried our dear ones in enormous mass graves.

Congratulations to the teacher Tamar Amarant, the living spirit of the sacred work of memorializing the Jewish communities.

Our heart felt thanks go to the management of the school for their encouragement and assistance.

Dvinsk Natives in Israel

[Page 6]

The Memorialization of the Dvinsk Community 1974

You delve into the memorialization of a community by studying its life, character, and people. You interview people, the survivors of the community, and you learn of a vital and productive community, one that was active, living and breathing.

A community which developed praiseworthy cultural and social institutions, a community that took pride in its animated daily life, until you reach the period of the terrible Holocaust which consigned the community, and its men, women and children to limbo.

And you stand and wonder:

Is such a horrible thing possible?

Is it possible that people were burned alive in furnaces? That women, infants and children were thrown into mass graves and the world remained silent?

That silence is atrocious in the eyes of a young person like me, who is growing up in this world, who is studying the past of his people and cannot reconcile himself to such a thing.

The horror penetrates my bones and demands: investigate and dig into the roots of this period of time, learn the lesson from the past for the future.

May the memories of the victims of the Holocaust be blessed!

Atzmon Ganor, Grade 8B

[Page 7]

The Community of Dvinsk
Prepared by Kol Yisrael Haverim Junior High School, Haifa Levana Hillel Grade 8

Published in Memorial Record #11, Yad Vashem, *Ponderings*

This year we worked on the memorialization of the community of Dvinsk-Dinaburg in Latvia, delving into the subject of the magnificent communities of Europe which once existed and are now gone. Hatred wells up in me toward the Nazi beast, which was able to destroy one third of our people in such a barbaric and cruel manner. How could a people reach such a loathsome state as to shoot people as they would a stray dog?

My brain cannot conceive of it. More and more I feel that we must not forget what happened: "Remember what Amalek did unto you!" The words reverberate within me and give me no peace. As I study the community I feel pity for those victims of the Holocaust, who were my brothers and sisters in the Diaspora. I feel I am a link in the chain of our people, who were persecuted only because they were Jews. I feel pity for the small children who barely had a chance to live before the Nazi butchers slaughtered them.

It is as if I am living the life of the community I am studying, hearing about, writing about, and coming to understand. I try to put myself in their places, and think, how would I behave? Would I run away from the ghetto? Would I join a group of vengeful fighters? Would I perhaps attempt to hide, in order to conceal my Jewish appearance from the eyes of the Nazi beasts?

I think that in every school in Israel time needs to be set aside for the study of the Holocaust so that we will learn, know, and never forget what happened. Knowledge and awareness will prevent a second Holocaust, God forbid, from taking place. The fact of knowing and identifying with communities connects us and proves that all children of Israel are brothers, and each is involved with the other.

[Page 8]

The Youth Television Broadcast on Dvinsk

We were very excited about appearing on Youth Television. Who wouldn't want to be on television? It's what most young people want most.

For two and a half hours they filmed us. We interviewed people from Dvinsk, asked them questions, and got very emotional.

The director, Leah Byrech, told us exactly when the program would be broadcast and we looked forward to watching it. We were on television for fifteen minutes. After the broadcast, I spent some time thinking about the matter. Would the students who saw us at work memorializing the community of Dvinsk follow in our footsteps one day?

But I realized that I myself had learned a lot from the work, which was done in the after-school hours.

For the most part I went to interview people, survivors from the community. I heard directly from them about the past of the community, and I was amazed: how did the Jews in the Diaspora know how to create such fine cultural institutions in their communities? How did the community know to preserve the unity of the Jews? How did they battle against the foreign rulers for each crumb of autonomy, and win?

The community took care of its own, providing food for widows and orphans, obtaining aid and assistance for the needy, and it seemed to me the warmth enveloped me as I listened to the survivors from the community telling me what life was like in the foreign and hostile Diaspora.

I understood the expression: "All Jews are responsible for one another."

I identified with the innocent victims of the Holocaust who were destroyed through no fault of their own, only because they were Jews. The martyrization of the Jews, which can be traced through many generations, instilled pride in me; here I am, a Jew living in my own land, and I want to give her my very best.

Shula Apotker, Grade 8B

Dvinsk in the Past

Group of Immigrants to Eretz-Yisrael from Dvinsk in the year 1921

[Page 10]

Dvinsk in the Past

From the imagination of Atzmon Ganor
Student, Grade 8B

[Page 11]

When you conjure up from the depths of your memory the outlines of a Jewish city and mother, you remember Dvinsk. This is Jewish Dvinsk, crowded and teeming with Jewish life. And now, when you know her voice has been silenced, horror grips you. This is what the murderers did to this source of Jewish culture. That well-spring of Jewish creativity has been stopped up and will never flow again.

There is an obligation to leave behind a memory of Dvinsk for the generations to come, so the descendants of Dvinsk will know the source from which they came, so that they will have in the forefront of their minds the memory of our sainted ones, who were turned by the evil ones into fertilizer for their fields. Until the end of all the generations, the memory of the martyrs, whose bones were ground to phosphate and whose hair was taken for stuffing mattresses, must be preserved. That is the goal of the article.

~.

The Foundation and Development of the City of Dvisnk

The city of Dvinsk was founded in 1278 by the Knights of the Livonian Order and named Dünaburg [Dinaburg] by its founders, meaning the Fortress on the Daugava (for it was built on the western Daugava River, on whose banks the town rests). The town kept this German name for several hundreds of years, until 1893. The city lay, as has been mentioned, on the banks of the Daugava River at the junction of the Riga – Oryol and Leningrad – Vilna railroad lines. The city was therefore very attractive to occupiers, who always coveted the strategically-located spot. For the Livonian Knights it was a stronghold and a base for the broadening and strengthening of their rule over the Balticum area. More than once the Livonians, like the Russians, tried to attack the fortress (in 1315, 1403, and 1418), without success.

In the 16th century Dvinsk was captured and occupied by the Russians and was later formally passed into their hands by means of an agreement with the Polish king August Sigismund. With the destruction of the Livonian fortress in 1561, the city became part of the Polish-Lithuanian Commonwealth. The city went through many periods of changing rulers even after that. In 1577, the city was once again in the hands of the Russians; then later was re-claimed by the Poles. King Stefan Batory had the city surrounded with a strong, fortified wall in 1582.

In 1600 the city fell into the control of the Swedes; in 1635 by agreement it was transferred over to the Poles. In 1656 the city was taken by Tsar Alexis Mikhailovitch of Russia, who changed the German name of the town (Dinaburg) to Borisoglebsk. According to a new agreement, the city was returned to the Poles. During the Great Northern War of 1700 – 1721, the city continued to change hands.   *[Page 12]*   With the First Partition of Poland in 1772, the entire area was apportioned to Russia, but that did not provide the city with a long period of serenity. In 1795 the Poles attacked. They set fire to the city, which burned down completely. During the Napoleonic War, the city found itself for a brief time in the control of the French, and only in 1812, when Napoleon was defeated, was the city once again appended to Russia, in whose control it remained until the outbreak of the First World War in 1914.

For a short period of time during World War I, the city was ruled by Germany. With the signing of the Brest-Litovsk Treat early in 1922, Dvinsk fell within the borders of the independent state of Latvia. This situation continued until 1940.

With the German occupation in 1941 and during the course of the Second World War, the city was destroyed. The fate of the Jewish community is well known. Today, Dvinsk is part of the Latvian Republic of the Soviet Union. After World War II the city was rehabilitated, and quickly developed into an important industrial center, particularly in the lumber sector, which developed thanks to the geographic conditions of the city, which sits on the banks of the Daugava River. The river, which is more than 1,000 kilometers long, provides a convenient waterway for the transport of the lumber barges. Railway lines reaching the farthest ends of vast Russia pass through the city.

The many different rulers of the city left their marks on it. The population has many layers and is made up mostly of minorities: Belarusians, Malorussians, Lithuanians, Poles, and Germans. The Jews were the largest minority: until 1914 they made up 14% of the population.

It should be mentioned that even during the period of the establishment of an independent Latvia the residents of Dvinsk completely ignored the language of the country, the Latvian tongue, and continued to conduct their public activities, including meetings in the offices of the municipality, in Russian.

The Latgalians, and the Latvian tribe in the area around the city, were regarded as forming an inferior stratum of society. Their dialect was slightly different from that of their brothers from the Lapland and Courland regions, which were considered part of a "purer" race. The latter treated the Latgalians with contempt and called them by the derogatory name *Tsangalim*, which means inferior. The pure Latvians, seeing themselves as close to the superior German race, assimilated among them (they all spoke German, while the Latgalians were still using their own dialect of the Russian language). The Latgalians were behind in all areas of life and occupied the poorest, most backward level in every area. For example, while in Courland and Lapland the percentage of illiterates reached 50%, the illiteracy rate in Latgale reached 30% [sic]. In the beginning, they had difficulty with their own language, which lacked tradition and history. In 1860, the population of Dvinsk was 26,000, in 1892 73,000, and in 1913 it had reached 130,000. The developing industries in the city were lumber, leather, linen, tobacco, grain, and sweets.

[Page 13]

The Jews of Dvinsk

The Jewish settlement in Dvinsk first put down roots in the second half of the 18th century. As has been mentioned, there was a fortress in the city, but in 1812 the Jews were forbidden from constructing and living in a permanent residence there. In spite of that, in 1805 one would have found about 800 Jews in the city. The Jewish community in the city began to grow and develop. Later, Jews began to flow into the Pale of Settlement and continue onwards to Dvinsk, so much so that at the time of the 1897 census 32,400 Jews lived there. The Jewish population continued to grow. At the outbreak of World War I there were over 60,000 Jews living in Dvinsk, making up nearly half the residents of the city.

All of the Jews of Dvinsk knew how to speak and write in Yiddish. The city had an abundance of schools *(cheders)* and from every direction could be heard the voices of those who began their education by studying Torah as young children and completed their studies with *Gemara* and *Tosafot* [annotations to the Talmud]. By 1887, 208 students attended a handicrafts school for girls.

Two libraries were established in the city. The same year we also find three loan funds. According to the census of 1897, Jews made up 46% of the total population. Almost all commerce was in the hands of Jews. Of 1,370 merchants, 1,134 were Jews. On the other hand, only 168 of the Jews of Dvinsk worked in agriculture. The Jews also had a large part in the clothing industry: 4,769 Jews made their living in this field. There were 838 Jews working in the education system, and 805 in lumber processing. That same year, 692 Jews served in the army. At the time, there were 3 factories which employed 575 male and female workers. In 1901 the three public elementary schools for Jewish children that existed in the city (the language of instruction was Russian) were attended by 300 students. That same year, a school for enthusiasts of the language of the past (with instruction in Hebrew) was established; it had 81 pupils.

During World War I, which broke out in 1914, the city was depleted of its Jewish inhabitants. At the command of the bitter enemy, the Grand Duke Nicholas Nikolaevich (uncle [sic] of Tsar Nicholas II) who was commander in chief of the Russian army, the Jews were expelled from every spot along the front. They were considered an untrustworthy element and were suspected of spying. Tens of thousands of Jews were forced to abandon their property and wander from place to place deep within Russia, even reaching as far as Siberia. Then the deeply-rooted Jewish Dvinsk of the people was revealed, in all its glory.

As one man, the Jews contributed to helping one another like brothers, to an unimaginable extent. The resources for a normal life were blocked. Hunger and diseases were rampant and the city emptied of its residents. Everyone who could do so fled, trying to get as far away as possible. Even the pride of the community, the Rogatchover Gaon, left; a fact which depressed those who remained. All remaining eyes fell upon the great light, the learned Rabbi Meir Simcha, who stubbornly ignored all of the insistent pleas that he also distance himself from the danger, and not just temporarily. "For as long as there are nine Jews in the city, I will remain as the tenth for a minyan," was his reply. [Page 14]   Although the Gaon, together with his flock, suffered the same misery as the other Jews in the city, for the duration of the war he refused to leave. He was as Rabbi Damta and as a father to his children.

The City's Rabbis

The city of Dvinsk was fortunate to have been served by some of the most brilliant rabbis of the generation. Among the splendid company that made the city of Dvinsk a byword in the Jewish world in the rabbinical field, there were three whose names were especially glorious.

The first of them was Rav Reuvele Dunaburger, one of the greatest geniuses of his generation, from whom the Rav Kook, may his righteous memory be blessed, learned Torah. (The Rav Kook himself was a native of Grïva, which was located on the other side of the Daugava River which flowed between Grïva and Dvinsk. Dvinsk had a profound influence on HaGaon Rav Kook).

The other two geniuses, who were the crown jewels in the rabbinate of that generation, were: Rav Meir Simcha HaCohen and the Rogachov (Rav Yosef Rosen). The two of them brought glory to the city and to Torah Judaism everywhere. These two men were the teachers of a generation and it is thanks to them that Dvinsk attained world-wide renown.

Rav Meir Simcha served as rabbi for 39 straight years, and the Rogachover – like Rav Damta – served honestly for fifty full years. The city of Dvinsk did not experience any sort of division between Chasids and Mitnagdim. Aside from "baruch sh'amar" and "yitzmach porkana" there was no perceptible difference between the Chasids and Mitnagdim in the city. The two streams lived side-by-side without any division between them. Although HaGaon HaRav Meir Simcha, the leader of the Mitnagdim, and the Rogachov Gaon, rabbi to the Chasids, were in their internal worlds quite far from one another in their temperaments and way of life, they were close in terms of their knowledge of Torah and their brilliance.

The erect and regal stature of the Rav Meir Simcha spoke eloquently of honor and majesty. He interacted with those around him, with a pleasant manner and measured speech, and was accepted and admired by all, including the non-Jews of the city. The latter believed with all their hearts in the magical spirit of the rabbi. I recall, in the days of the flood, when the

Daugava overflowed its banks and was on the brink of bursting the dam, both goyim and Jews swore that they saw Rav Meir Simcha stand on the dam, glance briefly at the raging waters, then murmur something. The waters then subsided and the danger passed.

His experience as a merchant in his younger years had given the Gaon the knowledge of how to smooth over the disagreements that arise in daily life.

In contrast, the shepherd of the Chasidic flock, the Rogachov Gaon, was short and agile with the face of an ascetic, his head adorned with curls which fell to his shoulders; he made an impression on all who saw him without even trying. Among his published books was the famous "Tzafnath Paneach." *[Page 15]* After an hour-long meeting with the amazing Gaon, our national poet, H.N. Bialik expressed his feelings thus: "From the brain of the Rogachover it would be possible to create two Einsteins; a dear man whose reality is unlike any other, who is an enormous spiritual asset to the nation. If it were possible to scientifically utilize all of his brilliant knowledge, it would be possible to enrich our culture with dozens of valuable books. If it were possible to draw his Talmudic knowledge from the wellspring of his mind, it would be possible to create a comprehensive culture." Those impressive remarks came from the mouth of Bialik after a meeting of only one hour's time. The city of Dvinsk was fortunate indeed to have rabbis who were among the most brilliant of their generation.

The Synagogues in Dvinsk

The Jews of Dvinsk were not extreme in their religion as were, for example, certain kinds of Jews in Poland, and were indeed far from similar to the Jews of the *Meah Shearim* neighborhood of Jerusalem. Rather, the vast majority were traditional Jews who observed the commandments without donning any special form of dress.

Although the *shtreimel* and the *kapoteh* were not to be seen, there were many synagogues and minyans in the city, and all were full of worshippers. The *Ker Shul* in the center of town on Petrogardska Street was especially noteworthy, with its splendid building and its opulent furnishings. The synagogue drew many worshippers who wanted to hear the cantor and chorus, whose pleasant voices appealed to those of discerning taste. This was where the secular "believers" gathered...

A famous cantor who lived in the city made the *Ker Shul* his home, and those who were knowledgeable in the field of music could appreciate his singing.

On the other hand, there was the Planover minyan, where the Rogachover prayed; a place of prayer for dozens of minyans who came to pray in turns, starting with the early-birds and ending just before noon. This synagogue was always full to overflowing with worshippers. One minyan would complete its prayers and the next would begin. Also well-known was the house of study called *Der Kahal Sha'ar"* where Rabbi Meir Simcha prayed. Here everything was more relaxed; there were fewer worshippers and everything was calm. Rabbi Meir Simcha prayed for an extended period of time, and the worshippers would wait respectfully until he had finished the *Shmoneh Esreh* and had stepped back. This was in sharp contrast to the Rogachover, who would be the first to finish the *Shmoneh Esreh* and rush to the house of study where he would study Torah day and night.

Those were the best known minyans of the city. In addition, there were many dozens more, such as: *Der Ketzbisher, Die Schneidershe Shul, Der Farbisher Minyan,* and so on. In each one a large crowd of worshippers would gather. On Yom Kippur, all of the voices would fill the streets, and the entire city became as one huge prayer, coming tearfully from the heart.

Such was Dvinsk, a Jewish city always, on weekdays as well as holidays. There was also a yeshiva in the city, where about one hundred boys studied. Day and night they studied the *daf yomi*, or daily page [of the Talmud]. Some of them were extremely intelligent. The head of the yeshiva was *Der Kavener*, a brilliant man who captured people's hearts. The yeshiva was called Socha Horovitz after the generous and wealthy Reb Socha Horovitz, who established the yeshiva with his own money. *[Page 16]* The city of Dvinsk kept the Jewish traditions with great respect. Even the agnostics treated the believers with respect, and the latter in turn were tolerant of the former. It is worth remembering that Dvinsk was the cradle of the revolutionaries, the Bund, and the leftist Zionist movements. The two lived side by side in mutual respect, and even in the turbulent days, on the eve of elections, they kept to their own. This was the pride of the city, Torah and the belief that each way has its own merit.

The Political Parties in Dvinsk

Dvinsk was a fairly typical city insofar as poor people were concerned; within the majority there were concentrations of poverty where the people were barely able to make a living. In terms of social depression it was second to Vilna, the Jerusalem of Lithuania. Its poverty was relatively proportionate and the people took a lively and vigorous interest in every matter regarding the fate of the people and the struggle for a better future and a more just society. The Jews of the city took an active part in every struggle against the oppressive government which discriminated against the Jews. Thirty-five percent of the city's Jews were workers who earned daily wages, and the rest were craftsmen whose income depended on the mercy of God. The wealthy, even according to the standards of the town, were so few a child could tally their number. Most people made a meager living. It was no wonder that the population responded to any sign of revolt against the subjugation and always hoped for an easing of their condition. Thus we find that, by the 1880s, when there was an outbreak of government-approved pogroms in tsarist Russia, active resistance groups were organized. At the same time, various associations were founded in the city, such as: *Hovavei Zion* named for Moshe Montefiore, *Ahdut Zionit*, Young Israel, *Herut*, Socialist Zionists, and *Hatechiya*. All worked towards the same goal: fighting against the taskmasters and for freedom from the oppressive government. The first group of *Poale Zion* was established in the city in 1900 with the inspiration of Ber Borochov and Shimoni (Dvin), after about a year an official list was created for the political party *Poale Zion*. In 1903 a Dvinsk group led by delegates Alter Yaffe and Zalman Abramson appeared at a conference of *Poale Zion* in Vilna. The program clearly defined the awareness of the class war, and socialism as the principles on which the movement was based. During the bloody days of 1905 the movement's organizers were hit hard by the government, and by the time World War I broke out the movement had been substantially weakened. Only in 1914 did the movement begin to recover, and in the days of Karnesky it revived but only for a short time. The first commissar in the city was the chairman of the *Tzairei Zion* party Comrade Rosenvein, thanks to whom people could walk about on guard duty during curfew nights, with authorization papers in their pockets, serving as a militia which had been formed in the city.

Also in the general Zionist movement were outstanding Zionists from Dvinsk: the representative of the association *Hovavei Zion* in Dvinsk, the delegate S. Y. Zacks, participated in 1890 in the convention of the Odessa Committee where the first signs of the Zionist youth movement appeared. Dvinsk was the first city to witness the appearance of the youth association *Adamat Yisrael*. In 1903, the Zionist workers' movement began to effect group immigration of its members to Eretz Yisrael, and the first pioneers set forth to build and be built. One of the members was Sarah Malkin, who became well-known as one of the first female pioneers. Also in the group were Rachel Gutman, Antin, Tehiya Lieberson, Eliezer Tsadikov, and Baruch Kasteral. From these members the pioneer movement in Dvinsk grew and spread. Émigrés from the city can be found today on kibbutzim and moshavim, in rural communities, serving in the *Hagana*, and serving as commanders in the I.D.F. The first pioneers paved the way for the many that would come after them.   *[Page 17]*   The city of Dvinsk was one of the strongholds of the Bund. Mostly proletarian, its poor and impoverished strata were occupied by many industrial workers of the clothing and match factories, and others. The workers were drawn naturally to the Bund. They built their future on remaining in the Diaspora, and were satisfied with the demand for cultural autonomy for the Jews as an integral part of the S.D. party. In 1872 we find a group of revolutionaries led by the young Jew Eliyahu Snapp and the Russian Belyayev who was studying for the priesthood. In 1876, there were many arrests and almost the entire group was incarcerated; thereby effectively destroying the movement, which was called the Association of Socialist Revolutionaries. From 1893 – 1897 the city became a center for the outbreak of strikes for the improvement of work conditions and to ease the yoke of the political regime. The workers of Dvinsk celebrated the First of May for the first time in 1896. Representatives of the Bund in Dvinsk, led by representative Kaplinsky, played an active role in the Bund convention in Bialystok. In 1899 about 300 Jewish workers celebrated the First of May, and in 1902 the number of Jewish demonstrators had reached about 700. On the date of a demonstration in February 1905, the police clashed with demonstrators and 30 people were injured and killed. In memory of the victims of that bloody conflict, in 1925 a monument was erected in Dvinsk which became a rallying point for the members of the Bund.

During the trial of Beilis in 1913 the Jews of Dvinsk were in terrible anxiety. The name of the famous attorney Gruzenberg was on everyone's lips. People in the synagogues prayed for the libel charges to be dropped.

With the handing down of the judgment, the Jews were able to breathe comfortably.

During the trial, the Jews of Dvinsk did not flinch and organized a protest.

In 1915 the Bund planned a protest against the war. All of the participants were arrested and sent to jail.

At the outbreak of World War I in 1914, the wave of war engulfed the city and scattered the residents like chaff in the wind. The city emptied almost completely of residents. Only once the war was over did the residents gradually return to the city, which began to recover a little. With the establishment of an independent Latvian state, the Jewish community numbered twelve thousand, as compared with 60,000 before the war. Broken-down refugees returned to the destroyed city, which was a shadow of its former self. They rushed to rebuild their community, and upon its old foundations a vigorous new life began to emerge. They were aided in this by the broad autonomy given to minorities and guaranteed by the Geneva Convention; until the bitter enemy rose up and truncated Jewish life, and the Jewish city of Dvinsk was erased from among the people of Israel.

[Page 18]

Jewish Activity in Dvinsk

The Jews of Dvinsk saw themselves as thoroughly Lithuanian, for they had absorbed the industriousness and erudition of their neighbor Lithuania. Amongst themselves they spoke a Vilna dialect of a poetic and vibrant Yiddish. They were proud of their skill in this language and used it creatively. The children received their daily education in this language. It is no wonder that Letski-Bertoldi, the member of the Constitutional Assembly of Latvia, relied upon Jewish Dvinsk when explaining the necessity for recognizing Yiddish as the Jewish language. Also among the goyim there were many who spoke Lithuanian Yiddish as fluently as our own people. The Jews played a large part in the development of the city, and visitors could feel the special Jewish ambience that pervaded it. Although the Jews made up only 14% of the population, their influence on the economy and on all aspects of public life was considerable. This was caused by the fact that population was made up of a mixture of peoples: Poles, Lithuanians, Russians, Ukrainians and so on. The Jews made up the largest minority of the population. The three most important offices in the municipality were held by Jews: finance, administration, and economy.

After the war, with the creation of the Latvian Republic, the political streams were represented and led by the following people:

From the Bund:	Dr. Noah Mayzel, Yitzhak Levin-Shatzkas
From the General Zionists:	Glinternik, Storich
From Tzairei Zion:	Dr. Gordon
From Socialist Zionists:	Moshe Bliach (Amir), Dr. Zand
From the Merchants:	the Koplovski brothers, Bolbaka
From the Property Owners:	the Gorbintz brothers, Edelstein
From the Artisans:	Ravdin

They were the face of the city, its spokesmen, during the period of the independent Latvia up until the Fascist Revolution (1934). With the rise political parties in the framework of a liberal Latvia, the parties mentioned below came into existence and were active in every field, and Dvinsk once again became a center of vigorous cultural life. Pioneering youth movements such as *Gordonia, Hashomer Hazair, Netzach,* and *Beitar* were established, and the athletic divisions of the Zionist youth and the Socialist Zionists gained recognition. In spite of opposition from the Bund, the Zionist workers' Socialist Zionist camp was officially recognized and became quite influential.

[Page 19]

Industry and Commerce in the City

There were very few wealthy people in the city. Notable amongst the industrialists were: the Horowitz family, the Zacks family, the Grilicks family, and the Wittenburg family. They were dominant in the fields of beer, leather, lumber, matches and soap. The majority of the Jews were small shopkeepers, or small workshop owners where sometimes the owner was the only worker, or he worked with one assistant.

Most of the workshop owners were milliners, shoemakers, carpenters, and tailors – based on the rule that was forced upon them: "go forth and make your living from one another."

Among the small shopkeepers were those who were quite successful and made a tidy profit. With all of the liberalism of the democratic Latvian government, there were still economic areas in which there existed a certain taboo, that no Jew could set foot in them.

In all of Latvia there were only 21 Jewish government clerks out of a total of 5,291, or 0.4%, at a time (1925) when Jews made up 5% of the population. There was one Jewish policeman, who served in Riga, out of a total of 4,316 in the entire country. When he made his rounds everyone wanted to see the only Jewish policeman.

Among the 1,682 clerks in civil service there was not one single Jew. Only two Jews worked for the postal service, and thirty-three for the railroad.

Altogether, only about 200 Jews worked for the government of the Latvian democracy, out of 100,000 Jews in the country. That was the reward they received for all their help in establishing the creation of Latvia and designing the government.

It's no wonder that in the city of Dvinsk, full of Jews though it was, not even ten Jews, through whom their fellows could have received service, worked for the government.

The few Jews currently living in Soviet Dvinsk are not natives of the city but rather are Russian Jews who moved there.

Of the previous citizens of the city only a very few remain, because almost all of the city's Jews were annihilated by the Nazi beast.

The few who remain walk dazed through the city. In their letters to their loved ones, they still mumble: "Dvinsk without Jews. Inconceivable!"

On the paving stones of the city's streets where passersby set their feet, one can see the partially erased letters representing "Here lies..." These tombstones bear witness to the passing of the Jews of Dvinsk from one end of the city to another, where the Jews of Dvinsk would have their dachas (summer homes) under the murmuring trees where now live Latvians who killed the owners and inherited the homes in Pogolianka and Strop, where the bones of many murdered Jews are buried.

The red flag waves above the city, which is red from the blood of the slaughtered Jews to whom no memorial or tombstone has been raised.

[Page 20]

Cultural Life in the City

With the establishment of the country of Latvia, the cultural life of Dvinsk blossomed in every way. Six new schools were established in the city (two in Yiddish, two in Hebrew, one in Russian and one a religious school). There was a progymnasia [secondary school] in Russian, a municipal gymnasia in Hebrew, a night school in Yiddish, and an ORT trade school. Dozens of Hebrew classes were offered. There were lectures and symposia. Jewish Dvinsk was a leader in culture and language.

The Jewish Community in the City

Before World War I several different charitable organizations existed in the city, such as *Linat HaTzedek, Bikur Holim, Kimcha DePascha,* and *Gimilut Chasadim.*

The people of Dvinsk were generous and kept the *mitzvot.* Although there was an air of philanthropy involved, there were also good intentions and kind-heartedness.

With the establishment of the country of Latvia the Jewish community in Dvinsk developed a well-organized public life: democratic elections were held in which all of the public streams took part, a community board was elected and institutions were established that were managed and supervised by the board. A well-stocked library was founded near the community, as were a pharmacy and home for the aged. Thousands of the needy received food for Passover and other aid from the community. The community owned real estate; the municipal hospital *Der Yiddisher Shpital* was owned by the community. The community administration was housed in a spacious building on Miasnitzka Street. It also owned land outside of the city, which had been leased for a token sum to the *Histadrut HeHalutz.* The land and buildings were used as a preparation community for Zionists hoping to move to *Eretz Yisrael.* Thus it was possible for the *halutzim* (pioneers) to establish a kibbutz thanks to the community, in which all of the Zionist political parties were represented.

The first head of the community was the attorney Minkovitch (who later moved to Eretz Yisrael and lived in Jerusalem for the remainder of his life). The next leader was the attorney Tzvi. There were arguments, decisions were made, and the community of Dvinsk provided an excellent example of cooperation amongst all of the political parties with mutual respect and democratic process in the full meaning of the word.

[Page 21]

The Hebrew School in Dvinsk 1921

Haim Nachman Bialik's Visit in Dvinsk 1932

[Page 22]

The Self-Defense Organization in Dvinsk at the Start of the Twentieth Century

From the book "Yidden Eich Latland" by Mendel Buba

After the events in Kishinev and Homel, the Jews of Dvinsk began to organize a form of self-defense.

When the Tsarist police began to turn against the Jews, the Letts decided to attack the Jews, and planned their activities for a market day when most of the Jews would be in the city and the Christians would be a little drunk from their day's profits.

The self-defense of the Jews was supervised by Shlomo Pokroi, who divided them into groups of dozens, with each person armed with axes, clubs, cudgels and every other sort of cold weapon that could be concealed.

The Lett attackers began to loot the Jewish shops and to beat the shocked and frightened Jews. The self-defense youths began to forcefully attack the looters and murderers and chased them away. The strong, burly butchers with their knives in hand threatened the looters, who became frightened and ran away in fear of the Jews.

The pogrom propaganda was not successful in Dvinsk following the organization of the Jews. Many jokes and stories were told about the beating the looters got.

The self-defense program justified itself. With pride and a head held high, the Jewish workers of Dvinsk walked with a smile on their faces. They had stood their ground, defending their property and their lives.

The looters never again dared to try and attack the Jews of Dvinsk. Their unified, organized stand brought the Jews together against their harassers and prevented bloodshed.

[Page 23]

Jewish Cultural and Religious Life in Dvinsk at the Start of the Twentieth Century
From the book "Yidden Eich Latland" by Mendel Buba

The younger generation in Dvinsk was educated in the *Talmud Torah* and the *cheder*, some of which became "improved schools" wherein the students also learned mathematics, science and the Russian language.

Several trade schools supported by ORT and the Jewish Colonization Association (JCA) were established for girls as well as boys. In the three elementary schools in Dvinsk at that time, the language of instruction was Russian, and the younger generation of Jews was educated in that language.

The many synagogues and houses of study provided expression for the religious and traditional Jewish life in Dvinsk. At the center of Dvinsk was the *Ker Shul*, with the progressive Jews who visited there. There were also the Planover Minyan, where the Rogachover Gaon prayed, and the Community House of Study, where the *mitnaged* rebbe Meir Simcha HaCohen prayed. The simple people of Dvinsk, the various artisans, each prayed in their own special minyan: the Synagogue of Tailors, the *Schneiderayshe Shul*, the Butchers' Minyan, the Painters' Minyan, and so on.

The rabbis who ran the religious life of Dvinsk were the Rogachover Gaon Rabbi Yosef Rosen who wrote the "Tzafnath Paneach," and Rabbi Meir Simcha HaCohen, author of the book "Or Sameach." These men were considered authorities by Jews around the world. They were surrounded by a circle, not only of Jews but of members of the Christian population as well, which respected them, deferred to them and was considerate of them. There is a well-known tale of how the brilliant Rabbi Meir Simcha returned the overflowing Daugava River to its banks, thus preventing a flood that could have, God forbid, destroyed the city and caused a loss of life.

After a long conversation with the Gaon, H. N. Bialik of blessed memory said of him that if all of the Rogachover's knowledge was collected in one place, the world would be blessed with a treasury of scientific tomes.

[Page 24]

The Zionist Movement and the Youth of Dvinsk

By Mordechai Nieshtet, from the book "History of a Movement"
(Avraham Etay Mordechai Nieshtet)

Zionism was not so much an ideology for us, but rather simply a part of our character, something we drank in with our mother's milk; we absorbed it in the home and the *cheder*, at school and in the atmosphere on the street, from visiting teachers and emissaries from Eretz Yisrael, and in the libraries. The book *Ahava Zion* made quite an impact on the youth. From the age of the gymnasia, the ideologies of Shimoni were also influential.

It seems to me that if we analyze the components of our ideology to see which are results of the reality of Eretz Yisrael, and which are the results of our life in Latvia, we would discover that we were more influenced by Eretz Yisrael than by our daily lives. Zion was like a dream for us, an inseparable part of our souls. Sometimes we would count the remaining months and years until we could fulfill our dream of moving to Eretz Yisrael. In the climate of these ideas, the youth would not accept a Zionism of donations and gatherings; they responded more to a Zionism that took into its own hands a solution to the problem of the dispersal of our people in the Diaspora.

The youth read many books about the condition of the Jewish people; they were in search of a theoretical basis for the Zionist idea. Brener, Trumpeldor, and A. D. Gordon served as examples for the Zionist youth. They went to work in training camps in order to practice in reality the physical work that awaited them in Eretz Yisrael – to build and be built there.

The youth attended summer camps at which there were competitions, exhibitions which reflected the subject of labor. The youth movements, which attracted the best young men and women, were at the center of a lively, active and interesting life, full of awareness and saturated with lofty ideas regarding training, *aliyah* and achievement. Their fate was the same as the fate of all the sons of Israel who were murdered in the Holocaust.

[Page 25]

The Community of Dvinsk
Told by Mr. Moshe Hyal

Dvinsk, the third largest city in Latvia, is located on the Daugava River. Before the outbreak of World War II, there were 47,000 residents, of which 40% were Jews who lived mostly in the center of town.

There were five Jewish schools in Dvinsk and in a few of them the official language was Hebrew. In order to teach the language properly, there were teachers from Eretz Yisrael who came and spent several years at the schools. There was also a Hebrew gymnasia, and during the 1930s there was a training kibbutz, which prepared the Zionist youth from the Gordonia and *Hashomer Hazair* movements for performing agriculture labor.

The city was full of Zionist youth movements, which established youth clubs like the Borochov Club for youth and a Zionist Club for adults. The *Hashomer Hazair* movement published a monthly magazine called *Hamishol*. The youth of Dvinsk read and studied from the many books in the city library. The Zionist movements were very active, holding conferences, gatherings, and rallies which made quite an impression on the Jewish population.

When the pro-Nazi youth movement wanted to take over the streets of the city they did not find fertile ground. The city's butchers chased them out immediately, and forcefully.

Among the Jews, many of whom were merchants, there were various classes. The rich people who owned shops and warehouses were at one level, and the destitute at the other. Once a week, the latter would go from door to door begging for handouts just so they could survive.

At the head of the Jewish community were several go-getters, whose main concern was the welfare of the city. Most of them were rabbis, the spiritual leaders of the community.

The Jews of Dvinsk kept the traditions. The shops were closed on the Sabbath. On Sundays, the Christian Sabbath, some of the shops were open for half a day. The large factories were not inside the city. The Jews were merchants or artisans who toiled in workshops. Young men from wealthy homes would, upon graduating from high school, travel to Italy to study medicine. Other young people would help their parents in the family business or take over the business themselves. In the 1930s many Jews left Dvinsk, and the youth in particular went to Eretz Yisrael.

Dvinsk was famous for its hospitality and many visitors from Eretz Yisrael came there. H. N. Bialik of blessed memory visited Dvinsk and awakened a lot of interest. School children performed recitals for him in the large movie theater and Bialik was quite touched. Yechiel Halperin also visited Dvinsk and met with the youth.   *[Page 26]*   David Ben-Gurion of blessed memory was supposed to visit Dvinsk. The Jewish community busily prepared for that event, but before he arrived in the city David Ben Gurion was forced to return to Eretz Yisrael. Everyone was very disappointed that they would not be able to see and hear the famous man.

The annihilation did not pass over the city of Dvinsk.

The Nazis demanded that the Jews of Dvinsk wear three yellow tags on their clothes instead of the two most other Jews wore. The Letts cooperated and assisted in the destruction of the Jews of Dvinsk.

The tombstone on the mass grave says only: "Remember the victims of the Fascists."

Dvinsk, which is under the authority of Russia, was not able to raise a tombstone for the murdered Jews. It was not something the Soviet government in Latvia was interested in doing.

Interviewers:

    Levy, Zvi
    Hillel, Levana
    Apotker, Shula
    Students, Grade 8A

[Page 27]

Dvinsk, My City
As told by Mr. Simcha Katz, written by Sofia Grade 8A

Dvinsk was a large, effervescent community with a lively Jewish character. Russians, Poles and Germans also lived in the city. The mixed population became integrated into the general life.

The Jewish youth was aware of the general problems and of Zionist problems specifically. Between the two World Wars there were about 35,000 Jews in the city, though the community shrank as the city was close to the front lines.

The youth, who were educated in the Zionist movements, attended training kibbutzim and moved to Eretz Yisrael with the appropriate documents, which were called certificates.

Until 1934, while there was a democratic government in Dvinsk, the Jews did not suffer from discrimination. They were merchants, artisans and members of the free professions and contributed with their energy and initiative to the economic development of the city.

Only with the national revolution in 1934 did the situation of the Jews worsen, following the restrictions imposed on them. With the coming of World War II the Holocaust came also to the Jews of Dvinsk, and destroyed them.

Since the Jewish community of Dvinsk was surrounded by a hostile population, they could not defend themselves. No partisan underground was established there. There were very few Letts who aided the Jews in escaping from the claws of the Nazi. Here and there a villager might hide a single Jew or a Jewish family. Those who helped Jews escape from the cruelty of the Nazis will be remembered well.

[Page 28]

My City, Dvinsk
Told by Mr. Gur Shmuel

I was born in Leningrad and moved to Dvinsk, where I lived from 1924 until 1940 and worked as a bookkeeper.

I knew the Russian language very well. My family was made up of five people, and we were traditional Jews. I studied in an elementary school where the language of instruction was Hebrew. My teachers were typical Zionists, and they infused the subjects we studied with Zionist content.

Our studies were designed to develop a nationalist feeling in the students. The atmosphere of the school was very pleasant. The holidays were celebrated in splendid fashion. On Lag B'Omer we would go into the forest with bows and arrows. For Chanukah we arranged ceremonies at the school, and the songs we learned awakened the activist spirit in us.

Some of our teachers came from Eretz Yisrael. They were sent to their posts by the Jewish Agency, and performed their duties faithfully, telling us many stories about the developing and renewed Eretz Yisrael.

I completed elementary school and high school in Dvinsk.

In our free time after our studies, we would spend time together at the school.

We would organize debates on literature and various other subjects of vital interest in the world. Representatives from the various youth groups would participate in the literature debates, and the arguments would be lively and fruitful.

We attended summer camps and winter camps organized by the youth movements. We organized night games, in which we strengthened our bodies and spirits for the future. Each of us made plans for going to Eretz Yisrael.

To my sorrow, not many of us reached Eretz Yisrael. Only a few individuals survived the horrific Holocaust which befell the Jews of the Diaspora.

Interviewers:

> Hava Hapner
> Leah Barkovitz
> Students, Grade 8A

[Page 29]

The Community of Dvinsk, in Latvia
By Hava Hapner, Grade 8

In my Holocaust studies class, I couldn't help but wonder: how could the world have kept silent when it knew what the Nazis were doing to the Jews? As I interviewed the refugees of the Holocaust from Dvinsk, I came to understand how magnificent that community had been.

There were Jewish youth there who joined Zionist youth movements, and never needed to ask the question the youth of today ask: where shall I go to have some fun? They studied, educating themselves for a goal and strengthening their character, and during the horrific Holocaust showed their ability to save themselves in the ghettos, the camps, and the forests. I feel great love, admiration and respect for them that they were able, in those terrible circumstances, to survive without losing their humanity.

We must learn, and know, what happened to one third of our people. The many communities in occupied Europe which were destroyed knew how to create a magnificent culture, and glorious educational organizations, and produced many great people: writers, rabbis, poets, and artists. The community was an entity which took care of itself. I am filled with love and admiration for their activities.

The big, wide world was indifferent to the slaughter of our people, and we must warn against and expose that evil injustice. The Nazi – that barbaric beast – controlled all of Europe and crushed the pride of man beneath its boot.

The wounded, beaten and bereaved Jews fought for their lives every day and every hour. Chapters about the Holocaust must be added to the history books, telling of the cruel murder, the rebellion, and the uprising of the Jews in those horrible conditions. We are studying this community, and I am filled with pride that I belong to such a people, who knew how to defend their dignity, and I personally feel a part of them.

This article appears in the file Yad Vashem
In Their Memory
11 Tevet 5735 [December 25th, 1974]

[Page 30]

Dvinsk – City of the Jews by Moshe Amir (Beliach)
By Moshe Amir (Beliach)

From the memorial book – The Jews of Latvia – Tel Aviv, 5713 [1952]

With a trembling heart I take up my pen to attempt to make note of a complete Jewish community that was destroyed and no longer exists. Woe is me - that it has become my fate to bring up the memory of Dvinsk, the city of the Jews: my hand shakes and refuses to do my bidding. Shabbat: peace and quiet in the streets of Dvinsk. Even the goyim slow their steps, as if they too are reluctant to disturb the Sabbath rest. The joyful sound of prayers burst forth from dozens of houses of prayer. The most important of the minyans were the Planover Minyan and the *Ker Shul* on Opitzraskaya Street, where the two geniuses of the generation prayed, Rabbi Meir Simcha HaCohen and Rabbi Yosef Rosen, the Rogachover Gaon. The two men were far from one another in the way they lived, but were so close to one another in their genius.

The regal and upright stature of Rabbi Meir Simcha the *Mitnaged* spoke of honor and dignity. He was involved in the lives of the people, had a pleasant manner, and weighed his words carefully. On his way to synagogue one Sabbath day he encountered the son of one of the wealthy men of the city, who had a lit cigarette in his mouth. The young man became confused and was rooted to the spot, the cigarette dangling from his lips. "Good Shabbes to you, Meirel," said the Gaon pleasantly. "You must have forgotten that today is Shabbes. Yes, Meirel, today is Shabbes. 'Remember the Sabbath day and keep it holy.'" He continued on his way to the synagogue as if nothing had happened. The young man never forgot the lesson he learned that day.

I remember the turbulent days of October, when in the middle of the night people were awakened and forced out of their beds. Many people ran away, no one knows where or why. The hand of revolution cut people down indiscriminately…They arrested the rich man from Petranov, and on the way to the fort they shot him and threw his body in the river. They paraded Segal the shopkeeper through the town with a sign on his chest that said, "This is what we will do to the burghers and the speculators (scalpers)." The rabble tore him to pieces near the police station. Movshenson, the city engineer, was taken from his bed and in the morning his bullet-ridden body was found in the gutter. Suddenly a horrible rumor spread: "They're bringing out the rabbi!" Everyone burst out of their homes and saw the horrible sight of HaGaon Rabbi Meir Simcha marching down the street, his head held high, surrounded by Chekists with pistols drawn. He was taken to the infamous building, whose name alone inspired fear, *Hachika*, on Alayna Street. In spite of the great danger, thousands of signatures were collected, of Jews and non-Jews alike, on a petition guaranteeing the character of the rabbi. Even more than that, "the undersigned dared to declare that the arrest of the Rabbi would cause general unrest amongst the inhabitants of the city," as it was written in the petition. The same day, the rabbi was released and never again harmed.

The other great spiritual leader was the shepherd of the Chasidim, the Rogachover Gaon, short of stature and agile in his movements, the embodiment of "All my bones shall say..." From the first light of morning until late at night he paced back and forth in his room, completely immersed in his studies. He had thousands of questions and answers, about everything and for everyone. He was the teacher of the greatest minds of the generation. *[Page 31]*   On his way to the synagogue, the Rogachover would continue pondering the issue at hand, oblivious to his surroundings. He would run down the middle of the street, bumping into anyone who got in his way. Everyone moved aside when they saw him coming. Drivers would stop their wagons, and the peddlers their carts, women would rush to the sides of the street, and all followed the small figure of the genius of his generation with looks of love and admiration. In the synagogue he was always the first to complete his prayers, and would become annoyed with the one leading the prayers, "What is taking him so long? Why is he prolonging his singing before the Master of the Universe? He knows, He knows everything, even without his singing! Faster, faster!" And even before the tallises had been folded, he had dashed off back to his study, which he would not leave day or night.

I remember the graduation celebration at the yeshiva named for Sotcha Horowitz. In addition to the parents of the students rabbis from the surrounding area were in attendance. We, the graduates, studied the daily page. Suddenly there was silence. HaGaon Rabbi Meir Simcha had risen to make his concluding remarks. His homily was short and sweet. He didn't "move mountains": he knew how to get straight to the heart of the issue. In his clear and sharp mind he separated the important from the unimportant as with a scalpel, presenting the former clearly to all. Everyone was listening attentively, when suddenly the Rogachover Gaon jumped up amidst general confusion with outrage blazing in eyes, to defend G-d. Rabbi Meir Simcha simply stood by quietly, with a forgiving smile on his face, and continued as if nothing had happened. The Gaon of Rogachov calmed down and mumbled, "Go on, go on." Rabbi Meir Simcha continued with his speech, bringing it to its conclusion. When he had finished, the Rogachover Gaon jumped up and, without addressing the words of Rabbi Meir Simcha, he began to argue vehemently, and it seemed that the Shechinah shone out in rays from his face. Everyone thirstily drank in his words, and Rabbi Meir Simcha listened with enjoyment and was impressed.

These were the spiritual leaders of the Dvinsk community. They did not involve themselves in secular matters. All day to day matters were left to the community institutions and those elected to serve in them; it was they who determined the public character of the Jewish community in the city.

The educational system in Dvinsk was a broad one. There were five municipal elementary schools. In the first there were about 700 students; the principal was M. Beliach, and the language of instruction was Yiddish. The second had about 400 students, the principal was Ginzburg, and the language of instruction was Hebrew. The third had 350 students, the principal was Dovrin and the language of instruction was Russian. The fourth had 350 students, the principal was Levinburg and the language of instruction was Yiddish. The fifth also had 350 students, the principal was Kitski, and the language of instruction was Hebrew.

There was also a high school with 500 students. The first principal was Lipshitz, who was followed by Gorfinkle, and the last, who perished together with his pupils, was Kopilov. There was also a Central Jewish Schools Association high school that met in the evenings, which was attended by 300 students. An ORT trade school with some 200 students was run by the principal Bloom. *Agudat Yisrael* ran a private elementary school under the direction of principal Nieshul, with 100 students. All of those lives were cut short. The innocent voices of these fledglings were silenced by death in the ruins of their nest. My tears for them will never run dry. *[Page 32]* I also recall the splendid public institutions: the municipal hospital called Der *Yiddisher Hospital* and its devoted doctors: the chief physician Dr. Gurvitz, scion of a rabbinic dynasty, the chairman of the *Keren Hayesod* (he poisoned himself in the ghetto); Dr. Z. Gordon (he died in Jerusalem); Dr. Rozenberg (he died in a car accident in Haifa); and the experienced medic, Pyrenov. The banks: the Community Bank, which was supported by the Joint and gave assistance to thousands of its members; the bank for artisans: the *Kupat Am* Bank, which everyone called Stark's Bank, after the manager Stark of blessed memory who was a Zionist and a noble man. He made the bank what it was and was devoted to it. I remember the city's large library, which contained some 30,000 books, and Miss Brook who dedicated many years of her life to that institution, and the nearby public pharmacy that served the needs of the community, run by the white-haired pharmacist Karrol the Bundist. The Chevra Kadisha was located in the same building. The force behind that organization was Zalman Boaz, a noble soul with the face of an intelligent student, who was not disturbed by the work he did as an undertaker for so many years (he has a son and daughter at Kfar Giladi and Kfar Blum, and a son at the Foreign Ministry in Jerusalem). His right hand man was the elderly Rabbi Baruch Aginski, a former merchant who went bankrupt and took comfort in the holy work he did at the cemetery (his sons live in Kiryat Chayim...).

How could I forget the community institution for the lonesome elderly, the home of the aged, which was located outside the city limits in a quiet, soothing spot surrounded by a pine forest? The manager, Miss Berman, was like a mother to them (she now lives in South Africa). Close by was a lively neighbor, the farm of the *Hechalutz*, a large building surrounded by fields. In this place the young generation grew wings as it trained and prepared for moving to

Eretz Yisrael. Every morning happy groups would set off for work, with a song on their lips. The "immodest" young people would roll up their shirtsleeves and wear short pants that exposed their thighs; this behavior set off a stormy controversy in the city. The children of the respectable folk of the city and surrounding towns received their training at this farm. When they set off each day for their work in the city, their tools on their shoulders, axes and saws for chopping down trees, or shovels for clearing snow and for other "goyish work," they were followed by thousands of eyes, shaking heads, curses, and even some who watched with secret pride. The Jewish heart beat strongly; and deep in the soul there was pride and respect for those "immodest" youth.

There in the pine forests the pioneers would gather around a bonfire. They were joined by the Borochov Youth, *Hashomer Hazair*, *Natzach*, and various other young men and women. All would eagerly listen to the words and the messages offered by the counselor or by the emissary from Eretz Yisrael who might happen to be there, about the working society in Eretz Yisrael.

Sometimes there would be stormy arguments that lasted until morning. From here the pioneers would make their way to Eretz Yisrael, where today they can be found in all parts of the country: in the city, on the moshav and on the kibbutz, especially in places like Shefayim, Mishmarot, Kfar Blum, Kinneret, Afikim, Ashdot-Yaacov, Ein Gev, Kfar Giladi, and others. The places of those who had gone were taken by more young people from *Hechalutz*, the Borochov Youth, and the Shas Youth, who would gather at the community building at 80 Zelyona Street.   *[Page 33]*   The building, the place where those who would realize their dreams got their starts, and the street would be filled with people every evening. The very walls absorbed the urge of the youth, the movement to Eretz Yisrael, and a life of labor. It was from this place that the proud Jewish athlete with the symbol of the Star of David on his chest set forth to take his rightful place on the teams of the Latvian Social-Democratic Sport Organization. Within the walls of that building the Labor Union was founded. From that place the nationalist flag was first raised, together with that of the First of May. It was later recognized by the S. D. (in spite of the protests of the Bund).

From the threshold of this building the Zionist-Socialist manifesto spread out into the working people. It came into opposition with the powerful Bund, which had deep roots in the city, and with the Communist Youth, and was particularly successful in its propaganda for the Zionist-Socialist idea. The youth flowed into the ranks of the *Hechalutz*, who were the children raised at the knees of the elders of the Bund. Among the speakers of that esteemed movement were the following young people: Alter Goldman, Mordechai Chaikin, Muliya Brodbeka (now in Shefayim), M. Shvalav (Lieutenant Colonel Drori), Liobka Levy, Bella Beliach (Herzliya), Golda Pipkavich of blessed memory, Borka Goldin (among the dead in the Shefayim massacres), Issar Halperin (Harel), Chaim Shenkin, Yehuda Stoll of blessed memory, Boyerski, Donna Nachman, and many others. Many other young people gathered around them, putting the life of the Diaspora behind them and happily leaving home and moving to Eretz Yisrael.

Such devotion to the lofty ideal! Such youthful fervor! Such daring aspiration to change the status quo! What a stubborn position the youth held, that broke away from a tradition of many generations and rebelled against what was accepted. And all of those who remained and imagined they would put down roots in the place, were buried under the avalanche.

And the days of immigration to Eretz Yisrael: unforgettable! Each immigration of pioneers was an event, and each day of departure was like a holiday for the Jews of the city. From the first morning light the streets surrounding the station were full of people, all accompanying the pioneers. All the barriers to the train were broken, the excitement was tremendous. Tears of joy mingled with the tears of mothers and relatives. A single tear trickles down the face of a father, sinking into his beard. Every youth movement came, in uniform and brandishing flags, to give a send-off to its members who were leaving. The train moved away to the notes of *Tehezakna* and *Hatikvah*. From every side voices called out their longing and the hope that they would soon meet again in the Jewish homeland. The wheels of the train rattled, the national flags decorating the train with a festive atmosphere fluttered, and even the goyim waved and called out "Du Palestina!" Suddenly there was the sound of many voices calling out together, "Who will build the Galilee?" and many voices answering, "We will build the Galilee!" For awhile the sounds of voices singing "Anu Olim Artza" could be heard until at last the distance swallowed the sound.

"When will it be my turn?" many asked in their hearts. The tension dissipated, only emptiness remained, and disquiet. Eyes scanned the sky for signs of the train's smoke in the distance, where the pioneers were traveling to the Jewish land, to create and work.

Yes, those were unforgettable days. Many were able to leave in time, but many more remained behind and were killed.   *[Page 34]*   When I remember the *Hechalutz*, the youth of the Zionist movement, and the camp of the Zionist-Socialists, I cannot fail to remember the three crown jewels of the movement, the three who accompanied us like faithful shepherds in every stage of our work, our dear friends Saragovich, Moshele Zarodin, and Yosef Smoshkovich.

Saragovich, who came to us from some far-off place in Russia where he had served a punishment for his membership in the Z.-S. On his way home to his family in Finland, he came to our city and remained there. He carried on his thin shoulders the burden of the entire movement. Lonesome and without family, he lived in a tiny room, two meters square. Under his head were packages of releases, and other writings of the movement from the Diaspora. A crust of bread and a thin pallet were his portion, and in his slender body there burned a holy soul.

He never slowed down in his work. Although he had no official title, he was in reality the center point for all the various strands of the movement, until he moved to Eretz Yisrael. He didn't have the physical strength for the fight to reclaim the land, nor against the ravages of malaria; the disease took over his body and he didn't want to become burden.

We were shocked to read the note he sent, "Now I put an end to my life." No, no, don't fear! I still believe. I am still as I once was. Continue your lives here – come!" And we immigrated and continued. His last wish was fulfilled to its fullest, and the place that the pioneers of Latvia founded was named after him – Kibbutz Saragovich, known today as Shefayim.

And the second – Moshele Zarodin. This young man's name was on everyone's lips. He was a sensitive, delicate Yeshiva student. He gave everything to the movement. We knew his days were numbered. His pale appearance bore witness to the disaster that was sure to come. He also recognized his fate, and therefore he rushed to do as much as he was able in the time that he had; to give the maximum, as much as he was able, before the end. *Hechalutz*, the labor union, the Borochov Youth, his involvement in all of them was an unbreakable bond. He was much loved and respected, though he left us when he was only 28 years old.

And the third and last – Yosef Smoshkovich. He was an extremely fine artist. There was no form of craft that he could not master. There was no painter like him; he always had many artistic ideas and broad horizons, and both dreamed and fulfilled his dreams. He was devoted to the movement and was among the finest of activists, up until the end. He also fell ill with malaria and was taken from us in the prime of his life at age 40.

Those three were the ultimate pioneers. All three dreamed of Eretz Yisrael, but only one made the journey and actually set foot on the longed-for land; and then he fell. The other two were warmed from afar by the light of the Jewish land though they died in the Diaspora.

As I write about the movement *Eretz Yisrael Ovedet*, I particularly remember the stormy period which was expressed through the bitter and stubborn struggle between the Zionist-Socialist front and the anti-Zionist workers' camp. This was the first battle of the Zionist-Socialist camp. After stormy debates, and after endless discussions between the Bund and Z.-S. on the question of the appearance in the First of May demonstrations, a third person came, the chairman of the Latvian Social Democrats. A representative of the gentile Sejm, Boimeister, decided in favor of the Z.-S., which received permission to march as a special Zionist company under its own Zionist flag with its own symbols and slogans. It was a great victory for the Z.-S. and a defeat for the Bund, but the former were obligated to appear without humiliating their foe.   *[Page 35]*   It was necessary for the first time for the Zionist-Socialist movement to show its proletarian face to the outside world. Both camps, the Bund and the Z.-S., prepared in secret so that, God forbid, the rival would not learn of the other's "secret weapon." In the matter of the leaders of the camps, there was no argument – both were equally accepted, though neither was truly what one could call a "proletariat." That of the Bundist camp was a clerk in the health insurance company, and the other was the principal of a municipal school for the children of laborers. Thus everything was settled, and the biggest question remaining was, who would be the flag bearer for the movement in the parade?

It was known of the Bund that they had candidates for this prestigious task who had on their side both tradition and the right to carry it out: the painter Yitzhak Nochimovich, who lost an eye in the battles of 1905, and his two assistants: the mechanic Reiner and a senior laborer, a printer. Each of them had seniority and a history in the proletariat that could not be disputed. The competition was fierce and the young Z.-S. movement had a big problem.

The "day of judgment" arrived. The people formed lines and, to the call of the trumpets the flag-bearers appeared at the head of the parade. The huge crowd was surprised – shocked even, for a moment – then waves of applause washed the street. The new flag of the Z.-S. was waved proudly in the hands of a wondrously beautiful flag-bearer who had braids down to her knees. She was not chosen for her youth and good looks, but rather for her unusual profession. She was a welder! She could be found day after day working alongside her father in the forge. She would beat the white-hot iron with a mallet and sparks would fly up; she performed her work with the ease of experience (she is now in Kiryat Hayim). A Jewish girl – a welder! Who could question her proletarianism? Any who might wish to complain had no grounds to do so. Her assistants also had unimpeachable qualifications – on the one side the experienced weaver Hyatt who was born in the mill where the thread was spun, right next to the machinery, a fact he was quite proud of, a proletariat from the day he was born (he died at work in the Beit Hamoreh in Tel Aviv). On the other side was the painter, a day laborer every day of the year, Yankele Fisher, a man of the line devoted and faithful. They formed a trio to be proud of.

The movement met the challenge!

At the head of the procession was the Z.-S. committee, Dr. Zand (a poor youth who fought his way to the title of doctor, purchasing his status with years of hunger and suffering: an ear doctor and a simple man, he died in Siberia), Yosef Smoshkovich, Moshele Zarodin, Yodele Friedman, Chaim Shenkin (Holon), Yehuda Stoll (*Shemen* Haifa), Chaim Geller (died in Shefayim), Yosef Boyerski (Tel Aviv), Aharon Eidus (Shefayim), Shapira (Shefayim), the Donda brothers (one in Haifa), the Blair brothers, the Elisbok brothers (South Africa), Nochimovich, Y. Traub (Eshkol – Kfar Giladi), Yosef Margalit, Alter Goldman, and many others – a unified, honorable group.

After them came many more members of the Z.-S., young men and women – *Hechalutz*, *Hechalutz Hazair*, the Borochov Youth, the S. D. athletic group; all of them strong young men bearing badge with a Star of David on a red background on their chests.   *[Page 36]*   Then came the rearguard of the preparation company, wearing their work clothes and carrying their tools. How our hearts pounded the first time it was announced, "The representative of the Zionist-Socialist party will now speak." "There, marching under the blue sky of Eretz Yisrael," he began in an enthusiastic voice, "there they are marching as we do today, singing traditional working songs, the pioneers of the people of Israel, establishing the rule of labor and socialism, in their own country." We extend our laboring hands across the borders to our friends…

Long live Zionist Socialism! Long live the working Eretz Yisrael, and long live the Hebrew worker!

There was great excitement, and surprising renewal; the ice was broken, since they had stopped arguing. Z.-S. had taken its rightful place in the Labor movement in every field as an equal. There were still troubles from within. I recall the circle of Hora dancers spinning faster and faster, when suddenly a voice ripped the sky: "Thieves! Kidnappers of children! Give me back my son!" This was the bitter cry of the father of Velvel Kramer (of Shefayim) when his son was given approval to move to Eretz Yisrael. Similar scenes took place almost every day.

Complaints, pleas, and threats of the fathers and mothers were rife, to leave the sons and daughters with their parents, not to take them to *Hechalutz*, which was tantamount to making aliyah. Many snuck out of their homes in the middle of the night, leaving a note saying "I'm traveling to Riga" which in reality meant, "I'm moving to Eretz Yisrael."

If an emissary from Eretz Yisrael arrived, it became a major event. Shops were closed, work came to a halt, and thousands of Jews dressed in their holiday best filled the station to greet the guest. They would carry him to his hotel, and he would be forced to make an appearance on the balcony so everyone could see his face. He was treated like a king, for he brought with him the atmosphere of Eretz Yisrael. Even the non-Jews of the city would be on their best behavior; in their interpretation, the "minister of the Jews has come from Palestina."

The theater, near the train tracks, could not hold all of the people who came to hear the speaker. Cramped and squeezed, all stood and listened with awe and reverence to the words of one who was a true eyewitness. And everyone responded with a generous hand, sometimes beyond their ability to pay, to every fundraising effort in support of Eretz Yisrael: *Keren Hakaymet*, *Keren Hayesod*, Bank *Hapoalim*, and *Kupat Poalei Eretz Yisrael* (the Workers Fund for Eretz Yisrael). Every fundraising campaign sent its own emissary, and each one was greeted warmly and with fondness. The city won the hearts of those emissaries with their love, and they never skipped the city on their tours. Dvinsk was a stop on the journey of the Prisoners of Zion from Russia to Eretz Yisrael, and for emissaries from Eretz Yisrael to Russia; their road was fraught with dangers. Z. Aronovich, Bar-Yehuda, Yehuda Kopilovich, Baba Edelson, Zeev Hayam, Dr. Adler, M. Lichtman, and dozens of others passed through the home of the writer of these lines.

In conclusion, a few words about the political and public streams in the city. The most influential parties were the Bund and the Z.-S. party. The unified Bund had deep, long-standing roots in Dvinsk. The cradle of the 1905 revolution was there. Its influence was widespread. Its leaders were prominent, zealous, and talented. Among them was the representative to the Sejm, Dr. N. Maizel. He was a fiery speaker, a prominent mover-and-shaker. Yizhak Levin Shetzkiss of the sharp pen was clever and quick, zealous, and consumed with every particle of his being with Zion. *[Page 37]* Peretz Meiksin, a powerful organizer. These three men were surrounded by experienced workers and devoted intellectuals. For years, the Bund held the keys to all of the public institutions in the city; it had almost no competitors amongst the workers in the Jewish community until the Z.-S. movement began to infiltrate the territory of the Bund. Their representatives began to appear in the Health Service, the municipal offices, and in the labor union; for the first time a Zionist-Socialist speech was heard on the First of May. *Hechalutz* marched in the parade carrying both the national flag and the red flag.

All of the above shaped the character of Jewish Dvinsk. But where are they today?

The beast arrived in the magnificent Jewish community.

Her babies were smashed against the walls by strangers. The best of her young men and women were led naked to massacre; her elderly dismembered before the eyes of all. The sacred Jewish community was dispatched to Hell.

Alas for those we have lost and will never forget.

[Page 38]

Dvinsk Today

[Page 39]

How Does Dvinsk Look Today?
An Interview with Mr. Yitzhak Gorevich

If I wanted to compare the Dvinsk from before the war with the Dvinsk of today, I would be hard-pressed to find the words. Dvinsk was once a city full of Jews, active, creative and working; the Dvinsk of today is foreign to me.

Only a monument remains, on which it is written: "Here are buried the victims of Fascism." There is not even a hint on the monument that an entire community is buried there. The monument has no national character. Every single spark of nationalist Jewish culture was destroyed, and the Soviets are quite familiar with that type of work. This is one of the links in the chain of the assimilation of the Jews in the Soviet regime. Today there only remains one synagogue, and a ruined cemetery.

There are hardly any native Dvinskers left today. There is a small Jewish community in Dvinsk today, most of whose members came from eastern Russia and settled there. Those Jews have no connection to what once was. There is not a single school – not one whose language of instruction is Hebrew, nor one in Yiddish. There are no Zionist youth movements, and no political movements; it is a cultural wasteland. The Nazis physically destroyed the Jews, and the Soviets finished them spiritually.

After the war there was still a Jewish theater and a drama class, but during the 1960s the regime also got rid of those. "Why do you need a Yiddish theater?" they asked. "None of the population understands that language." And so the drama class and the Jewish theater were closed.

The Jews do their best during the holidays, Rosh Hashanah and Yom Kippur, to refrain from working, even going so far as to feign illness in order to stay home from work and go to pray in the synagogue.

Some of the Jews who try to follow tradition and *Yiddishkeit* try in any way they can to obtain an aliyah permit. The Jewish population works in the many factories that opened in Dvinsk. The remaining youth tries to study in the universities – but after completing their studies they have difficulty finding the jobs they want, because sometimes Jews are rejected from jobs that come with a high level of responsibility, such as managers or chief engineers. The Jews try not to become assimilated, and to remain a cohesive group. They don't live together in a separate quarter as they did in the ghettoes of the days of the Germans, but the older generation wants their children to marry Jews, not *goyim*. They try to keep the embers of Judaism glowing.

Edited by: Leah Berkovich, Grade 8, Kiah School
Written by: Shula Apotker, Sarah Inger, Hava Hafber, Sofia Kastel,
              Ganor Atzmon, Dovrit Blimenfeld, and Eitan Sela.

[Page 40]

Dvinsk Then and Now
As told by Mr. Aryeh Madelya, Written by Shula Apotker, Grade 8A

In Dvinsk before the war there were many Zionist youth movements, namely: *Hashomer Hazair, Gordonia, Herzliya,* and *Beitar,* and also Yiddishist youth movements from the Bund stream. Dvinsk was once an important community. Natan Bistritsky visited there and taught the youth their first Hora. Thus the youth learned to dance the *Hora,* until he said "Long live Bistritsky and his *Hora!*"

When the Nazis entered Dvinsk, they killed many Jews. In November 1941 there was an aktia of children: they dug a huge hole and threw the murdered children inside. Today there is a marker on this grave that says only, "Here are buried the victims of Fascism" without any mention of the fact that they were Jews. World War II, and the Holocaust that befell the Jewish people, killed 98% of the Jews of Dvinsk.

The Nazis destroyed the Jewish cemetery. After the war it was possible to find tombstones that had been used to pave roads or to rebuild destroyed houses.

The Soviet regime in Dvinsk does not currently work to develop the Jewish culture of the city. Only a few of Dvinsk's Jews remain. The Jews who are located there came from vast Russia, after wandering from place to place until they settled in that city. Only one synagogue remains, and it is difficult to gather a minyan of Jews there for prayers. In the large aliyah in the 1960s most of the Jews immigrated to Israel, and the once splendid Jewish culture of Dvinsk no longer exists.

[Page 41]

Dvinsk Today

Madelya, Aryeh is a former Prisoner of Zion who arrived in Israel a year ago. After his release from Siberia, where he was imprisoned for 14 years, he arrived in Dvinsk in 1947 and remained there until 1972.

After the Holocaust about five thousand Jews gathered in Dvinsk, most of whom were not natives of the city but rather were from cities in central Russia.

The city had been destroyed during the war and was rebuilt. The city featured many tall buildings and all of the government shops were located there.

The first thing we did was organize a Yiddish-language theater.

The shows were the fruits of the pens of S. Aleichem and A. Goldfaden. Most of the Jews came to see a show in Yiddish, because they wanted to hear their language.

A large factory for synthetic thread was built in the city, and employed about 15,000 people. Most of the Jews of Dvinsk left the city and moved to Riga. In 1970 about 70 families from Dvinsk moved to Israel.

No Jewish school exists in Dvinsk. The children study in comprehensive schools where the dominant language is Russian. Before the Six Day War there was a Jewish cultural group which was closed by the government.

In the city there remains a small synagogue where a few minyans occasionally gather. The Christians throw rocks at it and the Jews mostly avoid going there. There is no rabbi. There is a shochet (ritual butcher) who fulfills all of the religious functions: he is the synagogue manager and the beadle in the synagogue.

The 18th century cemetery was destroyed in 1972 on the orders of the city government. When a Jew passes away he is buried in the general cemetery, and only a Star of David on his tombstone indicates that a Jew is buried there.

The young generation that has grown up knows only the Russian language. No Jewish holidays are celebrated. The Jewish youth is becoming assimilated into the existing society. There are no Jewish weddings; there is no *mohel* to bring Jewish babies into the covenant of Abraham. Books in Hebrew or Yiddish are not to be found. The once-splendid Jewish culture has vanished from that city, which was once brimming with life and creativity, and filled with activity before the war. There are no Jewish representatives in any of the government institutions. There is no Jewish newspaper, though there is a Russian one. How is it possible to create cultural Jewish life when the government line of the Soviet regime in Latvia has been to uproot everything that was Jewish? *[Page 42]* Sometimes a cantor comes from central Russia, from Odessa or Vilna; then the Jews gather who are yearning to hear a word in Yiddish. But those performances are rare, and only happen before holidays.

Lately the Jewish youth are in the habit of gathering around the synagogue on Simchat Torah and dancing the *Hora*.

The police do not look favorably upon such gatherings of Jews in one place, and always disrupt the dancing.

The police view the dancing as a bad thing and are afraid it will inflame the depressed spirits and inspire a rebellion.

Dvinsk – a home to the Jews before the war – is now, after the war, a monument to the ruination and destruction of Jewish life. The Soviet regime continues to suppress every spark of Judaism.

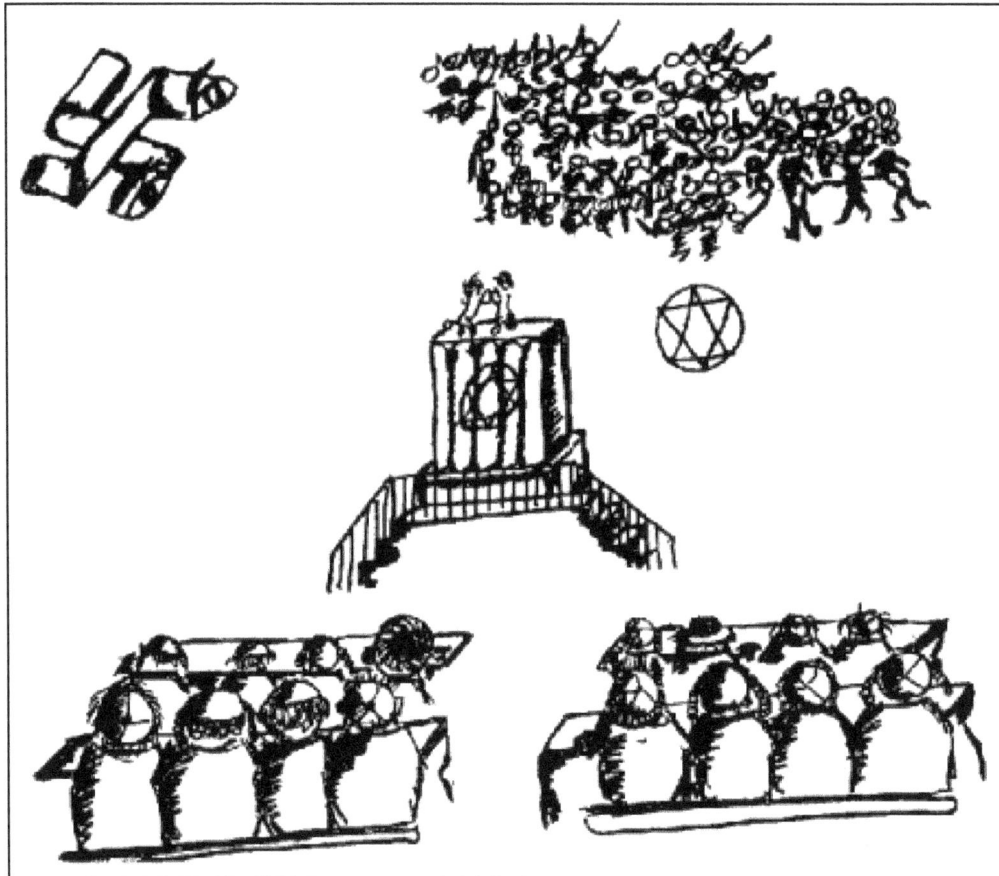

[Page 43]

Dvinsk During the Holocaust

[Page 44]

The Ghetto in Dvinsk
From the Book: Jews in Latvia (Yiddish) By: Mendel Buba

The Germans entered Dvinsk on 29 June 1941 after a heavy bombardment that demolished many of the houses and aroused panic, especially among the Jews. On 21 July 1941 an order was issued, directing all men up to age 60 to assemble in the market square. After being kept in suspense for a full day, they were taken to the central prison. Some were led straight from the square to the Strop Forest where they were slaughtered.

Those who were imprisoned were sent out to do various jobs, and some of them never came back from those tasks. The Latvian populace was as cruel as the Nazis, and cooperated with them in the slaughter of the Jews.

On the 15th of July the large synagogue was set on fire, as were the smaller synagogues and houses of study, afterwards. Only the House of Study of Rabbi Meir Simcha, which was turned into a warehouse for foodstuffs, and the Planover Minyan, which became an old age home for Aryans, remained standing.

On the same day, a decree was issued that ordered all Jews to wear a yellow badge on their chests and backs. Men were also required to put the patch over their left knee.

On the 26th of July all of the Jews were imprisoned in the ghetto in Riga, a city which is located on the other side of the Daugava River.

The "ghetto" was created in an ancient fortress from the days of the Tsars, the greater portion of which was a destroyed barracks and a stable for horses.

They also put the Jews of the smaller towns surrounding Dvinsk into that ghetto; in all they crammed in some 15,000 people, into a horribly overcrowded space with atrocious sanitary conditions. Supposedly to alleviate the overcrowding, the Germans ordered the preparation of a list of elderly people with the intention of moving them to a special camp.

The same thing was said about the Jewish people who had arrived from the surrounding area who had been expelled from their homes with nothing; they would be moved to a "new camp."

The "new camp" was located not far from Dvinsk, about 8 kilometers, in a resort suburb called Pogolianka, where they took the poor souls and murdered them in a cruel and sadistic manner.

They were forced to undress and arrange their clothing neatly, then stand before holes which had been dug in advance and into which they fell after being cut down by machine gun fire.

We are the remaining, living memorial; we are the sons, and the sons of the daughters, of the murdered. It is our sacred obligation to perpetuate their memories, and to engrave their images upon our hearts, and to tell the sons of our sons the stories of the magnificent community of Dvinsk, which once was and is no longer.

Living institutions must be created, monuments of stone, books telling the stories must be published, to leave a reminder for the coming generations.

[Page 45]

In the beginning of November work permits were distributed to tailors and shoe makers, who worked in German workshops. From the seventh through the ninth of November they removed the remainder of the Jews from their homes and took them to "convalescence in Pogolianka." The *Aktion* lasted for three days and afterwards, only 1,000 people remained in the ghetto.

Only 400 Jews remained in the ghetto after its destruction on the first of May, 1942. On the same day, they wiped out the heads of the *Judenrat*, the hospitals and their doctors and nurses. Only Jews who were of use to the Germans remained alive. They were employed because of their trades and housed in their workplaces. Some were housed in the fort by the river.

In the ghetto, three women were killed "according to the law"; one was shot and two were hanged. The formal charges against them were:

One impersonated an Aryan, the second sold things in the ghetto, and the third was accused by a Lett homeowner of violating the law against "defiling the pure race." The homeowner suspected that she knew about the vast property that he had stolen from the Jews and hidden away, and thus he got rid of the eye witness.

The death sentence was carried out in the presence of all of the ghetto's residents, from children to the elderly. In one case, the commander of the "Jewish police" was forced to execute the sentence. One of the women was left hanging for three days to serve as an example to the Jews.

On the 26th of October the final remnants of the Jewish population, 350 people, were taken from the ghetto and sent to the Kaiserwald concentration camp near Riga.

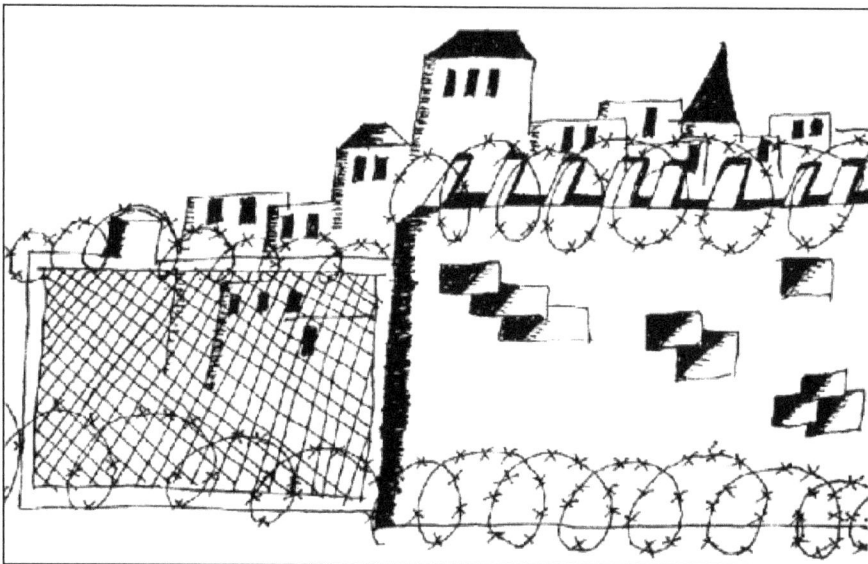

[Page 46]

The Dvinsk Ghetto

On 22 July 1941, World War II broke out.

On 29 July 1941 the Nazis gathered all of the Jews in the center of the city (opposite the Lett department store). They took the men away and sent the women and children home.

For a week we sat at home. Then they imprisoned us and our wanderings began. My mother, my sister, and I went by way of the Planover Synagogue. The prison in Dvinsk is where they murdered most of the Jews. Only a small group of 300 young men and women left the prison alive. They moved us to the Dvinsk ghetto, which was filled to capacity.

The ghetto was once a fortress for the Lett dragoons, well-fortified on all sides, earthen ramparts, wire, fences and swamps near the Daugava on the Grïva side. On the other side of the river on the ramparts were observers and policemen in their command posts. The ghetto was about half a kilometer long. In one corner of the ghetto was the office of the commander, who excelled at cruelty.

Just before this office was the exit from the ghetto, through which the workers went out. Most of the women and children stayed in the ghetto and didn't go out. Those who did work, like me, were gathered in the morning near the gate. The German soldiers would come and take us to work. Those who went out to work were young, healthy, and strong.

The Jews performed forced labor without recompense. The work was difficult and exhausting. There were also Jews who worked in their trades, like shoemakers, tailors, and carpenters who built garages for the heavy military equipment. They also needed female workers for cleaning, laundering and cooking. A group of men and women worked regularly in the military hospital; among them were Ichilov Sheinka (who moved to Israel from Australia), Sima Yaffa, and Isaac Yaffa (her brother, who currently lives in Ra'anana).

They always took me to work. My mother and sister didn't work. My brother Shaul worked in a military unit where a few dozen other Jews also worked. They built garages and did carpentry work.

Those who remained in the ghetto and did not work were subject to aktia. The first was the aktion of the elderly. The German commandant told the Judenrat – whose members were Mowschensohn, Dr. Vaspi, and Dr. Gurwitz – to provide 200 elderly people for a camp. Dr. Gurwitz volunteered to accompany the group.

The camp was called: "The second concentration camp for the elderly and out of work."

Dr. Gurwitz wished to accept that summons, and went to check the conditions of the camp; he set out with the group of elderly people and never returned.   *[Page 47]*   In this manner, the Germans deceived the Jews and the Judenrat. No one knew where the work camp was, or whether it even existed.

The Jews who had work permits were temporarily protected and were called "useful Jews."

There were also Jews from the surrounding towns such as Dagda, Kārsava, Preili, Zilupe, and Rakliani Krāslava in the Dvinsk ghetto. These were the Jews who, at the outbreak of the war, found temporary sanctuary in Dvinsk and were later killed in the ghetto. Among them there were also Jews from abroad, from France or Poland, who had come to visit relatives before the war, who were then trapped in the ghetto and killed.

It sometimes happened that Jews went to their deaths even with viable permits. They said they were tired of life, and preferred death.

In one of the aktia, we returned from work under the supervision of soldiers, for whom we had been working. In that unit were: the teacher Gurwitz, Bleich or Bleichman (from Eglaine – her husband was a veterinary doctor), and me; there was one permit for all of us. As we got closer to the ghetto we saw that all of the Jews were standing in the courtyard, grouped together in families.

I, of course, immediately ran to my family and stood at the head of our group. With me were my mother, my Aunt Leah, and her children. Two children approached our group, one an 8 year old boy and the other a 7 year old girl. They told me, "We will stand in your row, say we're part of your family." I added them to our family group.

A Gestapo man walked among the rows wearing a black tie and carrying a whip in his hand. He decided who would live and who would die. He approached my family and when he saw that I did not have a work permit, he began to beat me all over my body.

I didn't shout or cry, but simply said, "I work in an army unit and have a collective permit with two other women; there they are." The Gestapo man looked at me, amazed by my audacity, and said, "Where does this Jewess get the boldness to speak?"

All eyes turned to us, then the teacher Gurwitz rushed forward with the permit. The Gestapo man checked it, and all of my group and my family were sent to the side of the living. We were lucky that time!

During a different aktion, I was in a room with my brother Shaul – he rolled up like a ball on the bed and I covered him with a pillow and lay down so that I was hiding him. The Lett police went through the rooms, shouting and taking people out of the rooms to the yard and then onto trucks, to be taken no one knew where.

I, with my blond hair, seemed to take them by surprise – "What is this *shiksa* doing here?" Apparently they mistakenly thought I was a non-Jew, and they never laid a finger on me or my brother.   *[Page 48]*   During the month of October I didn't work. All of my former classmates would gather and sit together on the benches from times of the Lett dragoons, and weave dreams for the future. In that group were Sheinka Gendel (killed) Hindake Levy (killed), Sima Yaffa (now in Riga), Isser Hyatt (killed). We would talk about the hoped-for liberation and the end of the war that perhaps, one day, would come.

Someone asked me, "Rachel, do you think we'll be able to stay alive?"

I answered, "Of course we'll stay alive. See, the sun is shining and warming us, that's a good sign." Most of those sitting there never were liberated. Their bones are buried in the Bezia sands. In 1961, on those sands was built a big chemical factory.

The 7th of November came. My brother went to work, but I stayed in the ghetto. The ghetto was surrounded by a living chain of Lett policemen. Together, all the young people ran to the *Judenrat* and cried out, "Help!" but the people of the *Judenrat* were hopeless. At one in the afternoon, as I stood by the *Judenrat* a young woman I did not know approached and said, "What shall I do? My friend went to work at the military hospital this morning and left me her work permit on the condition that I return it to her this afternoon. But I'm scared to go out; there are so many policemen around! What shall I do? Help me." I answered her, "Give me the permit – I will take it to her." The permit was in the name Bella Potsh (I learned later that she was from Chagda and didn't return to the ghetto). I took the permit and ran to say goodbye to my mother and sister. I told my mother that I was going to try to run away, and that she should hide under the pallet.

My mother parted from me with tears in her eyes, and told me that if I survived I should tell the world how they murdered the Jews, and that I shouldn't forget the address of Uncle Leib in America. I went out through the ghetto gate waving the red permit. At that time, no one could leave the ghetto; only those who had a permit in their hands and who knew the password, which was given out by the German commandant. Everyone watched me as I went to the office of the commandant. I waited in the yard for an hour and then left. The policemen thought I had been with the commandant and not delay me. I passed through all the guards. Only one was left. It seemed to me he had fallen asleep, but he suddenly shouted a question at me: where was I going? I replied that I was going to the military hospital and that I had a permit, that the doctor had given me permission to come to the ghetto to see my mother, who was sick. The policeman looked at me and said, "Oh well, then say the password." I answered, "Mr. Policeman, I've forgotten it. I'm so worried about my mother's illness, I've forgotten." The policeman gave me a look and said, "Go quickly, and God be with you!" I quickly crossed the bridge and entered a small forest. I removed the yellow Star of David and buried it in the ground. I went to the place where my brother was working. He hid me in the factory and in the evening left with the other workers and returned to the ghetto. He never left there again. When he reached the ghetto the policemen forced all of the Jews out of their homes and into the yard. On the steps, he met our sister Sarah and together they and the rest of the Jews set off on their final journey... *[Page 49]* My mother, who had hidden under the pallet, was discovered by the policemen, and stabbed with a bayonet.

A bloodbath, she wallowed in blood as she fell in the yard. My brother Shaul was able to cover her with sand. I learned what befell my family later, from an eyewitness.

At eight in the morning my brother Shaul hurried to work. At the gate he was stopped by two detectives who knew him to have been an activist in the communist movement before the war. He went together with the teacher Steinman.

The head of the secret police, Motznik, who stood by the gate, pointed at my brother Shaul and said, "That is the communist commissar Friedman from the high Soviet Lett council." The thing was, in 1940 when the Soviets controlled Latvia, they had elected as commissar 40 year old Feibish Friedman who had been an underground communist (he is now in Riga). The head of the secret police claimed that my brother was that Friedman, although he was only 22 and his name was Shaul, not Feibish. But why should he concern himself with such details as the proper name? It was obvious that Friedman was a communist, and after all the family name was the same.

I ran away to Breslau. The Jews of Dvinsk were exterminated on the 7th and 8th of November, 1941. The few remaining remnants were taken to the Dvinsk fortress, from which they were taken out to forced labor. Later, they moved them to Salaspils (not far from Riga), and from there to German and Polish camps.

Only a few individuals survived and returned.

I continued to run and to wander. Through the villages and towns, I came in contact with the partisans and joined them.

In February 1943 I crossed the front lines, and reached Moscow on the 14th of April. There I was received warmly. They listened when I told them of the slaughter of the Jews of Latvia and my city, Dvinsk. In Eretz Yisrael, I found my liberty.

Rachel Friedman
A refugee of the Holocaust from the ghetto of Dvinsk

[Page 50]

The Ghetto of Dvinsk
From the book: The Story of the Netzach Movement in Latvia By: A. Eti and M. Nishtet

The ghetto for the Jews of Dvinsk and the surrounding area was established in July 1941 in the stable of the abandoned barracks next to the town of Grïva on the banks of the river opposite Dvinsk. During the months of August and September, the first *aktia*, in which thousands of Jews were killed, took place.

After a relatively quiet month of October, the biggest and cruelest massacre took place at the beginning of November. From the 6th to the 8th of November, thousands of Jews were taken to the forest of Pogolianka, where they met their deaths. After those aktia, there remained about 800 Jews. Those days in the ghetto have been described by Rachel Friedman (who made *aliyah* in 1971):

"I was trapped in the ghetto along with my family. My closest friends there were my friends from the movement. We would get together and talk about our uncertain future. One day my brother told me about a rumor he had heard regarding the presence of partisans in the forests near the town of Viški, not far from Dvinsk. It's doubtful whether there was any foundation to those rumors."

"When the big *Aktion* began early in November, my brother and I were outside the ghetto. We wanted to run away together, but my brother returned to the ghetto to try and get our mother out as well so she could join us. But my brother was not able to get out of the ghetto again. I ran away to Belarus, and I was put into the ghetto in the town of Breslau. Later I joined a partisan unit, and remained with them until the end of the war."

It would seem that Rachel Friedman was one of the only members of the movement who joined the partisans. A second incidence is that of Zevulon Krislav of blessed memory (Riga branch) who was part of a group that, at the behest of the Red Army, parachuted behind enemy lines on the island of Hazenholm in the Daugava estuary near Riga. The seven member group was active in the area around Riga for about two months. Zevulon K. was one of five members of the group who were killed after being betrayed. He was put to death after being brutally tortured. The reason for lack of members of the movement among the partisans is obvious: the Letts usually cooperated with the Germans in the slaughter of the Jews, and there was no reason to hope for help from the farmers at a time when so many of the Jews of Latvia were being exterminated. At the end of 1941 there were no partisan units operating on Latvian soil. Such units were founded or penetrated the Latvian border at a later date.

We will return to events in the ghetto. A few dozen Jews were used by the Germans in various jobs in the city; they were not locked up in the ghetto but rather were allowed to live in pre-arranged apartments in the city. As they left for work every morning and returned every evening to their apartments, they were not subject to strict inspections. Compared to the tragic situation of those in the ghetto, these workers were relatively well-off. They did not lack for food or clothing; they could have helped many of the Jews in the ghetto. But from December 1941 to February 1942 a strict curfew was imposed on the ghetto because of contagious illnesses that broke out amongst those imprisoned there. *[Page 51]* During that period many died from disease and starvation. At the end of February 1942 the quarantine was lifted from the ghetto. Then, all of the Jews who had been living in the city were expelled and forced into the ghetto, except for a few individuals who were allowed to continue living in the city. A few hundred of the last Jews still living in the ghetto worked in the fortress or the city. On the 1st of May 1942 the murders began again and the end came to the ghetto of Dvinsk. The handful of Jews still alive worked and lived in the city. That situation continued until the end of October 1943.

From time to time, attempts were made in the Dvinsk ghetto to organize and to obtain weapons for self-defense when the time came. The efforts came at the initiative of small groups of young people not necessarily based on participation in the movement, but rather based on long-standing personal acquaintance stemming from involvement in youth movements or from school ties. A number of members of the movement were involved in those actions. This is known through the testimony of members of the movement who had the facts.

Comprehensive and detailed testimony regarding events in the ghetto in general and including the accumulation of weapons was provided by Ita Rosenberg (now Ita Bell, a member of Kfar Blum):

"I joined the movement just a few months before the war started. I was about 14 years old when Dvinsk was occupied by the Germans. My mother and I asked to run away to the East with a large group of others, but in the end we weren't able to do so because my grandmother was old and weak. I estimate that about half of the Jews were able to escape. Until November of 1941 there remained in the ghetto a group of youths between the ages of 14 and 16; some of them were members of the movement. We worked in various jobs in the city. I worked cleaning houses and sweeping streets."

"In that bereaved atmosphere where one expected to die at any time, our friend Issar Hyatt of blessed memory had the best attitude in the ghetto. He was not my direct counselor, but was the leader of the company of scouts to which I belonged. Since he was slightly older than the rest of the group of young people in the ghetto (among them several members of the movement) he was a leader and a figure of respect, who encouraged us and tried to instill hope in us. He was unable to come to terms with the bitterness of reality.

Even during the brief Soviet regime, Issar continued to keep in touch with his protégés, in defiance of the instructions of older activists in the movement, who thought it best not to hold meetings at that time. In the ghetto he often told stories about the establishment of the kibbutz Ein Gev and about life in Eretz Yisrael. "If we stay alive – we'll immediately move to Eretz Yisrael." We would repeat that sentiment after him. One day, it was at the beginning of 1942, Issar was caught trying to sneak a loaf of bread into the ghetto and was shot to death on the spot by the murderous Germans."

Regarding the hoarding of weapons and practice with them, we have the account of Eliyahu Graber (now in the United States):

"Among the older members of the movement in Dvinsk, only a few were imprisoned in the ghetto. Most of them fled to the Soviet Union. I headed east but our group of refugees was not permitted to cross the border into Russia. We were forced to return to Dvinsk. That is how I came to be in the ghetto. I was one of those who lived in the city and not behind the walls of the ghetto. For awhile I worked in the fortress. At work I would see a friend my age from the movement – Gutman Yachnin." *[Page 52]* "We were a group of young people who obtained weapons, especially hand grenades and pistols. The underground tunnels of the old fortress were a safe place for us to practice with the weapons. We didn't create a formal group, nor did we have plans for initiating resistance activities. We thought we would be able to use the weapons, either each one of us on his own, or as a group, according to the way events unfolded. As it turned out, we did not have a chance to use the weapons, which were smuggled into the ghetto."

Regarding the accumulation of weapons and their concealment in the ghetto, Moshe-Menashe Vapna, who spent some time in the Dvinsk ghetto, said:

"We were a group of four boys, ages 10 – 14, which was part of a unit that served the German army. We worked driving wagons, transporting building materials. One of the four was Gutka Yachnin. We did not live in one of the buildings in the ghetto, but rather in the stable, near our horses. Gutka was disabled, and had walked with a limp since he was a baby, but he was as nimble as a ghost. His unusual agility, in spite of his limp, saved him from death more than once. Many times he was able to escape from a dangerous spot. Several of the Jews in the ghetto obtained weapons in various ways. The best place for hiding the weapons was in the stable. With the help of a young man named Bubka Fuks, Gutka installed an iron crate in the ground in which the weapons were hidden. The owners of the weapons promised Gutka that when the day came that they would remove the weapons in preparation for escaping to the forests, they would take him, and us, with them. But those who made that promise did not keep it."

The last Jews of Dvinsk did not delude themselves. They knew that every day brought the danger that the Germans would suddenly come to take them away to some unknown destination. Many of them prepared for that day in their own ways.

As Ita related:

"Every day that passed and we remained alive was considered a victory. The months passed until it was the summer of 1943. One day we received word of an uprising in the Warsaw ghetto. We saw tanks full of wounded soldiers being transported from the front lines to the rear. It was the German soldiers themselves who revealed the failures at the front, the existence of partisans in Belarus, and about the uprising in the ghetto of Warsaw. The last event awakened in us a spirit of courage and hope. "If they can do it, why cannot we also?" we said to one another. We thought to defend ourselves with weapons, but we didn't think we had any hope of staying alive. In our wildest dreams, we didn't imagine that a single one of us would survive."

"A few young men accumulated some weapons and made various plans. One of them was the member of the movement, David Bleier of blessed memory. In the beginning, he told me in utmost secrecy that a number of Jews had weapons. Later I saw them with my own eyes, and I held the pistols and hand grenades in my own hands. According to the plan of David Bleier and the small group he organized, we were supposed to escape to the forests at the last moment before the Germans came to take us away. We didn't want to run away earlier than that because of the warning the Germans had given, that for each Jew that ran away, ten Jews would be killed."   *[Page 53]*

"David had established contact with several farmers, who promised us shelter when we reached them. As time passed, the plan began to seem more and more real. We waited for the right moment. In preparation for that opportunity, we sewed warm pants and prepared blankets and food. We thought to escape from the city in groups of two or three, or perhaps individually. But the way events unfolded, our plan could not be put into action. The bitter day at the end of August 1943 came unexpectedly. Policemen and the Gestapo surrounded the area where we were living. All of the Jews were ordered to come out. A few were able to escape. A few Jews committed suicide rather than fall into the hands of the murderers. My mother, David Bleier, a woman named Hava Zilberman, and I ran away over the roofs until we reached the house of a Christian woman, who hid us in a closet; later she went to the police and turned us in. We were taken to the procession of people walking to the train station. While we were walking, David tried to run away. The policemen ran after him and shot at him. David stopped, and shot and killed a German who approached him. He then took his own life on the spot."

"That was the end of my friend David Bleier of blessed memory. As far as I know, David was the only Jew of Dvinsk to shoot and kill a German. He was 17 when he died."

There ends the account of Ita.

~.~.~.~.~.~.~.~.~.~.~.~.~.~.~.~.~.~.~.

Some of the last Jews of Dvinsk were moved that same day to the local prison, where they remained for a few weeks until they were taken to the Kaiserwald camp near Riga. A few dozen of the prisoners were released and returned to the city, where they remained for awhile. The vast majority were taken to the train that day and sent to Riga. Gutka Yachnin, who was one of those crammed into the train car, once again showed his agility. With the help of others, he removed the wire that secured the small window and then squeezed through the opening and managed to safely jump out of the train without the guards noticing. When he realized that he would not be able to find shelter, he returned to Dvinsk and turned himself in. He was taken to Kaiserwald; from there he was taken, together with the last Jews of Latvia, to a death camp in Germany. Gutman Yachnin of blessed memory most likely found his death in the Stutthof death camp. Among the others who successfully escaped that day was Eliyahu Graber.

He related the story of his experiences of that same day and through the end of the war:

"Armed with weapons we ran off, my friend and I, away from the Germans who had come to take us away. They chased us and shot at us. My friend was shot. We were both caught and taken in a wagon to the prison. On the way, I was able to escape, and I hid in the ruins of a burned-out building, of which only the foundation remained. I crawled inside the chimney. My pursuers did not discover my hiding place. After a day or so I escaped from the building and joined a group of Russian captives, who worked outdoors. I introduced myself as a Lett. I was a free man. I worked for the Germans as a mechanic. My work took me to army camps, and I acquired a lot of information about the deployment of various units. When the Germans began to withdraw I ran away from my workplace. After facing many life-threatening dangers, I reached the front lines and presented myself to a patrol of the Red Army. *[Page 54]* I gave them important intelligence information and convinced them to believe me. After I had obtained their trust, they enlisted me in the army. I served in the Red Army until the end of the war. In 1945 in one of the battles near Warsaw, I was injured."

Those are the eyewitness accounts we have obtained up to now. They are few and fragmented. Obviously, they do not present the whole picture, but there is enough there to bear witness to the fact that the young people of the movement, who were faced with the most horrific test one can imagine, dealt with the situation to the best of their abilities.

*   *   *

*   *

[Page 55]

The Camp Ganbin and Liberation
From the newspaper of the Jews of Melbourne, Australia

An employee of the newspaper, Mrs. Sonia Slobo experienced as a child the seven circles of hell in the Dvinsk ghetto, and the camps of Riga and Stutthof, in Germany. Shortly before liberation, she was moved along with about 1,000 other women to Ganbin, a village in Germany, where she worked extremely hard.

Only 60 remained alive after the liberation.

Mrs. Sonia Slobo wrote the lines below immediately after the liberation, on 11 March 1945:

(Loosely translated)

~.~.~.~.~.~.~.~.~.~.~.~.~.~.~.~.~.~.

In the wilderness far from any settlement, we remember the women who suffered cold, hunger, and filth in the crowded granary, exposed to the cold winds. The women lay on filthy straw, burning with fever, their parched mouths murmuring, "Water... water... give me just a little snow and I'll give up my share of the bread."

The women lie there, nearly unconscious and wishing for death to come and free them from their great suffering. Their teeth chatter from the cold. The body twitches with fever. Quiet! The cart with the potato soup is approaching.

The guards force the poor women out of the granary. They can barely stand to receive their meager portion of soup.

The tumult and confusion are great. The women are forced to stand in lines of five, with the ones who are ill supported by their friends.

The first course is a blow to the head from the guard's baton. The blood flows down the face and into the eyes, blurring the vision.

A shout is heard from the granary: "Who wants to trade a portion of soup for a bit of salt?" The guard sends the women back into the granary, as the sick ones stumble and the thin soup is spilled. There is no place to stretch out, and the shouts are heard: "Help! My leg! My leg!" The cries are accompanied by pinches and slaps.

In the middle of the night we hear a shout: "Is there a nurse here? Quickly, quickly!" "What happened?" "My daughter is about to give birth," answers the mother in an anguished voice.

From the mother-to-be neither a moan nor a groan is heard, so that the guard, G-d forbid, won't hear anything and learn what is happening. *[Page 56]* The newborn was wrapped in a bloody scarf, with the Star of David showing in the folds. In the two granaries lay sick women, their bodies swollen with starvation, preparing themselves for death. Despair cuts short the last thread of life. The body is a skeleton walking on two legs. The lice eat the skeleton and the few scraps of flesh still on it. They drink the last drops of blood.

There is no one to show mercy. We must make due with the two potatoes and the cup of murky water that is called coffee. No one is capable of moving or standing up. The gaunt bodies, burning with fever, are covered with rags.

The straw is filthy and wet. The women lie with half of their bodies rotting. The legs are frozen. There is no spark of life in them. They wait and wait.

Silence in the granary. The poor women have fallen asleep, and those who still live step on the dead. There is no feeling, there is no hope – "all is lost." No one has the bravery to shake off the despair.

One morning I go out, barely take a few steps and see – there is no guard. From afar the sound of rolling rocks. "What is that?" It is machine guns, attacking the Nazi enemy.

Three figures approach from the distance. Is that the German guard? It's hard to see from so far away. Slowly I take a few steps forward. From far off I hear a shout: don't be shocked – "People, you have been liberated."

People? Up until now I had been a number. Am I still a human being? The voice from afar grows closer. It is warm and friendly.

The ill and the healthy slowly get to their feet and walk towards the word "people." Those whose legs will take them walk to the village. Across from us travels a soldier of the Red Army. His face shows surprise and friendship. He was shocked by the cries that greeted him.

"Don't cry – you are free – you must get strong, the whole world is winking at you." Those were his words, "the world winks." What world? Does such a thing exist?

We slowly entered the village. We spread out into the houses which were empty of people. We took food, drink, and clothing. It all seemed like a dream.

Yes – we must give thanks to the Red Army, who liberated us from the camps and from four years of slavery.

Only the great sorrow gnawed at us. Only a few remained alive. Most are gone and will never come back. The mounds of ash are scattered by the wind.

Our brothers, our sisters, our parents are hidden in those ashes. Only a few remain.

The tears close my throat. No matter where I go, I see the rows of five skeletons with their pale faces and their hopeless eyes.

[Page 57]

The Metamorphosis of a Young Man of Dvinsk from the Old Left
By: Mordechai Neishtet

The article appeared in *Shadmot*, #38 1970

The city of Dvinsk was home to the Jews until it was wiped out in the Holocaust. It sits on the banks of the Daugava River, on the way from Western Europe to Moscow, close to the border with Poland. The Jews did not make up the majority of the population, but they were a clear presence in the city. On the Sabbath and on special Jewish days the city came to a standstill. The shops on the commercial streets were shut and locked. The peace of the Jewish holiday spread throughout the entire city.

Two of the great Torah geniuses who shared the light of their brilliance with the large and respected Jewish community were Rabbi Meir Simcha HaCohen (called the Gaon of Dvinsk for he had lived there since his youth), and Rabbi Josef Rosen, who was known in the Jewish world as the Rogachover Gaon, who settled in the city in the 1920s. On the other side of the river opposite the city there stood a small settlement called Grïva, not really a town and not really a village, with a tiny Jewish community that obtained all of its necessities from the big city on the other side of the river, was born the Rav Kook. From now on, say that we are dealing with a place of Torah and the roots of Judaism. The Jewish community in Latvia was an entity unto itself but was also an important part of the impressive Russian Judaism.

Most of the Jewish children were educated in Torah and *mitzvot* in the various *cheders* in the city. Each *cheder* had its own *minyan* in the city, and there were perhaps more. The *cheder* in which I studied was next to the large synagogue, where the Gaon of Rogachov used to pray. Some mornings the Gaon would arrive accompanied by his servant for quick prayers. Why quick? The Gaon had a habit of being somewhat ill-mannered in prayer. He resented every moment that he did not spend immersed in the Gemara. We impressionable young men of the *cheder* would peer into his sacred room to observe the light shining out of the face of the Gaon.

Rabbi Peretz Gusman did not seem too old in the eyes of his pupils, but there were among us some students who were the sons of his pupils from the previous generation. My father of blessed memory would tell his sons that he, too, studied in the *cheder* of the same rebbe. He was a good Jew. He tried to restore *Yiddishkeit* to the hearts of his pupils, but in keeping with the times. There existed something known as an "improved" *cheder*, that is to say a *cheder* that also offered some of the subjects taught at the public schools such as mathematics, writing, and grammar. They introduced the practice of giving out printed diplomas, just like in the other schools.

I made a very good friend in Rabbi Peretz's *cheder*. We were faithful friends throughout the years. He was the son of a large, wealthy, and respected family in the community. Most of the sons of the family received, per their parents' wishes, a nationalist education. Some of them were the students of Rabbi Peretz; they studied in the Hebrew school and joined the *Hashomer Hazair* youth movement, *Netzach* (an abbreviation for Pioneer Zionist Youth), which drew the best of the youths. That family was among the first pioneers from our city to leave for life on a kibbutz in Eretz Yisrael. Today, after forty years, they and their descendants are among the senior and founding members of half a dozen *kibbutzim*. *[Page 58]* My friend did not have a happy childhood; he was orphaned from his mother at an early age and remained the only son of his father, who because of the demands of his business could not care for him as he should. Since we were such close friends of the heart and soul, he spent many hours and days in my family's modest home, and our friendship grew stronger and deeper despite the fact that an important connection was lacking – school. For some reason, he was sent to a Jewish school where the language of instruction was Russian. Understandably, we were not taught the same things. After we reached thirteen, the age of bar mitzvah, we no longer studied at the *cheder*. In spite of that, during that time a new base was added to our friendship. We both joined the youth movement and became part of the same educational group. The movement deepened our friendship still further, and added the background of common expectations and experiences.

Even before we reached the age of *bar mitzvah*, we wanted to be free of the *cheder*. At that time I already saw myself as a complete skeptic. I already knew there was no G-d. In his place was the pioneering ideal: and to live there as a farmer for the rest of my days. The Hebrew school also prepared us for pioneering.

Not all of the community's Jews, or even most of them, were supporters of Zionism. The Bund had deep roots in the city, which was the home of one of the first cells of that youth movement. Most of the poor and the workshop owners were members of the Bund party.

From the 1930s on, the strength of the communists increased in the Jewish community. More and more of the youth were caught up in the extreme left. The soil was fertile and the timing was right for such ideas; at school we eagerly studied the classics of Russian literature. Many people spoke Russian at home. We would devour the works of Sholokhov, Ehrenburg, Babel, Mayakovsky and others, and delighted in them.

The socialist background took over the communist idea and ideal, and of course was clear and undisputed. Thus communism in Latvia in the 1930s continued to spread. The young and naive, formed from the same material from which was forged the pioneering element, took the Marxist doctrine into their hearts and souls. They knew what they could expect – expulsion from the gymnasia, torture by the secret police and arrest – but they were unafraid.

The first mission of every young person who became involved in the *comsommol* (Russian youth group) was to try to bring all of his friends into the illegal movement, as well. They would deliberately start ideological arguments at every opportunity. They would single out their friends in the pioneering movement in particular. "What is there for you in far-off, hostile Palestina?" they would ask. The struggle for just government in the world was a common topic. The enemies of the Jewish people were Latvian fascism and German Nazism. There was only one force in the world that could stand up to them, and that was of course the Soviet Union, the country that had realized socialism as a way of life. Every one would have to prove personally exactly where he stood. What self-aware young person could fail to join the camp of the righteous fighters? No less irritating was the conceptual assault of communism – the despondency over the bitter reality: a difficult economic situation, the people of Israel held captive in poverty, immigration to Eretz Yisrael almost non-existent; for that they sat at the training kibbutz for two years, or three, or more. *[Page 59]* The shocking list of the events of 1929 was still fresh. Parents did not wish to see their sons getting gangrene in the prison of Dvinsk, and there were Zionists who were not happy to send their sons to far-off Palestina, which promised malaria, poverty, the hatred of the Arab majority, and an uncertain future. And so from time to time some of the boys would drop out from the movement and join the *comsommol*. Even among the Zionist families, black sheep were revealed. It brought on a deep depression and a temporary embarrassment within the local chapter of the movement. It was known that those who were ensnared in the *comsommol* were ordered not to leave immediately, but rather to continue their clandestine activities in order to draw in additional young people, sometimes from among their own protégés in the movement. Those who remained alive (who were not killed in the war or executed as "spies") and those presently living in Latvia, feel a depression like a dark chasm, and are jealous of their friends who are living a free life in Eretz Yisrael. One day, my friend left the movement and joined the enemy camp. It was clear that he would become a fanatic; for some reason that step seemed obvious to me. Our friendship had already weakened, and its end came as a natural progression. But after a certain amount of time had passed, my friend once again began to come around to my house. But the cat was soon out of the bag. His intention was to draw me away from my beliefs and to quickly pull me into the *comsommol*. Then the arguments began. He would not leave me alone, and put pressure on my weakest points. For an hour he filled my ears with his claims, but I soon turned things around with my reasoning and opinions. "Even if you are right and the truth is on your side, it doesn't make a difference to me. It's not my truth; personally I decided long ago to move to Eretz Yisrael. That's my path, and I have no other. Enough of this pointless argument." And with those words I sent him away. The pioneering consciousness of most people came from the presence of an emotional source which had been engraved on their hearts from an early age, namely the education they received: in their parents' homes, in the Hebrew school, and from the teachers from Eretz Yisrael and the lessons in Hebrew literature they provided. In my opinion, two works did the educational missionary work in those days: "Ahavat Zion" by A. Mapu, and "Masada" by Yitzhak Lamdan. Last but not least, the *Chumash* and the *Talmud*, which we studied in the *cheder*, influenced me. After the break with my friend, and up until today, we rarely saw one another. Our paths went in completely different directions. By rights, one of us would move to Eretz Yisrael and live on a kibbutz. And the other, after activity in the *comsommol* and a period of imprisonment, would become free in 1940, thanks to the Soviet army that "liberated" Latvia. After that, his fate would be bitter and awful. The facts of the matter were completely different. He moved to Eretz Yisrael before I did, and that mystery is inexplicable to me. What was the sequence of events that caused him to give up on the communist fight in Latvia? Why did he abandon the communist path he had chosen and travel to Palestine, of all places? I will never know, but I can guess; he received a permit to immigrate as the owner of a fortune; he certainly did not obtain a pioneer certificate. He certainly arrived here as a faithful communist. He probably continued his communist activities in secret, something that without a doubt carried with it the danger of arrest by the Mandate government.   *[Page 60]*   In 1937 my former friend, like other communists from Eretz Yisrael, volunteered for the International Brigade, which fought against Franco in Spain. There he fought for the victory of socialism in the world. Based on an article in the Israeli press, which was published a full thirty years after the Spanish war, it is known through trustworthy evidence that he was the one and only of hundreds of Jews who set sail from Eretz Yisrael to the Spanish front, who returned home in one piece. When he returned he resumed his political activities, and from then until now he can be counted among the top echelon of the Israeli Communist Party (Maki). For many years he filled an important role in the offices of the newspaper of that party.

If I am not mistaken, he published his writings under an assumed name that he most likely was given during his days in the underground.

Everyone remembers the gaping chasm that existed between the Jewish settlement and the government in the early 1950s, in the days of the plot against the doctors, and the Slánský trial, when great danger circled over the heads of our brothers in the Soviet Union. At that time, Maki was a communist-Stalinist party in every respect, so it would have been impossible to have a meeting between old friends.

The years passed, and much water passed down the Jordan River and the Daugava. What intelligence could not accomplish, time did. Maki is no longer a viable communist political party. Who would have believed that there could be any common ground between Maki and the Zionist labor movement?

As it is known, political facts have personal ramifications. Who could have believed that two paths that diverged back in Dvinsk would begin to come together again in the state of Israel in the 26th year of its existence?

It would be strange and unexpected if we were to meet suddenly one day, to perhaps sit together over a cup of Russian tea and summarize for ourselves what happened, and why. I am very curious to know how it happened that a communist made aliyah to Israel. It's possible to guess at the simple, rational explanations for the things that happened. I would be likely to reject any such type of explanation; it is easiest for a man to offer the simplest explanations for the twists and turns his life takes.

Nonsense! One always needs to look for another, more complete explanation. I would say that my former friend was able to come to Eretz Yisrael thanks to the fact that he studied in the *cheder* of Rabbi Peretz, may he rest in peace. The seeds which the rabbi sowed in us at the age of four or five bore fruit. And if the first harvest was destroyed, what remained grew up later. I am prepared to repeat my claim, even if I seem to be a deceiver in his eyes, and yours.

No matter what, these lines will serve as a memorial candle for the rabbi of my father of blessed memory, and mine, and for the community and those same simple Jews, praiseworthy, loyal and anguished, the believers and the skeptics, who perished.

(Ein Gev)

[Page 61]

Yizkor [Memorial Prayer]
Appeared in the Australian Yiddish language newspaper in 1967 to mark the passage of 25 years since the destruction of the Jews of Latvia
By: Sonia Slobo

25 years have passed and gone
Since our loved ones were slaughtered.
I cannot forget you,
For I dream of you.
My dear father and mother,
My pleasant brother and sisters,
My children bear your names.
I continue to tell them
About the murderous Nazis,
Who cut short your lives.
It is engraved in my heart,
Like a stone.
And if I am smiling on the outside
Inside the tears flow and flow.
Our children have no grandfather or grandmother.
After all the many generations
Only a few remnants remain.
The gas chambers and the furnaces swallowed everyone;
They threw you in while you were still alive.

And only once a year do we gather
To say *Kaddish* over the common grave.

25 years have passed and gone
And the wounds have not yet healed over.
We do not know where the graves are
We can only count the years of memorial prayers.
Before my eyes stand your living shadows.
And I see how they threw the children into the ditches.
or the Nazis it was a game of bullets for dolls
With the skeletons laid out in rows and piles.
I can see my little brother –
Taken from the arms of my screaming mother
She tries to hold fast to her children.
No cries or tears and lamentations can help.
The murderers' hearts are like stone.
A deep and eternal hatred burns in my heart
For those who slaughtered one third of my people.
From the heavens I hear my mother's whisper

Avenge us, my daughter: Revenge! Revenge!

[Page 62]

Yizkor [Memorial Prayer]
29 years after the destruction of the Jews of Latvia

Sonia Slobo from Dvinsk – from an Australian Yiddish-language newspaper

Your image, Mother, has been erased from my memory
29 years have passed.
I recall how with your gaunt frame, you shielded
Your children from the fear of terrible death.
So the young children would not see
The tears of their mother falling.
So they won't see the murderous Nazis
Brandishing their weapons.
You stood, Mother, and waited for the order:
"Left, right, left, right…"
Dear Mother! Now I understand
How your heart filled with fear and dread.
When you drew your children close
As if you wanted to absorb them into your very being.
Your image – I still see today. Alas!
Tormented with pain and anguish
I gaze through the hospital window
And follow you who are going with a last glance.
Like shadows before my eyes you pass time and again.
And thus millions of Jews were murdered!
And the world saw and was silent, silent,
From seven children in the family
I alone remain.

I hope they will say *Kaddish* and *Yizkor* after them.
Millions were murdered in *Kiddush Hashem*
Because of their wretched existence as Jews.
And the six burning candles
Are a symbol for the generations to come.
In my heart there will always be hatred for the murderers
Who turned millions of Jews – to piles of ash.

[Page 63]

To Them!

How could you look upon that plague, which destroyed the best of the life of man?

Why were you silent? Why did the heavens not blush red from shame? Genocide was done before the eyes of the world – which turned its face from us.

To whom will we turn now?

The heart cries and howls – who can understand this Holocaust? Who will take revenge on the murderers who cut down our families in cold blood?

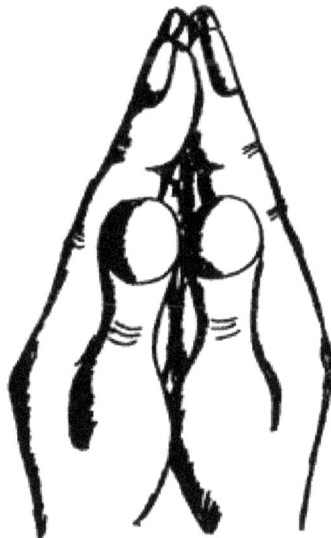

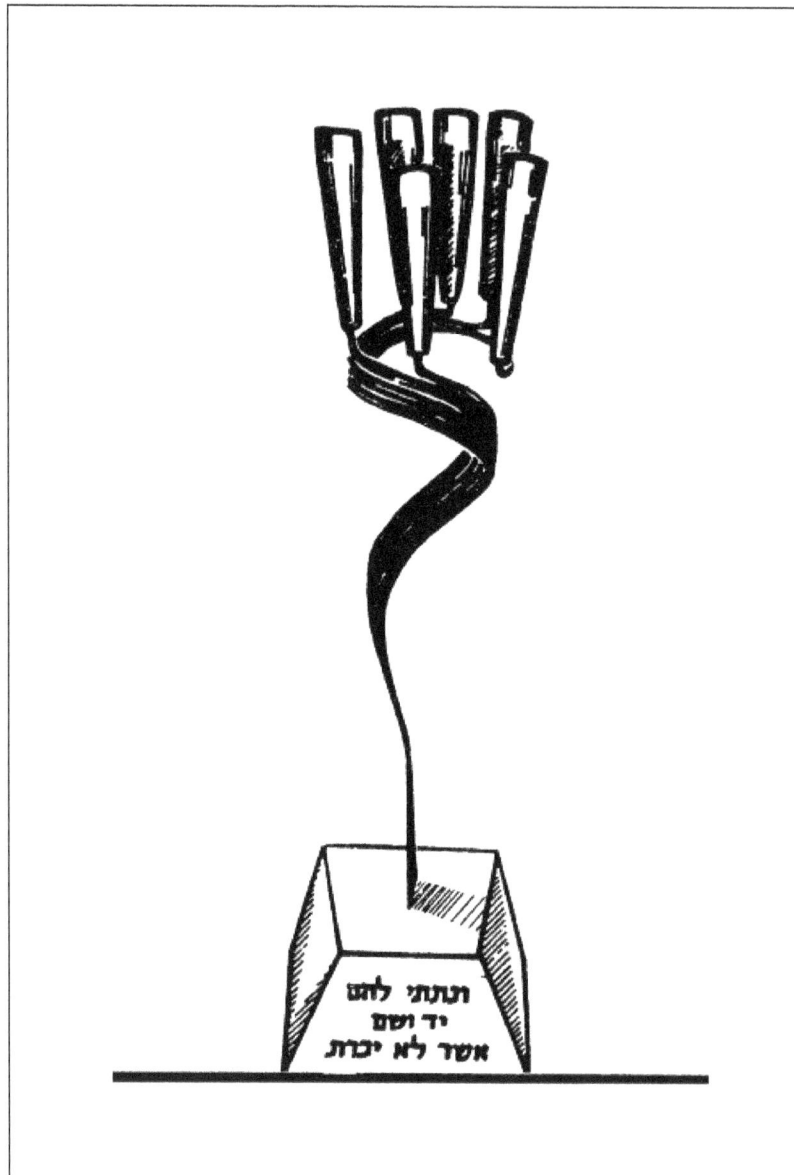

This Appendix of images from Dvinsk is a replica of the web site
http://www.eilatgordinlevitan.com/dvinsk/dvinsk.html
Courtesy of Eilat Gordin Levitan

Meir Simcha of Dvinsk (1843-1926) was a rabbi and prominent leader of
Orthodox Judaism in Eastern Europe in the early 20th century

The Rogachaver Gaon, Rabbi Yosef Ruzin

1903 "A modern family in the old country... Yeshaye Bloch, a well-known lawyer... his wife and children. This picture was sent in by Mrs. Rose Weinberg, of Detroit." (From a 'Forward' photo essay, 1933: "...The Vogues Of Yesteryear...")

Members of Daughters of Zion, a women's Zionist organization, Dvinsk, Russia (now Daugavpils, Latvia), 1904.

(The Institute for Labour Research in Memory of Pinchas Lavon, Tel Aviv)

Scheva (left) and Lijas Neisloss (Neisxloss), about 1910

Yeshua Hessel Kretzmer

Yoshua Hessel Kretchmer   Birth ~1845 in Birzai Death 1925 in Jerusalem

Dvinsk, 1917; Dave and Jack PoKempner standing on the ladder at a Zionist rally. Flags say Land of Israel, to the people of Israel, Palestine for the Jews 1917. Marlene Kempner Dobrin Family names Kempner, PoKempner, PaKempner, Mirvis, Rief, Westerman, Melman, Zox, Sachs, Krechmer, Litt, Lunch, Meyerson, Marovich, Shanker, Herzog, Hillman, Fleischman, Segall, Friedman, Dobrin, Schuman, Fuxman

Joseph and Rosa Sosin of Dvinsk about 1920

1922 Daugavpils; After the flood Photographer Reeksts, J.

1922 ; Daugavpils After the flood. Photographer Lapins, M.

1922. By The Drugstore after the flood

The year 1922; Dvinsk after the flood

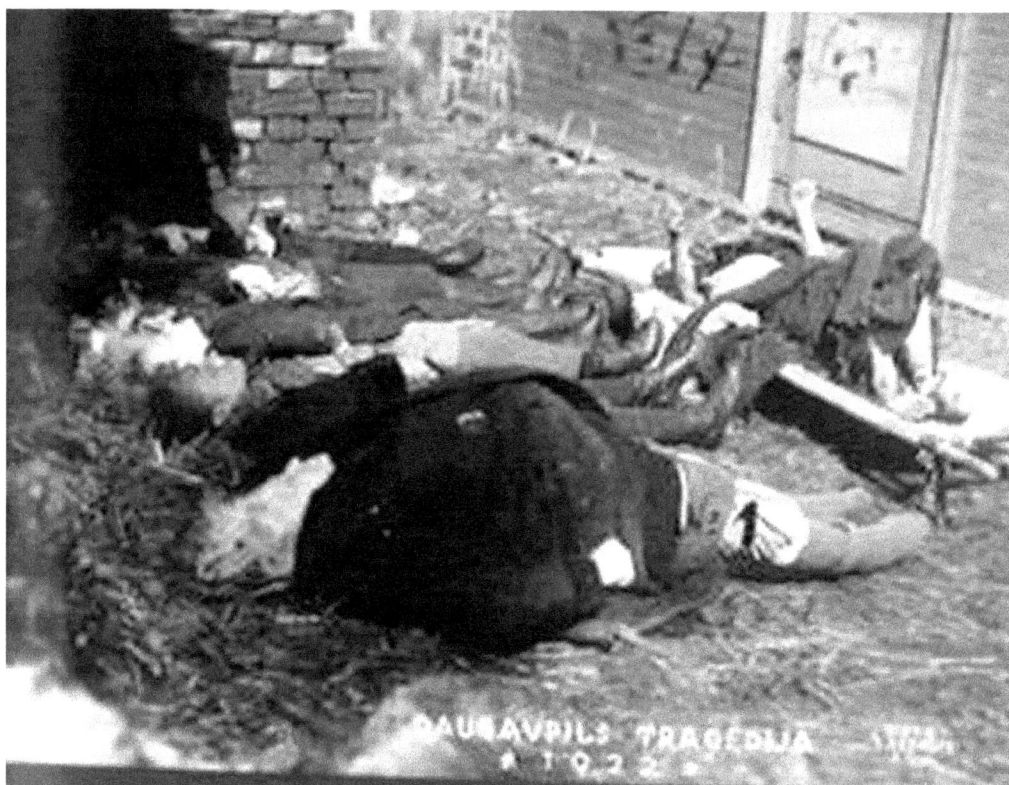

Corpses laid out on straw-covered ground after the flood of 1922 in Dvinsk

pub. Dec. 14, 1924 Daugavpils/ Dvinsk 'Jewish Daily Forward' caption in Yiddish: "Sholem Mark, the shames of the 'besmedresh' of the Apter 'rebe' [leader of a Hasidic sect]... and eight of his grandchildren"

1933

A meeting of members of "Galil Gimel," Dvinsk district of the youth
movement Netsach (Pioneer Scouting Youth - 1933

A balalaika ensemble in Daugavpils (Dvinsk), Latvia
Photographed in 1929 or 1930

A nature activity for members of the Borochov Yugnt youth movement in Daugavpils

Uncaptioned

A celebration inaugurating the dormitory center "Ma'on ha - Olim" in Daugavpils (Dvinsk). Before World War II

A meeting of members of "Galil Gimel," Dvinsk district of the youth movement Netsach (Pioneer Scouting Youth

Participants in a show entitled "Boom un Dreydl," staged by
pupils of the Yiddish school in Daugavpils (Dvinsk)

Pupils and teachers of the first Yiddish school in Daugavpils (Dvinsk)

General Evgenii Miller

Students in the Yiddish school in Daugavpils (Dvinsk), who set up a
cooperative for providing tutoring for needy pupils in the 1930s

Klive Moss site for Dvinsk

Pupils and teachers of the first Yiddish school in Daugavpils (Dvinsk). in the
1930s

9 ועד ה„בונד" בדווינסק
יושבים פ:מין לשמאל: י. רץ. פ. מייקסין. נ. מייזל. ג. לוין. וו. לונברג.
עומדים מימין לשמאל : ב. רינד. י. לוין. ש. גרובין. מ. קרמר.

Bund Executive in Dovinsk
Sitting, R. To L.: I. Ratz, P. Bayksin, N. Mayzel, G. Levin, V. Lonberg.
Standing, R. to L.: B. Rind, I. Levin, Sh. Grobin, P. Krebel

38. רופאים בדווינסק
יושבים מימין לשמאל : ד"ר ר. גורביץ. ד"ר ב. רוזנברג. ד"ר ז. גורדין
עומדים מימין לשמאל : ד"ר ב. וופסי. ד"ר מ. זנד.

Doctors of Dvinsk

68. קבוץ הכשרה של החלוץ המזרחי ברמנישקי (ע"י דווינסק)

Kibbutz Hachshara (training camp) of "HaChalutz Mizrachi" near Dvinsk (Ramnishki)

Sara Ziskovich? Zuskovits? (bottom row 1st on left), born 1915, moved to Riga from Dvinsk and then managed to get to Palestine in 1930's. If this photo 'speaks' to anyone I would be most grateful.

Alma Hall alma_hall@mac.com

Levitan, the principal of an ORT vocational school in Dvinsk

A pupil of the Yiddish school in Daugavpils (Dvinsk), who took part
in a show entitled "Boom un Dreydl," staged by the pupils

Jewish women and children in Daugavpils (Dvinsk), Latvia, who were forced by the Germans to bathe in the cold river during the Holocaust

Summer 1938 / Daugavpils

Golda - Genia Chaikin, a kindergarten teacher and school teacher from
Daugavpils (Dvinsk), Latvia

Group of children from Daugavpils with their parents depart for the OZE
(Society for the Protection of the Health of the Jews) Aronson summer
camp in Striap 1938

No Caption

Jews taken from the Dvinsk ghetto and assembled prior to their extermination in about 1942

Jews taken from the Dvinsk ghetto prior to their extermination

Jewish children and women of Dvinsk abused and forced by the Germans
to bathe in the cold river 1941-1942

Jewish women and children forced by the Germans to bathe in the cold river

Петербургская улица.

View of Petersburg Street, Dvinsk: a policeman and another man pose on the corner of a street of shops, 1908

Studio portrait of a group of young Jewish women, revolutionaries c. 1905. "They are all in America now" (From a 'Jewish Daily Forward' photo essay, 1932: "Jewish Revolutionaries Of The Past"

Published on April 8, 1923 Physical exercise in a public school in Dvinsk; Jewish Daily Forward

Likely an application for admittance to Palestine (1937) for doctor and wife

Latvia DAUGAVPILS Malkiel's SYNAGOGUE

From left; Roza Iss (1902 Riga- 1941 murdered by the Nazis), Gittel Nisselson (nee Jewelsohn 1880 Dvinsk- 1978 Israel) , Raitze Nisselson, Mane Nisselson, Scheina Armerman and Leiser Lurie at the grave of Josiph Nisselson From the album Asaf Lurie

Exterior of Jewish Trade School
DWINSK

Ida Nekhom nee Volkin with family. They perished in the Holocaust

Ilana Baird wrote; My Great-Grandfather Meilach Moshe (Moisei) and his
parents Abraham and Sara - where from Dvinsk Latvia.

A memorial to those who perished

INDEX of Pges 1-80 Only

A

Abramson, 22
Adler, 45
Aginski, 40
Amir, 38
Antin, 22
Arni, 4
Aronovich, 45

B

Bar-Yehuda, 45
Beliach, 40, 41
Bell, 62
Berman, 40
Bialik, 28, 30, 32
Bistritsky, 50
Blair, 44
Bleich, 58
Bleichman, 58
Bleier, 64
Bliach, 24
Bloom, 40
Boaz, 40
Boimeister, 43
Bolbaka, 24
Borochov, 22
Boyerski, 41, 44
Brener, 31
Brodbeka, 41
Brook, 40
Buba, 29, 30, 54

C

Chaikin, 41

D

Donda, 44
Dovrin, 40
Drori, 41
Dunaburger, 19
Dvin, 22

E

Edelson, 45
Edelstein, 24

Eidus, 44
Elisbok, 44

F

Fisher, 44
Friedman, 44, 60, 61
Fuks, 63

G

Gaon, 20
Gaon of Dvinsk, 70
Gaon of Rogachov, 39, 70
Geller, 44
Gendel, 59
Ginzburg, 40
Glinternik, 24
Goldin, 41
Goldman, 41, 44
Gorbintz, 24
Gordon, 24, 31, 40
Gorevich, 49
Gorfinkle, 40
Graber, 63, 65
Grilicks, 25
Gurvitz, 40
Gurwitz, 57, 58
Gusman, 70
Gutman, 22

H

Halperin, 32, 41
Hayam, 45
Horovitz, 21
Horowitz, 25, 39
Hyal, 32
Hyatt, 44, 59, 62

K

Kaplinsky, 23
Karnesky, 22
Karrol, 40
Kasteral, 22
Katz, 34
Kavener, 21
Kitski, 40
Kopilov, 40
Kopilovich, 45
Koplovski, 24
Kramer, 45
Krislav, 61

In Memory of the Community of Dvinsk

L

Levin Shetzkiss, 46
Levinburg, 40
Levin-Shatzkas, 24
Levy, 2, 33, 41, 59
Lichtman, 45
Lieberson, 22
Lipshitz, 40

M

Madelya, 50, 51
Maizel, 46
Malkin, 22
Margalit, 44
Mayzel, 24
Meiksin, 46
Minkovitch, 27
Motznik, 60
Movshenson, 38
Mowschensohn, 57

N

Nachman, 41
Neishtet, 70
Nieshtet, 31
Nieshul, 40
Nishtet, 61
Nochimovich, 44

P

Peretz, 71, 74
Pipkavich, 41
Pokroi, 29
Potsh, 59
Pyrenov, 40

R

Rabbi Damta, 19
Rav Kook, 19, 70
Ravdin, 24
Reiner, 44
Rogachov Gaon, 19, 20
Rogachover Gaon, 30, 38, 39, 70
Rogatchover Gaon, 19
Rosen, 19, 30, 38, 70
Rosenberg, 62
Rosenvein, 22
Rozenberg, 40

S

Saragovich, 42, 43
Segal, 38
Shapira, 44
Sheinka, 57
Shenkin, 41, 44
Shetzkiss, 46
Shmuel, 36
Shvalav, 41
Simcha, 19, 20, 21, 30, 38, 39, 54, 70
Slobo, 67, 75, 76
Smoshkovich, 42, 43, 44
Snapp, 22
Stark, 40
Steinman, 60
Stoll, 41, 44
Storich, 24

T

the Gaon, 19, 20
the Rogachov, 19
the Rogachover, 19, 20, 21, 30, 39
Traub, 44
Trumpeldor, 31
Tsadikov, 22
Tzvi, 27

V

Vapna, 63
Vaspi, 57

W

Wittenburg, 25

Y

Yachnin, 63, 65
Yaffa, 57, 59
Yaffe, 22

Z

Zacks, 22, 25
Zand, 24, 44
Zarodin, 42, 43, 44
Zilberman, 64

INDEX of APPENDIX

A

Armerman, 29

B

Baird, 32
Bayksin, 17
Bloch, 2

C

Chaikin, 21

D

Dobrin, 5

F

Fleischman, 5
Friedman, 5
Fuxman, 5

G

Grobin, 17

H

Hall, 18
Herzog, 5
Hillman, 5

I

Iss, 29

J

Jewelsohn, 29

K

Kempner, 5
Krebel, 17
Krechmer, 5
Kretchmer, 4

L

Lapins, 7

Levin, 17
Levitan, 1, 19
Litt, 5
Lonberg, 17
Lunch, 5
Lurie, 29

M

Mark, 9
Marovich, 5
Mayzel, 17
Melman, 5
Meyerson, 5
Miller, 14
Mirvis, 5
Moise, 32
Moshe, 32
Moss, 16

N

Neisloss, 3
Neisxloss, 3
Nekhom, 31
Nisselson, 29

P

PaKempner, 5
PoKempner, 5

R

Ratz, 17
Reeksts, 6
Rief, 5
Rind, 17
Rogachaver Gaon, 1
Ruzin, 1

S

Sachs, 5
Schuman, 5
Segall, 5
Shanker, 5
Simcha, 1
Sosin, 6

V

Volkin, 31

W

Weinberg, 2
Westerman, 5

Z

Ziskovich, 18
Zox, 5
Zuskovits, 18